ON THE ORIGINS OF HUMAN EMOTIONS

ON THE ORIGINS
OF HUMAN EMOTIONS

*A Sociological Inquiry
into the Evolution of
Human Affect*

JONATHAN H. TURNER

STANFORD UNIVERSITY PRESS
Stanford, California

Stanford University Press
Stanford, California

© 2000 by the Board of Trustees of the
Leland Stanford Junior University

Printed in the United States of America
On acid-free, archival-qualiy paper

Library of Congress Cataloging-in-Publication Data

Turner, Jonathan H.
    On the origins of human emotions : a sociological inquiry into the evolution of
human affect / Jonathan H. Turner.
        p.   cm.
    Includes bibliographical references and index.
    ISBN 0-8047-3719-3 (cloth : alk. paper) — ISBN 0-8047-3720-7 (pbk. : alk. paper)
    I. Emotions.   2. Emotions—Social aspects.   I. Title.
BF531 .T87   2000
304.5—dc21   99-086427

Designed by Janet Wood
Typeset by James P. Brommer in 11/14 Garamond

Original printing 2000

Last figure below indicates year of this printing:
09   08   07   06   05   04   03   02   01   00

To my wife, Alexandra Maryanski,

whose work gave me the key insight to start this book

CONTENTS

ILLUSTRATIONS

Language and culture are often seen as humans' most unique characteristics. In this book, however, I will argue that our ability to use a wide array of emotions evolved long before spoken language and, moreover, that expanded emotional capacities among early hominids represented a preadaptation for spoken language and culture among later hominids. Long before hominids could speak with words, they communicated through body language their emotional dispositions; and it is the neurological wiring of the brain for these emotional languages that represented the key evolutionary breakthrough. To develop this line of argument, I will draw on materials from diverse disciplines, including evolutionary biology, primatology, neurology, sociology, anthropology, and to a lesser extent, evolutionary psychology, psychobiology, and sociobiology. Obviously, this kind of interdisciplinary effort is fraught with the dangers of one person crossing so many intellectual boundaries, but if there is an area ripe for cross-disciplinary analysis, it is the study of human emotions.

Humans are evolved apes, and with this simple recognition we can ask: How did natural selection work on the basic ape anatomy and neuroanatomy to create the hominid line? My answer to this question is sociological, because if our distant ancestors were to survive on the African savanna, selection had to make them more social and organized. In order to increase sociality and organization among early hominids, natural selection had to overcome a huge obstacle: apes' propensity for weak ties, individualism, mobility, and autonomy. For apes are not monkeys who, in general, are highly social and well organized; and thus, selection had to change relatively low-sociality apes trying to adapt to open country terrain into better organized and more social animals who could coordinate food collection and defense. And, it had to do so in a punctuated time frame. Under these time constraints, natural selection forged a compromise by laying over biologically driven propensities for low sociality and individualism expanded abilities to use emotional languages for forging social bonds and solidarities.

Many will find my argument to be speculative, especially since it goes against many biases in the social sciences and, more generally, in philosophy about the innate sociality of humans. My view is that, at our older ape core, we are individualists who chafe against organizational constraint, but we are also an animal that can use a highly attuned emotion system to create social bonds and to sustain tight-knit social structures. By appreciating this compromise produced by natural selection on the hominid line in the past, we can better understand how humans use emotions in the present. An evolutionary story of how emotions evolved can, therefore, inform analysis of face-to-face behavior among the last descendants of hominids, *Homo sapiens sapiens.*

Jonathan H. Turner

ACKNOWLEDGMENTS

I would like to thank the Academic Senate of the University of California at Riverside for sponsorship of this research. As with all my research over the last thirty years, the Senate has been my chief means of support.

I should mention and acknowledge the year-long gathering of scholars at the Institute for Interdisciplinary Studies at the University of Bielefeld in 1993 for the explicit purpose of initiating a prolonged dialogue between scholars in the biological and social sciences. I was able to stay for only five months of the year, but during this time I learned a great deal about biology. Indeed, I am often surprised how much I absorbed by simply being around people who were oriented to biological reasoning. I wish to thank, in particular, Peter Weingart who was not only the organizer of this ambitious program but, at the time, the director of Institute as well.

I would also like to acknowledge the contributions of members of my Sociology of Emotions graduate seminar at the University of California at Riverside for reading the manuscript and making useful suggestions. The students in this seminar were David Boyns, Charles Levine, Barbara Cottrell, Davison Bideshi, and James La Valle. I also appreciate the anonymous reviews secured by Stanford University Press.

Finally, I want to thank my wife, Alexandra Maryanski, who not only gave me the key insight on which to build the argument of this book, but who also helped me review and organize the literature summarized and cited in Chapter 1. Without her help, the book could not have begun with such a strong empirical base.

ON THE ORIGINS OF HUMAN EMOTIONS

CHAPTER I

Ancestral Emotional Communication

Humans As Evolved Apes

Humans are really just evolved apes, but not just any ape. We are the only living species of apes that continues to prosper—indeed, to prosper so much that we are up against the inevitability of a Malthusian correction. Our hominoid cousins have been in decline for millions of years, and today only four genera remain—chimpanzees (*Pan*), gorillas (*Gorilla*), orangutans (*Pongo*), and gibbons/siamangs (*Hylobates/Symphalangus*). Compared to Cercopithecoidea and Ceboidea, or Old and New World monkeys, respectively, apes can be viewed as evolutionary failures, as can be seen in Table 1.1 on the respective numbers of extant genera and species within the suborders and superfamilies of primates.[1] The verdict is still out on humans, but, as Roger Brown so aptly put it, "the smart money is on the insects" in the long run and, one might add, the bacteria and viruses as well. I stress these points not merely to lament the decline of apes, as tragic as this is, nor the overpopulation of humans, as menacing as this is. Rather, the critical point is that we are apes at our core; all that is unique to humans has been piled on top of our ape heritage. We cannot, therefore, develop theories and research programs about humans without taking into consideration the biological legacy of our ape ancestry as it continues to influence human action and interaction.

The seeming detachment of the modern sociocultural world from human biology is an illusion, because interaction and social organization among humans are made possible by virtue of our hominoid neuroanatomy

I

TABLE I.I

Relative Numbers for Species of Apes, Monkeys, and Prosimians

Order	Suborders	Superfamilies	Number of Families	Number of genera	Number of species
Primates	Prosimii	Lemuroidea Daubentonioidea Lorisoidea Tarsioidea		16	45
	Anthropoidea	Ceboidea (New World Monkeys)	Callitrichidae	5	21
			Cebidae	11	32
		Cercopithecoidea (Old World Monkeys)	Cercopithecidae	16	78
		Hominoidea (Apes and Humans)	Hylobatidae	2[a]	9
			Pongidae	3[b]	4
			Hominidae	1[c]	1

NOTES: [a] Gibbons (*Hylobates*)
        Siamangs (*Symphalangus*)

       [b] Orangutans (*Pongo*)
        Gorillas (*Gorilla*)
        Chimpanzees (*Pan*)

       [c] Humans (*Homo*)

and physiology; and more fundamentally, interaction and organization are constrained by this biological legacy.[2] We thus need some understanding for how *Homo sapiens* evolved out of the hominid line that parallels the evolutionary lines of our few remaining hominoid cousins. Human capacities for thought and reason, for emotions, and for verbal communication are made possible by anatomical structures that facilitated the adaptation of our distant primate ancestors. We can no longer view this evolutionary heritage as a "black box" or as a given; instead, we must delve into our evolutionary history and see how it continues to influence, moment by moment, every face-to-face encounter among human beings.

The Evolution of Primates

Some sixty million years ago, early protoprimates began to climb the trees of dense forests; it is from these pioneers that the primate order evolved (Fleagle 1988; Campbell 1985; Gingerich and Uhen 1994; Conroy 1990; Maryanski and Turner 1992). The selection pressures of an arboreal habitat and its various eco-niches are what most scholars believe shaped the features of all primates, including humans.[3] What were these selection pressures?

One selection pressure was for better vision. Unlike most mammals who are olfactory dominant, higher primates are visually dominant (Campbell 1985; Forbes and King 1982; Rodieck 1988). Primate brains have been re-wired to subordinate other sensory inputs—haptic, auditory, and even olfactory—to vision. Such inputs are processed by association cortices in the brain that organize and integrate touch, hearing, and smell with vision. Selection for full stereoscopic (i.e., three-dimensional) and color vision would bestow upon primates enormous advantages for moving about rapidly in trees, since a poorly-sighted primate would have to move slowly, clinging to branches, whereas an animal with enhanced vision could leap and run across and between branches.[4]

Related to the emerging dominance of vision among primates was a corresponding decline in the olfactory bulb, although prosimians retain a well-developed olfactory sense (Radinsky 1974, 1975, 1977; Rose and Fleagle 1987; Beard, Krishtalka, and Stucky 1991). This reduction probably occurred because, at the neurological level, a highly sensitive sense of smell could interfere with visual dominance, especially since the olfactory bulb penetrates into the subcortical emotion centers of the brain. And so, for vision to dominate over other sense modalities, olfactory sensitivity began to decline among prosimians, with a dramatic reduction in apes and monkeys.[5]

Another selection pressure was for an enhanced sense of touch (Kaas and Pons 1988; Maryanski and Turner 1992; Maryanski 1997a). An animal that must move about in the three-dimensional world of trees requires either a set of claws to hang on or, if movement is to be rapid, a heightened sense of touch to feel texture, weight, and strength of branches. Without this haptic sensitivity, which is reflected in the prehensile hands and feet of monkeys and apes, vision would absorb the whole burden for guiding movements; and with only vision, miscalculations would be common and result in free falls to the ground—typically, to death.[6]

Other selection pressures were for retention of a generalized postcranial skeleton, especially the five digits on hands and feet, as well as a well-developed clavicle. With flexible hands, fingers, toes, and wrists, efficient movement in an arboreal habitat becomes possible, and thus, selection would retain and improve upon these skeletal features (Napier and Napier 1985; Tattersall, Delson, and van Couvering 1988; Conroy 1990). Primate adaptations also included a generalized digestive system and functionally differentiated dentition which gives most higher primates the capacity to chew and digest a large variety of foods. All of these features would facilitate a tree-living lifeway; imagine the difficulty a stiff-jointed, hoofed, or clawed animal with a restricted digestive system would have moving about and foraging in an arboreal environment.[7]

Finally, the primate arboreal zone favored selection for the expansion of primate brains, with the neocortex itself seen as "one of the hallmarks of mammalian brain evolution" (Jones 1990: 31) and as a "strong progressive structure that consistently increased in primate evolution" (Mesulam, 1983; Stephan, Baron, and Frahm 1988: 15). Most higher primates have larger brains, relative to body size, than most other mammals. Much of this increase in brain size was to the neocortex and was the result, in all probability, of reorganizing the brain for visual dominance as well as for expanding the capacity to remember and to think about the vicissitudes of an arboreal habitat in which one false step can mean descent and death (Jones 1990). A smarter animal can remember the distance, texture, and strength of branches; and it can think better and make decisions that will keep it moving in the complex three-dimensional environment of the forest canopy.

Thus, the basic features of primate anatomy reflect the work of natural selection on an earlier mammalian body form, shifting this basic design toward visual dominance, reduced olfaction, sensitive touch, and larger brains, while retaining the generalized skeletal features of primitive placental mammals. As we will come to see, human interaction cannot be fully conceptualized without some attention to these changes that began some sixty million years ago. Social interaction in the human measure is made possible, and continues to be circumscribed, by the selection forces that first worked on those early primatelike mammals seeking to adapt to arboreal niches.

About thirty-four million years ago, during the Oligocene epoch, early anthropoids or the monkey-ape grade of primates evolved in the arboreal habitat alongside prosimians. These prototype anthropoids exhibit a combination of primitive (ancestral) and derived monkey-ape traits and provide the models for reconstructing the ancestral lines that eventually gave rise to the earliest "stem" member or common ancestor of living Old World monkeys, apes, and humans (Köhler and Moyá-Solá 1997; Ankel-Simons, Fleagle, and Chatrath 1998; Gingerich 1990).[8] By the Miocene epoch, beginning about twenty-three million years ago, a large flowering of the first true hominoids appears in the fossil record, indicating that apes—and not monkeys, who were rare at this time—composed the first abundant adaptive radiation of higher primates (Conroy 1990: 248; Gibbons and Culotta 1997).[9] The fossil record also tells us that many early and middle Miocene apes were, like most hominoids today, relatively large-bodied, tailless, soft-fruit eaters, but that they were otherwise quite peculiar-looking for apes, with differences in dental, skull, and body parts, notably a "monkeylike" body plan and a locomotion pattern of above-branch leaping and running on all fours in the forest canopy (Rose 1993, 1997; Andrews 1996; Pilbeam 1997).

During the middle Miocene, about sixteen million years ago, new hominoid taxa (still with above-branch arboreality but with more derived, modern traits) appear in Africa and later in Europe, but this phase of the Miocene also ushered in a large adaptive radiation of Old World monkeys. Thus, by the middle Miocene both apes and Old World monkeys were well established in Africa, and a clear differentiation between the ancestors of present-day monkeys and apes was evident. Yet, as the Miocene continued, species of monkeys steadily increased while the many species of African apes that had radiated earlier went into decline and extinction (Conroy 1990; Ungar 1996; Andrews 1992).

The dramatic shift in the reproductive success of monkeys during the middle Miocene unquestionably came at the expense of apes, with one scholar recently underscoring that "many researchers have related a decrease in the diversity of non-cercopithecoid catarrhines in Africa since the early Miocene to an increase in the diversity of Old World monkeys" (Ungar 1996). Yet, how did monkeys triumph over apes? The current thinking is that apes and monkeys directly competed for food, and that monkeys won out over apes when they greatly enhanced their feeding efficiency through the evolution of dietary specializations based on increased abilities to tolerate and consume unripe vegetation (such as fruit) and on anatomical features such as storage pouches and distinctive cusps (found in Old World monkeys today).[10] Lacking a competitive edge, most ape species perished with the remaining ones left to forage at the tops of trees, the farthest extensions of branches, and the underside of limbs (for discussions see Andrews 1981, 1996; Galili and Andrews 1995; Temerin and Cant 1983; and Kay and Ungar 1997; Ungar and Kay 1995).

Whatever the explanation, the fossil record provides solid evidence that monkeys were replacing apes beginning in the middle Miocene and that during this replacement phase the few remaining ape species were undergoing dramatic skeletal changes found in apes and humans today. Yet this new adaptation to the less verdant niches of the arboreal habitat not only modified hominoid anatomy; it may have also led to distinctive behavioral and social propensities that, as we will see, still shape the flow of human face-to-face interaction and the dynamics of human social structures.[11]

What, then, distinguishes a contemporary monkey from a hominoid? Monkeys have a basic quadrupedal anatomy with immobile shoulder joints, a narrow rib cage, a tail, a small collar bone, and limbs of nearly equal or equal length. Monkeys are equipped (despite any secondary modifications) for four-footed walking on the tops of branches using their tails for balance (Napier and Napier 1985: 45; Conroy 1990: 75 ff.). Apes and humans, in contrast, have a distinctive torso with a short, wide trunk accompanied by mobile shoulder joints, no tail, specializations in the feet, hips, hands and wrists, and (for apes) arms much longer than legs or (for humans) vice versa (Hunt 1991). This unique morphology can only represent a response to such locomotor activities as climbing and under-the-branch suspension, using mobile but stable forelimbs for reaching, pulling, and arm-swinging from branch to branch. Apes and humans also share a more developed haptic sense, especially on their fingertips, with raised digital ridges (fingerprints) to enhance their grip on smooth surfaces (Napier and Napier 1985: 37). While these traits reflect a last common ancestors' adaptation to an arboreal habitat, contemporary hominoids have evolved secondary locomotor patterns for movement on the ground: orangutans (who are rarely on the ground) clump each hand to form a "fist-walking" gait; chimpanzees (who are half the time on the ground) and gorillas (who are mostly on the ground) bend each finger joint to fashion a "knuckle-walking" gait; and humans (who are always on the ground) lock their knee joints and stand on their feet to form a "heel-toe" striding gait for maintaining an erect posture (Napier and Napier 1985).

The hominoid brain is also much larger than the monkey brain, particularly in the cerebral cortex. In all probability, this difference results from a long and steady trend in hominoid evolution for large and elaborated brains, a trend that culminated in humans. The larger brain of apes, when compared to that of monkeys was probably initiated by the challenges Miocene apes faced when they were forced to shift from an above-branch arboreality in the early and middle Miocene to a below-branch arboreality in the late Miocene. For example, monkey-style four-footed movement is a mostly stereotyped pattern of locomotion; in contrast, the use of the hands alone among early modern-looking apes would have required many learned navigational skills, with selection favoring increased cortical control over motor movements, and precise calculation of egocentric distance. Selection would also favor more memory for learned secondary depth cues; and with a dependence on the prehensile hands for locomotion (and the corresponding loss of the back feet for support), selection would increasingly work to enhance tactile sensitivity to texture, vibrations, and temperature, as well as to what might lie under the surface of objects (Corruccini, Ciochon, and McHenry 1975; Holloway 1968; and Maryanski 1996b).

However striking the skeletal changes in Miocene apes, behavioral changes that influenced the nature of hominoid social organization must have been equally dramatic. For environmental zones dictate organizational patterns, and the massive extinction of apes coupled with the morphological changes for those that survived can only signal major upheavals in lifeways for Miocene apes. While hominoid paleo-environments undoubtedly varied throughout the Miocene (see Andrews 1996), the dietary preferences and functional morphology reflected in gibbons, the great apes, and humans point to a last common ancestor population who lived in a tropical forest canopy on a mostly frugivorous diet and who, as a result, evidenced a foraging pattern that included climbing, arm hanging, and under-the-branch arm swinging (or "brachiation"), along with a unique locomotor capacity to propel the body through space using the arms alone. Although difficulties arise in determining which locomotor activities dominated, the arboreal niche was likely narrow and peripheral, with limited resources (see Andrews 1981, for a discussion of diversity in Miocene monkeys and apes).[12] Under these conditions, how then might apes have optimized their foraging strategy for survival and reproductive success?

Alexandra Maryanski's (1992, 1997a) pioneering work provides hard data on what probably occurred millions of years ago. Maryanski conducted a comprehensive review of the data on primates in an effort to expose the underlying network structures of all living apes and representative samples of African Old World monkeys. From studies on these primates, Maryanski coded the behaviors reported for age and sex classes on the strength of social ties, and then, from this coding, she was able to expose the underlying network structures of each species and, more importantly for my purposes, to compare the dramatic differences between the social structures of apes and monkeys.

The social structure of most Old World monkeys is organized around intergenerational matrilines of related females and male dominance hierarchies, giving monkey organization a more tightly-knit and stable structure than is evident among apes. This structure is sustained over many generations because only males transfer out of their natal group at puberty, while females remain in close proximity to mothers and related female kin (Fedigan 1982; Jolly 1985; Napier and Napier 1985; Cheney, Seyfarth, and Smuts 1986; Wrangham 1980; Smuts et al. 1987). In all species of apes, however, adolescent females (and in most cases males as well) transfer out of their mother's group at puberty, thereby destroying any capacity to build structure through intergenerational matrilines (Moore 1984; Greenwood 1980; Pusey and Packer 1987; Maryanski 1992). Some male-male dominance exists among male apes but it is not as evident or clearly defined as that among male monkeys, nor is it the focal point of social interaction as it is with monkeys. From Maryanski's (1987, 1992) review of the data on social network ties among living apes, a pattern of loose and fluid structure emerges. Apes tend to develop comparatively few strong social ties; females normally leave their natal grouping at puberty, thereby destroying the capacity to build structure along kinship lines in which tight-knit subgroupings among females and their offspring provide a stable, intergenerational basis of organization.[13]

Among tree-living gibbons and siamangs, who are distantly related to humans and great apes, adult males and females form lifelong monogamous pairs, but at puberty a son is settled by the father in another area, where the son can attract a female mate, while the mother forces her daughter to leave and seek a single male who has established a residence in another territory. The orangutans make up such a loosely knit social structure that, aside from a mother and her dependent offspring, most orangutans move about alone in what can only be described as a near solitary existence. Our closest relative, the chimpanzee, moves about freely within a larger regional population, and like orangutans, chimpanzee society lacks stable adult groups, leaving individuals at the micro level to seek out their own supportive "friendships" that reflect personal likes and dislikes, although at the more macro level a bounded regional population of chimpanzees apparently enjoys an overall sense of community (see Goodall 1986; Wrangham et al. 1994). Gorillas live in groups but their social networks are still composed of only a few strong ties and many weak ties.[14] Thus, in general, apes reveal considerably more degrees of freedom, individualism, mobility, and autonomy than monkeys, along with relaxed status hierarchies and few kinship networks (for discussion on hominoid lifeways see Leighton 1987; Prevschoft et al. 1984; Rodman and Mitani 1987; and Tuttle 1986).

The Structure of Primate Societies

How, then, can we create a picture of the underlying structure of ape and monkey social organization? Table 1.2 attempts to visually represent the patterns of tie formation among selected Old World monkeys and the four genera of apes. In this schema, a + indicates strong ties, a o/+ weak to moderate ties, and a o weak or absent ties among age and sex classes. At first glance, it looks as if monkeys and apes have about the same proportion of weak, moderate, and strong ties, but a more careful inspection of *which* age and sex classes have strong ties indicates that monkeys have much greater capacities to build permanent social structures than apes. A comparison of *adult to adult* as well as *adult to adult procreation ties* for monkeys and apes reveals a clear difference: Among monkeys, strong adult female ties can exist for up to four generations of grandmothers, aunts, mothers, daughters, and female siblings, whereas among apes these ties are virtually absent. Monkeys create matrilines, which, when coupled with male dominance hierarchies, generate larger and more stable group structures. In contrast, apes cannot create matrilines because of female transfer from their mother's group at puberty. This fact—combined with apes' less-pronounced and

TABLE 1.2
Social Ties Among Monkeys and Apes

STRENGTH OF TIES[a]

		Among Representative Species of Monkeys				Among Extant Ape Species			
		Gelata	Patas	Macaque (most species)	Baboons (most species)	(Hylobates) Gibbon	(Pongo) Orangutan	(Gorilla) Gorilla	(Pan) Chimpanzee
Adult to adult	male-male	o	o	o	o	o	o	o	o/+
	female-female	+	+	+	+	o	o	o	o
	male-female	o	o	o/+	o/+	+	o	o/+	o
Adult to child	mother-daughter	+	+	+	+	+	+	+	+
	mother-son	+	+	+	+	+	+	+	+
	father-daughter	o	o	o	o	+	o	o	o
	father-son	o	o	o	o	+	o	o	o
Adult to adult procreation ties	mother-daughter	+	+	+	+	o	o	o	o
	mother-son	o	o	o	o	o	o	o	+
	father-daughter	o	o	o	o	o	o	o	o
	father-son	o	o	o	o	o	o	o	o

Code: o = weak or absent ties   + = strong ties   o/+ = weak to moderate ties

[a]All primates reveal an inherent propensity for preferential relationships within and between age and sex classes (see Cheney, Seyfarth, and Smuts 1986; Hinde 1983). In primate research the strength of social bonds is assessed on the basis of social grooming, food sharing, aiding and protecting, continual close proximity, embracing (excluding sexual contact), cooperative alliances, and the length of intensity of a social relation. Maryanski's analysis focused on the structural regularities in the patterning of relations among conspecifics and the emergent properties that characterize these relations. Distinct bonding patterns exist for all age and sex conspecifics (e.g., infant-juvenile ties) but only the key classes of ties are shown here because these are the core of any primate social structure. The scaling of primate bonds is a straightforward procedure because primate investigators typically agree on the degree of attraction among and between hominoid-cercopithecoid age and sex classes.

SOURCE: Adapted from Maryanski and Turner 1992 and Turner 1996a.

rather relaxed male dominance hierarchies—means that large and stable group structures are difficult for them to sustain. Thus, beyond those ties between mothers and their younger offspring (a pattern of ties common to all mammals), apes do not have as many strong and stable ties as monkeys to build social structures.

Using the data on tie formation among apes, Maryanski (1992, 1993) also employed cladistic analysis in order to uncover the likely relational patterns of the last common ancestor to present-day monkeys and apes. The cladistic methodology used by Maryanski is a standard tool for reconstructing the past in fields such as historical linguistics, textual criticism, and comparative biology (where it is called cladistic analysis). In these fields, the basic procedures involve an identification of limited groups of entities believed to be the end points or descendants of an evolutionary or developmental process. Then, an evaluation of the historical interrelationships of these descendants is undertaken with the idea that an "original" or common ancestor can be reconstructed through the detection of shared diagnostic or "derived characters." While the genealogical relationships are not directly testable, this methodology incorporates two testable assumptions: (1) a *relatedness hypothesis* that assesses whether or not the similarities found in a class of objects are due to a historical connection of descent from a common ancestor; and (2) a *regularity hypothesis* that assesses whether the modifications from the ancestral form to descendant forms are not randomly acquired, but evidence a systematic bias (Jeffers and Lehiste 1979; Platnick and Cameron 1977; Maas 1958; Hennig 1966; Gaeng 1971). A sister lineage, here Old World monkeys, is essentially used as a control group for comparing similarities and differences between this "next-most-closely related taxonomic group" (Andrews and Martin 1987) and those in the taxon of interest. This sister lineage permits the separation of primitive characters (or those inherited from a remote shared ancestor) from derived "evolutionary novelties" or sets of nested resemblances uniquely shared by a genealogical taxon. The great merit of the comparative/cladistic method is its utility in reconstructing ancestral patterns (Hass 1966), whether of an original text, a protolanguage, a biological lineage, or an ancestral social structure. Using this approach, nonhuman hominoids all reveal the following in common: ties among adult females are absent or weak;[15] mother–young daughter ties are strong; mother–young son ties are also strong; mother–adult daughter ties are weak or absent; father–young daughter ties are absent; father–adult daughter ties are absent; father–young son ties are absent; and father–adult son ties are absent. Orangutans and gorillas reveal either absent or weak ties between adult males, although chimpanzees do at times evidence stronger ties, especially among male siblings. Orangutans and gorillas evidence very weak or absent ties between mothers and adult sons, but again chimpanzees are the exception. Chimpanzees and orangutans have weak ties among adult males and females, whereas gorillas have weak to moderate ties among adult males and females.

This kind of analysis suggested to Maryanski that the Last Common Ancestor (LCA) to apes and humans probably had few strong ties. In all likelihood, the common ancestral population was a mobile cluster of individuals, perhaps making up a larger regional population like orangutans and chimpanzees today, but seemingly this ancestor did not form strong or permanent ties with conspecifics at the local group level. The only strong ties may have been those among mothers and young offspring; all other ties were, in all probability, absent or weak. What emerges, then, is an LCA population that is mobile, individualistic, autonomous, and not prone to high sociality or collective pursuits. If the ancestors of apes and humans were oriented this way, then it is reasonable to conclude that, at our hominoid core, we humans still possess these behavioral propensities to some degree. Such a conclusion flies in the face of arguments for the innate sociability of humans, but it is an argument supported by the data on primate social relations analyzed with established cladistic practices. And, as I will argue, the propensities of our ancestors have profound consequences for how we should think about human emotions and their effects on behavior.

Maryanski (in a personal communication) has recently speculated that tie-formation patterns among the great apes suggest community as the basic unit of organization among our common ancestor, but not community in the sense examined somewhat romantically by sociology's founders, who all appeared to lament the decline of cohesive, high-solidarity, traditional communities (conveniently ignoring, I should emphasize, the oppressiveness of these communities in terms of authority relations, morality, and other constraints—all of which would go against our ape ancestry's propensity for loose ties and individualism). If we examine organization among all apes, the larger regional population or community structure among chimpanzees is *the only unit* that endures over intergenerational time.[16] The profound difference in group continuity between monkeys and apes has to do with the monkey pattern of keeping females bound to, and knitted into, high-density female networks. This kinship-based recruitment assures the perpetuation of a monkey group over generations. In contrast, among gibbons, orangutans, and gorillas, both male and female dispersal from mother after puberty means that in the monogamous gibbon the tiny nuclear family structure dissolves with the death of the mated pair, in orangutans the matri-focal unit dissolves with the maturation of offspring (indeed, the near-solitary orangutans lack *any* other stable grouping), and in gorillas the group dissolves upon the death of the silverback male (who is the only stable member of a gorilla band, since males and females freely depart bands). Only for chimpanzees, both of whose sexes disperse at puberty from mother, does a stable structure persist. Although daughters move to another community, sons stay within their natal community—a solid block of forest, that is, ranging from fifteen to one hundred square miles where all chimpanzee adults move about freely in space. Community members recognize each other as part of their regional population as they move about alone or cluster together into spontaneous temporary parties within the population's territory. This is not a high-solidarity community, but rather only a recognition that others belong to a shared space. Humans, Maryanski argues, still carry this more general sense of community, perhaps heightened by the selection pressures that were to make humans more emotional. Modern humans seem to respond emotionally to the "locals" and even strangers who are perceived to be in their community; and in times of crisis, such responsiveness at the community level becomes particularly evident. What this suggests to Maryanski is that our ape ancestry lives on through this responsiveness to community, again not so much a highly charged sense of interpersonal solidarity but more of a general feeling of belonging to a place. Selection worked to make humans more emotional than other apes, and so this sense of community can be magnified to more emotional extremes, but these higher-intensity emotions cannot be sustained for long because they are too costly in terms of the physical energy expended and the affect mobilized; and, perhaps more significantly, these more emotional ties of sustained solidarity go against our ape legacy for weak ties, mobility, individualism, and fluid group structures.

If, at best, a general sense of others in a regional population, coupled with weak and loose ties in fluid groups, represented the structural basis of hominoid organization, then apes would not be particularly well suited for life in more open country niches. In these niches, hominoids who could develop more stable, cohesive, and organized groups would have selective advantages, especially against predation. And so, it is not unreasonable to conclude that the last common ancestor to *African* apes and humans would be rather poorly prepared for life in more open zones. In the niches of the forest habitat, the behavioral propensities of apes were fitness-enhancing, but with environmental changes that led to the movement of many primates from the trees to the woodlands and more open-country conditions, these behavioral propensities would appear maladaptive. This apparent lack of adaptive fit between the demands of less protected niches for tighter-knit groups and the behavioral propensities of the last common ancestor and the species of apes forced to survive in more open eco-zones may be the key to understanding how hominids and, eventually, humans became so emotional.

Adaptation of Apes to the African Woodlands and Savanna

During this retreat of the tropical forests,[17] especially in Africa, there were probably many open niches available to hominoids (Isbell and Young 1996; Hill 1998; Andrews 1989). Some remained arboreal; others probably moved into mixed niches in primary and secondary forests; still others like contemporary chimpanzees adapted to mixes of forest and woodland conditions; and some may have adapted to the forests at varying altitudes, as do contemporary subspecies of gorillas. Although there is debate over mammalian extinction patterns and just how dominant the grasslands became in east Africa (Kingston, Marino, and Hill 1994; and see McKee 1996), we do know that the wet rain forests began to recede during the late Miocene and that, as a result, many animals had to adapt to these dryer climatic conditions, or die (Malone 1987; Cerling et al. 1997; Agusti et al. 1998). Among these were hominoids and cercopithecoids who moved out to more open woodland environments, riddled with predators.[18] The ancestors of humans were one of these hominoid species. What did apes bring to these zones for natural selection to work on?

First, they brought brains comparatively large for a mammal, with cortical (voluntary) control over visual and tactile responses; and they brought an auditory cortex that was still very much wired into the emotional centers of the brain—loosely termed, the limbic systems (MacLean 1990)—and hence only partially under cortical control. Thus, when aroused, extant African apes will give off noisy responses, somewhat removed from control by the neocortex; and it is reasonable to assume that hominoids trying to survive in a bushland or woodland savanna environment also revealed this same propensity. Similarly, apes brought a poor sense of smell (the primary sense modality of most mammals) that projects directly into the limbic system, which was probably of little use in locating predators and prey, but which, if activated, might easily set off noisy vocal responses. Among these sense modalities, the anthropoid (i.e., monkey and ape) brain had been extensively rewired long ago for visual dominance, but full cortical control over emotional responses activated by other senses did not yet exist.[19]

Second, although apes brought skeletal structures adapted for niches in a tropical forest, they nonetheless took to a more open habitat a number of generalized skeletal features: flexible joints, short and deep trunks, no tails, limbs capable of sporadic bipedal locomotion, and flexible shoulders, arms, wrists, and hands (Hunt 1991; Swartz 1989). Apes also brought a primate dental morphology with teeth capable of holding, grinding, and processing a wide variety of foods.

And third, apes brought loose, fluid, and weak-tie patterns of social relations, without strong behavioral propensities for tight-knit social structures beyond the mother-child bond (common to all mammals). Moreover, they carried into these zones propensities for relatively relaxed male dominance, female and probably male transfer from the group at puberty, mobility among groups within a larger and more inclusive home range, and a tendency for personal autonomy and individualism (Maryanski and Turner 1992).

If we think about the ability of apes to adapt to open conditions with high rates of predation, hominoids do not look particularly well suited to survive. And indeed, most did not. A lack of control of emotions would make hominoids loud when aroused; and since noise attracts predators and scares away prey, a loud animal in open country without tight-knit organization for defense is soon a dead one. The skeleton had potential for new forms of locomotion, but a hominoid is not built for speed,[20] one means of defense against predators. And coupled with the loose, weak-tie nature of their social organization, hominoids could not capitalize on their organiza-

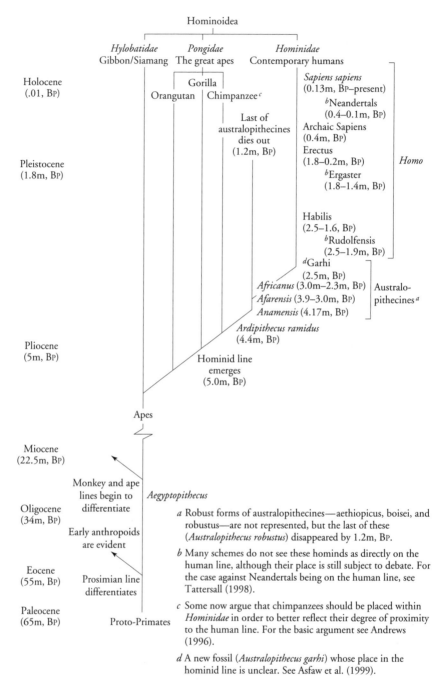

Figure 1.1. The evolution of primates

tion, as did such open-country monkeys as the highly successful baboons, to help in foraging for food collecting and in defense.[21] Apes are not organized around male hierarchies and female matrilines, and, indeed, the ancestors of contemporary apes and humans were at best rather loosely organized in regional populations without high degrees of group solidarity or cohesion to help in collective defense and food collecting. What, then, might hominoids to do when their anatomy and behavioral propensities seem so inappropriate for survival and reproductive success in Plio-Pleistocene Africa?

One adaptation was for modifications toward an erect bipedal gait. By the time of *Australopithecus afarensis* around 3.9 million years ago (White, Suwa, and Asfaw 1994), and perhaps before this (Leakey et al. 1995), early hominids were walking upright. There is considerable controversy on whether they were habitually bipedal in the human sense, and just why hominids were bipedal at all. Many hypotheses have been put forward as to how this adaptation emerged. One is that natural selection worked to make hominids bipedal so that they could see above the grasses and, thereby, find resources and avoid predators (White and Suwa 1987; Latimer and Lovejoy 1990); another is that bipedalism frees the hands for carrying food and weapons; still another is that bipedalism was more energy-efficient for long-distance travel as food resources became less plentiful (Isbell and Young 1996; Rodman and McHenry 1980); yet another is that bipedalism helped to secure high-energy food resources, especially fruit, from trees (Hunt 1994); another is that bipedalism reduces thermal stress by exposing less of the body to the sun (Wheeler 1993); still another hypothesis is that changes in the vestibular apparatus were critical (Spoor, Wood, and Zonneveld 1994); and so on. All speculations on when hominids became bipedal, as well as the morphology of early bipedalism compared to that of *Homo erectus* and humans, are open to debate. What is not in dispute, however, is that early hominids were bipedal long before dramatic increases in brain size beyond the ape measure occurred. Some have argued that the capacity for vertical climbing in the trees represented a preadaptation for bipedalism (e.g., Fleagle et al. 1981; Stern 1972, 1975); others see brachiation and vertical suspension as the key (Gebo 1996); and some see patterns of locomotion (i.e., knuckle-walking) as the critical preadaptation preceding bipedalism (Gebo 1992, 1996; Washburn, 1968). Since present-day chimpanzees can move about bipedally, at least for short periods of time in a "bent-knee" fashion (Crompton et al. 1998), selection clearly had an existing ability to work on, whatever the key preadaptation may have been. Hence, by four million years ago (Leakey et al. 1995), hominids were upright, although the full transformation of hip, leg, and feet joints, as well as musculature, to true humanlike walking had not yet evolved (see Crompton et al. [1998] for a review).

Other features of the hominid skeleton would also work in favor of fitness in less protected niches: dexterous hands would enable early hominids to pick up, hold, and carry food, while the ability to brachiate would facilitate throwing of objects to ward off predators or to kill prey. And the hominoid dental morphology and digestive system would also enable them to eat a great variety of available foods.

Yet, there must have been two very large handicaps for early hominids. First was their lack of cortical control over emotions. To survive in open country in the absence of the authoritarian and military-like structure of terrestrial baboons would seemingly require a rewiring of the brain for control over emotional vocal production to enhance survival and fitness. Control of the emotions potentially stimulated by olfaction would be less essential, since the size and sensitivity of the olfactory bulb was already greatly reduced in apes; and in fact, olfaction in present-day humans still projects directly to the limbic systems and is not directly under cortical control. Rewiring of the neuroanatomy for cortical control of vocal noise would perhaps be facilitated by the preadaptation for visual dominance and the already-in-place association cortices, such as the inferior parietal lobe, for coordinating and integrating auditory and tactile information under visual dominance. These association cortices could be connected via expanded neuro nets to subcortical limbic systems and thereby used to gain sufficient cortical control of noisy emotional outbursts. As control over emotionally-charged vocalizations was achieved, a more general control of emotions, per se, may have been a by-product of rewiring the association cortices for control over vocal emotional outbursts. If we accept this conclusion that selection could work on earlier rewiring for visual dominance to achieve control of limbic processes, the second stumbling block was the nature of hominid social organization. How was an individualistic, mobile, and weak-tie primate to create more cohesive, coherent, and tightly-knit structures of social organization for food collecting and for defense? As discussed earlier, monkeys had relatively little problem with making changes in social organization; selection simply magnified already-in-place propensities for male dominance hierarchies and female matrilines, thereby generating structures like those among yellow and anibus baboons (*Papio*), who march in large numbers and in military formation with dominant males in the lead, lieutenants on the flanks and rear, and females (who are much smaller than males) and their offspring in the center (see Rhine, Boland, and Lodwick [1985] for a full discussion). But apes could not use this mode of adaptation because the necessary behavioral propensies were not present, and therefore were not subject to selection; indeed, the organizational propensies so typical of monkeys had been selected out over millions of years as species of apes and monkeys differentiated. What, then, did selection have to work with?

One possibility would have been dominance hierarchies. Great apes do reveal tendencies for some male dominance, although this tendency is not as prominent as in monkeys. Indeed, captive or confined chimpanzees evidence much more pronounced male hierarchies than their counterparts in natural settings, and thus, the behavioral capacity for increased dominance was perhaps evident in those apes who had to adapt to more open-country niches. Yet male dominance alone could not sustain tight-knit social structures; indeed, individualistic hominids would react against such efforts at domination, escalating conflict and decreasing solidarity. But more fundamentally, without the complementary intergenerational connections among related females, half of what makes monkey organization so successful is missing. And since all female apes transfer from the natal group at puberty, a behavioral propensity for selection to form into the equivalent of monkey matrilines is not there for selection to act upon. It may be that selection among most species of hominoids on the savanna took the male-dominance route to getting organized, only to discover that this did not promote fitness. As a result, apes would have begun to die out. Yet for one or perhaps several lines of early hominids, selection took a different route and elaborated emotional capacities, and from this line the *Homo* lineage emerged.

The Evolution of Emotions Among Hominids

The rewiring of the hominid brain to gain control over emotions could become a preadaptation for stronger emotional ties, which, in turn, allowed those early hominids in the human line to build higher levels of social solidarity. But such rewiring of the brain is complicated, involving important changes in already enormously complex structures. Large mutations, which Fisher (1930) documented long ago, are generally harmful and maladaptive; and large mutations of such a sophisticated structure as hominoid neuro-anatomy would be disastrous. So relatively small changes had to occur, working on already existing characters and probably within a punctuated time frame. The avenue that the remaining hominids appear to have taken, I hypothesize, was a reorganization and elaboration of subcortical limbic structures, and their rewiring to neocortical and brain-stem systems, so as to produce an animal that could use and read a wide variety of emotional cues for enhanced social bonding.

Thus, when early hominids were confronted with the challenges of an open ecological zone, selection on the basic neuroanatomy of apes could operate on visual dominance and primal limbic-system assemblies for generating aversive and assertive responses, while perhaps also mobilizing hominids for emotions like satisfaction-happiness and disappointment-sadness. The essence of my argument, then, is this: First came control of emotions to create a relatively quiet primate; next came additional selection on this cortical control to expand the repertoire of emotions that could be used in interaction to forge bonds of increased solidarity and, thereby, more stable local group structures. These are, of course, speculative hypotheses, but they are nonetheless informed speculations that will guide my argument in the next chapters.

Hominids would thus embark on a new way to build strong ties and solidarities. Instead of relying on matrilines or pronounced male dominance, they would become emotional primates by using their complex neuro-anatomy and especially their highly sophisticated visual modality to read each other's emotions. Among monkeys, who are highly social, there appear to be dedicated and specialized neurons for visual recognition of the emotions revealed by face (Gross and Sergeant 1992; Rolls 1995; Sanghera et al. 1979; Brothers 1997: 35–37). These neurons are located primarily in temporal lobe cells and, in general, appear to be dedicated to heightened visual awareness of the social environment. Apes have not been well studied in this regard, and their neural assemblages may not be so task-specific, but if they are found to have similar neurons, then selection would have a structure on which to work, making the ancestors of humans highly sensitive to facial cues and alert to body movements in terms of what they reveal about social relations. The use of visual cues was supplemented, no doubt, by auditory, haptic, and olfactory cues, but vision, I think, was the key to building new forms of strong-tie associations. Language, culture, and the other features of humans that get more intellectual attention were, in my view, late evolutionary arrivals that supplemented and enhanced the effects of visual readings of emotional cues (Turner 1996a, 1996b, 1997a, 1997b, 1998). Indeed, I will even go so far as to argue that early increases in brain size of hominids from australopithecines to *Homo erectus* were more for rewiring emotions than for spoken language and culture. Linguistic communication and the building of culture would extend the solidarity-producing effects of emotions, but they could not supplant them. Granted, these assertions are controversial, but it is useful to see where they take us in explaining humans' unique emotional capacities.

The Primate Legacy and Human Interaction

Before turning to the details of human emotions, it may be useful to review how interaction processes are still very much influenced by the adaptations that primates made in the trees and that hominids subsequently made in the niches of the African savanna, bushlands, and woodlands. Some of these may seem so obvious as to not be worth mentioning; however, as I hope to demonstrate, they are nonetheless significant.

First, I will consider anatomical features. One of humans' most visible traits is bipedalism, which means that individuals expose not just faces but full bodies to each other in most interactions. To see how radical a change this is from the mammalian pattern, imagine two horses trying to expose their underside during interaction; this is, of course, just what humans do, and so body language is, as we will see, perhaps the dominant feature of human interaction—more important for solidarity-producing interaction than spoken words. Another anatomical feature is the dexterity of our hands and our comparatively flexible wrists, elbows, and shoulder joints, which allow for the use of a wide range of visual gestures to communicate with others, giving body language a doubly powerful set of interpersonal tools. Still another anatomical capacity is the ability to position and reposition upright bodies in ways that communicate meaning.

These abilities are still used by us in ways that approximate their use

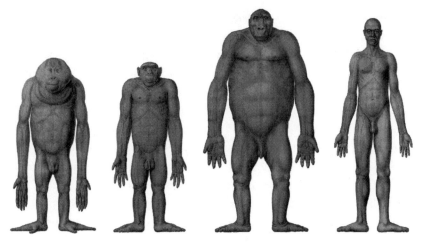

Figure 1.2.   The great apes and humans. Great-ape males and a human male. *From left to right: Pongo* (orangutan), *Pan* (chimpanzee), *Gorilla* (gorilla), and *Homo.* Each hominoid is set to the same scale in an erect position without body hair and with the lower limbs straightened for comparison. Reproduced from A. Schultz 1933. Courtesy of E. Schweitzerbart'sche Verlagsbuchhandlung.

among early hominids. Often visual and tactile body language is considered a supplement to verbal and auditory forms of communication, but I believe the reverse to be the case: visual body language is the more primal and basic aspect of face-to-face interaction. Auditory cues simply fine-tune the emotional overtones communicated through the visual sense modality; our brains are wired to see and to subordinate the auditory to the visual, and it would not be surprising that such is the case in human interaction. And this tendency, as I have already discussed, is a direct descendent of our arboreal origins and, later, our ancestors' forced occupation of the niches in more open-country ecological zones.

Second, and following from this emphasis on the visual, is stereoscopic and color vision, an ability that we obviously share with our primate cousins. But binocular, color vision is accompanied by our capacity to control emotions and, at the same time, to signal and interpret a wide variety of emotions visually. As primates, we are automatically alerted to visual cues, subordinating all information to the visual; and this visual intake of sensory information means that human interaction involves fine-grained reading of cues emitted by face and body.[22] We can use our visual senses, first evolved to move about in trees, to attune responses in ways not typical of most mammals, who tend to rely on olfactory cues. Moreover, because we expose our full bodies to visual inspection and because our facial movements are generated by striated muscles rapidly activated by the emotion centers in the brain (a topic to be pursued in Chapter 4), interpersonal attunement is achieved primarily via the visual senses, with other senses—touch, hearing, and olfaction—being secondary.

Third, human interaction and patterns of social organization are still influenced by our ancestors' propensities for individualism, weak tie formation, and autonomy. These propensities have been augmented by humans' capacity to develop a sense of self and to see self in relation to objects and others in one's environment, but more fundamental is the need for humans, as for our ape cousins, to have some degree of autonomy from others and the group. The brain was rewired and, along with the body, used to create emotional bonds that strengthened ties and promoted solidarity. Older and more primal tendencies for weak ties and autonomy, however, were not replaced; rather, they were simply supplemented by humans' enhanced emotional capacities. Language and culture further extended humans' emotional facilities and ability to build social structures, but these did not replace our basic ape behavioral drives for individual autonomy. Thus, interaction is always double-edged: we recognize emotional cues that signal associative tendencies, but at the same time we generally seek to avoid interpersonal immersion and, thereby, attempt to sustain autonomy of self and a certain interpersonal distance. Emotional bonds among humans are thus always in tension; they can burst apart rather easily or be difficult to forge in the first place. The fact that humans must use rituals in all interactions, in the sense argued by Erving Goffman (1967) and Randall Collins (1987, 1988), attests to how hard we must work to keep the tie-formation going, lest it fall apart under inputs from the neuroanatomy that we still share with the African apes and our last common ancestor.

The fourth and final way in which our interactions are still influenced by the adaptations of early primates has to do with our brain size, since humans' large brains, especially our asymmetrical and lateralized neocortex, make possible many embellishments to interaction: we can carry an image of ourselves; we can remember past interactions with great detail; we can carry and invoke all kinds of cultural content to facilitate the flow of interaction; and we can use language. Though a debatable conclusion, this latter ability was made possible, I believe, by two preadaptations: bipedalism, which helped to free the vocal track and to lower the larynx so that enunciation of speech became more readily possible (Aiello 1996; Negus 1929; Hill 1972); and reintegration of the brain under vision, which, as Norman Geschwind and Antonio Damasio have argued, created the association cortices that would allow hominids to use language at some point in their evolution (Geschwind 1965a, 1965b; Geschwind and Damasio 1984). Without these preadaptations in humans' anatomy and neuroanatomy, how could language ever have evolved? If we construct a thought experiment and assume that, by chance, one animal of a species could suddenly speak, what would happen to this animal? It would probably be selected out because it would have no one to speak to and would, no doubt, not attract mates to carry forth its genes. Thus, language was piggy-backed onto changes in hominid anatomy that were selected for reasons having nothing to do with language facility. Moreover, verbal language could not have evolved without earlier alterations in the brain to facilitate the use of visually based language, relying on visual readings of body cues. This wiring for a visually-based language perhaps built on the early rewiring of association cortices among apes in the arboreal niche, a rewiring that made apes visually dominant and that, thereby, required integration and subordination of other sensory inputs to the visual (Geschwind 1965a, 1965b). Later, as the prefrontal cortex expanded under selection pressures for emotional control, for expanded use of vocal symbols and for elaboration of cognitive abilities (Povinelli and Preuss 1995), the full neurological assemblages for sophisticated language were in place, most likely for use by *Homo erectus.*

Selection for spoken language could thus only occur with a considerable amount of the necessary wiring already in place, and this early wiring revolved around making primates, first of all, visually dominant and, second, on making early hominids more emotional animals communicating through a visually-based language revolving around emissions of signs through body cues. This earlier form of language is still, I believe, the more basic in emotionally-laden interaction, because it evolved for this very purpose. Of course, spoken language can supplement this more primal language system through inflections and intonations, but it cannot supplant it. Indeed, even the most emotionally charged talk carries relatively little emotional weight without the corresponding visual cues; and in fact, to respond emotionally to only verbal cues often requires that we construct visual images of what the other looks like as they emote with voice alone.

The Anatomy of Human Interaction: Preliminary Conclusions

To summarize my points thus far: human interaction in face-to-face encounters is possible because of our primate anatomy, as this was first honed
by adaptations to the arboreal habitat, then by the separation of apes from
monkeys, and, finally, by the adaptations of hominids to the African savanna. The result was a large-brained animal who can store a great deal of
information and retrieve it, who can see self as an object in its environment, who can anticipate its own actions and the actions of others, who
can read visual cues and gestures with great acuity, who can expose body
and face to signal visually fine-grained messages, and who can signal and
interpret a wide variety of subtle and complex emotions.

Other abilities for signaling and interpreting with words and language
came, I argue, much later in hominid evolution, building on the base of an
animal that sustained social ties through the use of emotional cues associated with a visually-based language. Auditory signals were no doubt part of
this language system—since calls are a very effective way to communicate
—once hominids had achieved some ability to control their emotions and
use them to overcome the handicap of being a noisy and loosely structured
primate trying to survive on the African terrain. Selection had enough to
work on if language abilities increased fitness. The brain had already been
rewired in the niches of the rain forest to create necessary association cortices for a linguistic primate, as is amply documented by the language abilities of African apes, especially bonobo chimpanzees (Savage-Rumbaugh et
al. 1993), who reveal an elementary language facility if allowed to "speak"
via their haptic and visual sense modalities.[23] And during early hominid
evolution, the brain was further rewired to control and use emotional cues
in a visually based language system, supplemented by auditory signals.
Thus, a verbal language could increase fitness by adding new dimensions
to communication and, hence, social organization—*given* selection pressures to get better organized. This happened, perhaps, during a period
when species of hominids began to compete intensely with each other.[24]
Under these conditions, the more organized hominids would be the most
fit to survive.

Yet I cannot stress enough my point that verbal language came later, and
that therefore it is less primal than visually based communication. Language
adds much to interaction, but by itself it is not particularly effective in gen-

erating solidarities. Too much microsociology focuses, I believe, on speech or talk, and associated activities such as intonation, sequencing, rhythm, and turn taking. These are very important forces in microencounters, but these, too, are supplements to those body cues that signal states of emotion and affect that are more primal and more essential to the flow of an interaction. This, at least, is my argument, and as such will organize a great deal of the analysis in this book.

From this premise, which obviously is debatable, it is necessary to explore in more detail how humans' emotional capacities first evolved. We have part of the answer: emotions were used to overcome apes' propensities for weak ties and individualism. What is now required is more detail on just how selection operated to make humans the most emotional animal on earth.

NOTES

1. Classification is subject to change; thus, the numbers in the columns of Table 1.1 are only approximate. The goal is to visualize *relative* numbers of genera and species as can be seen by looking down the last column on the right. Both apes and humans represent the end products of the superfamily Hominoidea, a lineage that flourished beginning about twenty-two million years ago in the early Miocene epoch. Yet, after this adaptive radiation of apes in parts of Africa, Europe and Asia, many hominoid species underwent a dramatic decline while monkey species who were once rare greatly multiplied. Conroy (1990: 248) notes that the widespread extinction of hominoids and the concomitant adaptive radiation of monkeys during the Miocene suggests a probable "causal relationship between these two evolutionary trends." Today, only a handful of ape species remain in specialized and highly restricted environments, with living apes often labeled "atypical relict forms" (Corruccini and Ciochon 1983: 14) and "evolutionary failures" (Andrews 1981: 25; Temerin and Cant 1983). For the present, humans are the only successful hominoid.

2. Primates can be physically distinguished by morphology and locomotor patterns. Monkeys share a quadrupedal gait, with secondary modifications that include leaping and arm swinging, with limb portions nearly of equal length. In contrast, the anatomy of apes and humans evidence adaptations that emphasize forelimb flexibility and suspension, with their bones, joints and muscles allowing for a wide range of mobility in all directions, reflecting an ancestral adaptation to some form of "brachiation," or propulsion dominated by the front limbs.

3. Primate roots go back to the Paleocene (ca. 60 million years ago), but to date only in Eocene beds (ca. 55 million years ago) have well-defined primate fossils been uncovered (Martin 1990a, 1990b). All extant primates are believed to be the evolved descendants of these early primates, beginning with Prosimii, or the lower primates. In the late Eocene or early Oligocene (ca. forty million years ago) primitive monkey-ape forms or generalized anthropoids made their first appearance (Simons 1990; Tuttle 1988). Most scholars attribute the morphology of primates to an arboreal adaptation, but see Cartmill (1974) for an alternative hypothesis.

4. The primate order is noted for its highly specialized neocortical equipment, with a great heightening of the visual cortex and a pruning of the subcortical olfactory cortex. Selection for the expansion of the primate visual center is already evident in the cranial anatomy of *Tetonius homunculus*, a fifty-five-million-year-old primate that is considered "remarkably advanced for its time," with an enhancement of both occipital and temporal lobes and a reduced olfactory organ. Later primate endocasts continue this trend toward visual dominance (see Radinsky 1970).

5. Contemporary lemurs still reflect a basic hand and foot locomotion for movement in a three-dimensional zone, a locomotor pattern that is best suited for wrapping around tree trunks, using the hand for grasping and the foot for propulsion. This prosimian type of muscular movement required an increased reliance upon visual equipment in ancestral prosimians, although these lower primates still rely on their olfactory organ for communication (Napier and Napier 1985). In contrast, monkeys and apes use vision for perceiving the intricate details of objects and scenes as well as for communication (see Conroy 1990).

6. The prehensile hands of monkeys, apes, and humans are highly refined and complex, allowing the sensitive fingertips to perceive impressions about the properties of the outside world. In apes and humans, haptic touch is so sophisticated that it can even be used to locate and recognize objects in space by stringing together independent chunks of information in succession (see Maryanski 1997b for a discussion). And only apes and humans have complicated fingerprints with above-the-surface ridges to amplify tactile stimulation (Napier and Napier 1985: 37).

7. Primates share the characteristic mammalian dentition, which involves four distinct kinds of teeth: incisors, canines, premolars, and molars. It is thought that primitive mammals had three incisors, one canine, four premolars, and three molars in each quarter of the mouth (or forty-four teeth in all). In the course of evolution, primates have lost incisors, premolars, or both. For example, hominoids and cercopithecoids have lost one incisor and two premolars in each quadrant (giving them thirty-two teeth). Present-day hominoids and cercopithecoids can be distinguished by the cusp patterns on their lower molars. Hominoids tend to have five cusps separated by a Y-shaped fissure pattern (a Y-5 cusp pattern) while cercopithecoids have four cusps arranged in two pairs, each linked by a loph (a bilophodont

four-cusp pattern). Current thinking is that the hominoid Y-5 cusp pattern represents the more primitive catarrhine condition of the stem ancestor of hominoids and cercopithecoids, while the Old World monkey bilophodont pattern is the more derived. This derived bilophodont monkey pattern will take on significance in my later discussion of the dietary adaptations of Miocene apes and monkeys. In constructing phylogenetic relationships dental anatomy is extremely important because teeth are normally under strict genetic control, and they are the most likely part of an organism to be preserved in the fossil record.

8. The only major site for Oligocene primitive anthropoids is the Fayum Depression about 150 kilometers from Cairo, Egypt. Several taxa are currently seen as candidates for reconstructing ancestral-descendant relationships including the long-snouted *Aegyptopithecus*, a well-known, considerably documented, early catarrhine with a calendar age of thirty-four million years. Recent postcranial materials indicate that this species was a "robust arboreal quadruped," which is widely viewed as the baseline locomotor pattern for early anthropoids, while a recent interpretation of this fossil's cranial morphology also suggests that it represents a plausible generalized template for the basal catarrhine condition (see Ankel-Simons, Fleagle, and Chatrath 1998; Köhler and Moyà-Solà 1997). Although the fossilized remains of the Fayum primates make it possible to separate prosimians from early anthropoids, a consensus has not yet been reached on the definitive character states that make up the common anthropoid ancestor of both monkeys and apes. For discussions see Köhler and Moyà-Solà (1997); Andrews (1996); and see Conroy (1990: 149–53) for a detailed and comparative account of the morphological traits of higher primates at the Fayum. See Conroy et al. (1998) for a discussion of endocranial structures of early hominids.

9. The Miocene was the heyday for hominoids, a time when a huge and diverse array of apes appeared. Currently over thirty genera are formally identified (Ward 1993; Begun, Ward, and Rose 1997; Begun 1992, 1995). The first adaptive radiation took place in Africa during the early Miocene with the arrival of such forms as *Proconsul*, *Afropithecus*, and the intriguing *Morotopithecus*, a taxon whose newly recovered postcranial materials seem more derived than other early Miocene apes, suggesting to Gebo et al. (1997: 403) that perhaps "it is the sister taxon of all living hominoids." However, more postcranial materials are needed before the status of *Morotopithecus* can be determined.

10. A complete and undistorted skull of *Victoriapithecus* (a middle Miocene Old World monkey) provides evidence that the *earliest* Old World monkeys were adapted to a frugivorous diet (Benefit and McCrossin 1997). Anatomical indicators also show that apes were also adapted to a frugivorous diet, with Andrews (1992: 645) stressing that "the majority [of hominoids] were arboreal frugivores occupying much the same niche as equivalent-sized monkeys today." Galili and An-

drews (1995) proposed that monkeys evolved certain derived immunological and biochemical processes that gave them a dietary edge. In 1981, Andrews proposed that monkeys evolved a specialized digestive tract to consume unripe fruit, a thesis he underscored recently by emphasizing that "the evolution of the colobine stomach has been put forward as a cause of the shift of cercopithecines to a more frugivorous diet, with destructive consequences for apes, which declined from 81% catarrhine species diversity in the early Miocene of Africa to 27% in the late Miocene to only 8% today" (Andrews 1996: 268). Temerin and Cant (1983) also claim that cheek pouches along with bilophodont molars aided Miocene cercopithecines by enhancing their digestive efficiency over apes.

11. It is well established in primatology that environmental variables, and especially a species' fundamental niche, act to constrain the size and ranging patterns of all primate societies. In paleoanthropology, the anatomical features of primates are useful for inferring foraging patterns that, in turn, provide information on the social organization of a species. See Hunt (1991); Napier and Napier (1985); and Andrews (1996) for discussions. Also see Maryanski and Turner (1992) for an analysis of the relationship between niche survival and shifting organizational patterns.

12. Right now, the Miocene fossil record is in flux because of recently discovered fossil specimens, with contradictory interpretations of molecular and fossil data being published—seemingly almost weekly. *Kenyapithecus* is still considered the most numerous East African large-bodied hominoid, an important genus because it helps to document ape positional behavior from the early to middle Miocene, a newly discovered skeleton linking it to *Proconsul*—notably "monkeylike" traits that suggest arboreal quadrupedalism as its locomotor mode (Benefit and McCrossin 1995: 246). *Kenyapithecus* also has a number of derived traits in the elbow and foot suggestive of a greater grasping ability (Nakatsukasa et al. 1998). During the late Miocene, the appearance of such European apes as *Oreopithecus*, *Dryopithecus* and *Ouranopithecus* are now a source of contention. For example, recent postcranial findings suggest that *Dryopithecus* has traits that lean toward the African ape orthograde locomotor posture (see Moyà-Solà and Köhler 1996; Andrews 1992; Ungar 1996). And, most surprisingly, *Oreopithecus*, who does closely resemble modern hominoids in anatomy but who is otherwise enigmatic because of certain bizarre characteristics, has now been reassessed by Harrison and Rook (1997: 347) as being "phyletically closely related to the extant hominoids." Meanwhile, Kay and Ungar (1997: 148–49) recently proposed that monkeys may have "pushed hominoids to increase their digestive efficiency" when some escaped to Europe, noting that *Oreopithecus* (unlike other apes) has derived "shearing values within the cercopithecoid range." And, Stewart and Disotell (1998) recently attempted to link Miocene European hominoids, such as *Ouranopithecus*, to African hominoids with "an out of Africa to Europe and back to Africa" scenario which,

they claim, eventually initiated a lineage that contained the LCA of living hominoids. See Gibbons (1998) and, for a recent overview of Miocene hominoids, see Begun, Ward, and Rose (1997).

13. In all primate societies, one sex departs the natal unit at puberty. With few exceptions, all monkey societies have male-biased dispersal, with females staying and forming tight-knit matrifocal lineages composed of up to four generations of mothers, grandmothers, aunts, and female siblings. For this reason monkey societies are often called "female-bonded" societies. Among apes, both males and females depart at puberty (with the exception of the male chimpanzee, who no longer remains in daily contact with his mother but does stay within his natal community). I should emphasize that female-biased dispersal at puberty is rare among primates (and also rare among mammals), but it is universal among apes (Pusey and Packer 1987; Greenwood 1980; Andelman 1986). Female exogamy among human hominoids is also favored by the overwhelming majority of studied human societies (Ember 1978; Murdock 1967). See also Wrangham (1987) and Foley and Lee (1989), where an emphasis is placed on the LCA hominoid structure as a model for understanding hominoid organization.

14. Gorilla groups are typically composed of one silverback male, a number of females, and dependent offspring. Yet, some groups (or bands) have up to four males with four or more gorilla groups sharing an average home range of fifteen square miles, and with resident groups occasionally meeting up, traveling and even bedding down together (Fossey 1972; Yamagiwa 1983; Schaller 1962). Within gorilla groups relations are casual and fluid. Although tolerant of each other, familiar adult males are self-contained, engaging in few overt interactions. Adult females also interact only rarely, although they are tolerant of each other (Harcourt 1977, 1979). Some research suggests that gorillas may also have a community form of organization, although the data are not definitive on the issue (Emlen and Schaller 1960; Imanishi 1965; Reynolds 1966: 44; Maryanski 1987, 1993, 1997a).

15. Maryanski used only common chimpanzees in her network analysis. However, there are two species of chimpanzees: the widespread common chimpanzee and the bonobo, who is a smaller and more isolated species. Bonobo chimpanzees are similar to common chimpanzees in organizational patterns (e.g., female transfer) but there is a greater female-female affiliation. This affiliation is the result of selection on females for a unique "genital-to-genital rubbing" or "GG rubbing," whereby two females make physical contact by rubbing their genitals together rapidly as they ventrally hold each other. This behavior, according to Furuichi, is very different from monkey-type cohesion and is not a bonding behavior per se. Rather, it helps to relieve tension among unrelated females who must feed in close propinquity because of the distribution of food resources (see Furuichi 1989 for a discussion).

16. Only chimpanzee females move *between* communities, but all adults freely move about *within* their own community, either alone or in momentary "social" circles whose composition is ever shifting, lasting a few minutes or several hours. With few kinship obligations, members turn to "friends" or choose to be aloof. Adult females, for example, spend about 70 percent of their time alone with only their dependent offspring for company. But the lack of stable micro-groupings is counterbalanced at the macro level because this freedom from tight-knit cliques allows a weakly tied social structure to share a common ranging area, linking together individuals who feel an overall "sense of community." Only the community endures over intergenerational time. See Wrangham et al. (1994) and Goodall (1996), who were instrumental in uncovering the "spirit of community" among our closest relatives.

17. Cerling et al. (1997) maintain that between eight and six million years ago (the dividing lines between the Miocene and Pliocene epochs), a significant change in vegetation occurred (i.e., a global expansion of plants or biomass with a significant C4 component), which is disclosed in the fossilized tooth enamel of equides, elephants, and other large-crowned mammals (i.e., the carbon isotope composition of enamel points at this time to a dietary shift from C3 to a C4 plant biomass). In addition to dietary changes (i.e., a C4-dominated diet is usually associated with grazing), a period of faunal turnover ensued with more open-country faunas appearing in the fossil record. In east Africa during the terminal Miocene, the change occurred very rapidly as "open wooded-grassland habitats replaced the earlier less seasonal woodland/forest habitats" (ibid.: 156). The Pliocene ushered in "a sharp increase in seasonality with the faunas evolving a savanna-mosaic character" (ibid.). In fact, the flora and fauna shift was so dramatic that "grazing antelopes and hippos replaced chevotains and anthracotheres as the dominant artiodactyls" (ibid.). And, as the authors emphasize, during this time hominoids again declined when "monkeys underwent a major radiation, replacing the diverse early and middle Miocene hominoid assemblage" (ibid.). See also Van Der Merwe and Thackeray (1997) for confirmation of stable carbon isotope analysis of Plio-Pleistocene ungulate teeth.

18. An open-country habitat is dramatically more dangerous than a closed-canopy habitat. In primary forests, males and females can move about alone on the forest floor, with the knowledge that escape to the trees is always there. But open-country living limits this option. In her review of primate predation, Connie Anderson (1986) found that the higher the predation, the less likely were male primates to wander about alone, while female primates in a predator-ridden environment were *never* found alone.

19. The hearing equipment of monkeys, apes, and humans is nearly the same. The auditory system among these primates evolved to detect instantly brief but

sudden sounds such as the cracks, pops, thuds, snaps, and cries that signal predation and threat (Masterton 1992). Once alerted, the visual system then normally attends to the object in space (Khanna and Tonndorf 1978). This auditory sensitivity in higher primates is so essential to their survival that, according to Masterton and Diamond (1973: 431), "it is virtually impossible to truncate the central auditory system in such a way as to make an animal incapable of responding to a brief sound."

20. Patas monkeys (*Erythrocebus*) who live in regions of dry African woodland savanna rely upon their speed to avoid predators and have the typical quadrupedal four-limb pattern of locomotion of monkeys that selection had worked upon to generate a cheetahlike gait of patas clocked at speeds of thirty-five miles per hour (Napier and Napier 1985: 146; Hall 1967). Like *Homo sapiens*, patas walk with a long stride and have the longest limbs of any nonhuman primate (Isbell et al. 1998).

21. Early hominid and baboon fossils during the Plio-Pleistocene have been uncovered in the same locality (Simon and Delson 1978), denoting that both faced similar predation and other selection pressures. Contemporary baboons (*Papio*) in open-country environments can number up to two hundred individuals with regular progression in troop movements that put vulnerable females and young in the center and mature males with large canines in the front and rear of the group, clearly an impressive challenge to predators (Rhine, Boland, and Lodwick 1985). In each baboon troop, males typically form a dominance hierarchy, with material genealogies making up the core bonding networks in baboon society (Melnick and Pearl 1987).

22. Since both monkeys and apes can already use visual cues of face and body for fine-grained communication (Maryanski 1997b: 196–98), selection had something in place to work on; and so, selection simply enhanced the ability of hominids to engage in fine-grained signaling and interpreting with visual cues. In addition, as noted earlier, if hominids had the neural assemblages of present-day monkeys that orient conspecifics to visual reading of facial gestures, then selection could work that much more rapidly.

23. Moreover, bonobos can easily understand via the auditory channel, without formal training, naturally spoken human syntax when they are simply exposed to a language-rich environment during their primary years. This indicates that their brains are wired for language potential (although they cannot use their vocal track to speak).

24. There were a number of hominids coexisting on the African savanna (see Figure 1.2) up until at least a million years ago (see Andrews [1995] for a discussion); at some point they may have come into contact, leading to competition and conflict. Under these conditions of direct conflict for resources, the better organized would surely win out.

CHAPTER 2

Forces of Selection and the Evolution of Emotions

Let me recapitulate the argument thus far: as apes were forced to live under savanna conditions, they faced the problem of how to become better organized. Highly structured social relations would be fitness-enhancing because group-oriented primates could gather and share food collectively, while coordinating activities to defend a comparatively slow and weak animal from predation.[1] Yet, Alexandra Maryanski's (1987) coding of field studies on primates for patterns of tie-formation among present-day apes and her (1993, 1992) cladistic analysis of the last common ancestor to humans and present-day apes indicate that the distant ancestors of today's hominoids could not become monkeys; they simply did not have it in their neurological wiring to be highly organized in the matrilines that would increase inter-generational solidarity and, hence, fitness in an open, terrestrial habitat, filled with predators. True, when forced to live in close proximity in caged situations, present-day apes do form male dominance hierarchies and clique formation (DeWaal, 1996),[2] but they also reveal considerable conflict under these conditions, which would decrease fitness in an environment dictating *cohesive* group structures. Selection pressures were intense, forcing a punctuated process of very rapid change in the behavioral and organizational propensities of apes, if they were to survive. Most did not, but somehow the ancestors of hominids were able to reproduce themselves by becoming more tightly structured at the group level. The key to this process, I hypothesize, was gaining some degree of neocortical control of subcortically-generated emotions (see Chapter 4) and, then, expanding both the cortical and subcortical abilities of our distant ancestors to communicate visually a wide variety of emotional dispositions. Out of such communication came new, stronger bonds that allowed hominids to adapt to the niches of the African savanna.

In this chapter, my goal is to examine the process of natural selection on the hominid anatomy, especially neuroanatomy, that created an increasingly emotional animal who could use its expanded emotional abilities to communicate visually. I will group these under two headings: *indirect* selection forces and *direct* selection forces. The indirect forces can be visualized as necessary preadaptations[3] that gave the direct selection forces something to work on during the evolution of emotional communication among hominids.

Indirect Selection Forces

HOW DID THE ABILITY TO USE LANGUAGE EVOLVE IN PRIMATES?

Norman Geschwind (1965a, 1965b) had a brilliant idea in the 1960s: Could the capacity to use language simply be an unselected by-product of the need to integrate the sense modalities under visual dominance among early primates adapting to the arboreal habitat? Much of the neocortex is composed of cortices governing the sense modalities and association cortices for integrating sensory inputs.[4] Arboreal primates needed to be visually dominant, a significant deviation from the basic mammalian design of olfactory dominance; and in a three-dimensional environment, there had to be integration of the sense modalities so that auditory and tactile information was consistent with visual impressions. Selection produced mammals with visual dominance and the ability to integrate sensory inputs; and this rewiring of the neuroanatomy is what created the capacity in primates to use language. As noted in the last chapter, this neurological rewiring had nothing to do with communication; rather, it evolved to facilitate movement through, and adaptation to, the arboreal habitat.

There is enormous controversy over whether or not chimpanzees and other apes such as the gorilla and orangutan display the rudiments of language abilities (e.g., Terrace et al. 1979; Bickerton 1990; Savage-Rumbaugh et al. 1993). It is difficult to straddle the fence on the debate; and so, I take the side of Sue Savage-Rumbaugh and her collaborators that bonobo chimpanzees can learn a vocabulary of perhaps one thousand words, understand these words in naturally spoken syntax, and construct through their visual-tactile sense modalities very crude and simple sentences that have meaning to humans. While certainly debatable, I see these capacities of bonobo chimpanzees as language. Moreover, studies with common chimpanzees reveal the same linguistic facility (Gardner, Gardner, and Cantfort 1989). Obviously, apes do not use this kind of language in their natural habitats, but when pressed they can evidence language abilities of two- to three-year-old human children. They can do so because Geschwind is probably correct in his insight: the basic wiring for language came with the transformation of primates to visual dominance and with the growth of the ape neocortex relative to that of monkeys.

Even if we do not accept Geschwind's hypothesis, recent work by Patrick Gannon et al. (1998) indicates that the areas of the chimpanzee brain that generate ape-language are the same as those areas of our brain that are responsible for human language. Along the planum temporale, the same asymmetries between the left and right side of human and chimpanzee brains can be found, although the human asymmetry is somewhat more pronounced. Data from MRI and immunocytochemical analysis indicate that this area is used to process communication, regardless of its source or form, whether gestural-visual or vocal-auditory. For chimpanzees, as for the last common ancestor to humans and chimpanzees, visual gestures of the face and body as well as occasional use of tactile modes of communication dominate over vocal signals, but nonetheless, these forms of communication utilize the same areas of the brain as humans use for vocal communication. Gannon proposes that the last common ancestor to chimpanzees and humans not only possessed these centers for communication along the left temporal lobe, but that they evolved in both hominoids and hominids, eventually becoming vocal for humans and heightening the amazing abilities of chimpanzees to communicate visually. Other data on hand use and gestural communication by chimpanzees show an overwhelming bias toward right-hand use, which, like their human cousins, means that the left side of the brain regulates gestural communication by the hands (Hopkins and Leavens 1998). Thus, it is the left side of the brain in apes and, no doubt, in the last common ancestor to apes and humans, that was available for selection to enhance nonverbal communication.

My view is that initial selection along the hominid line worked on these areas of communication to make hominids more attuned to reading visual gestures in a kind of emotional language that would increase solidarity among low-sociality animals. Only later, as the selective advantages of communication increased, did a shift occur to a more vocally based language. And as I will argue further in Chapter 5, human speech is built upon the emotional languages that preceded human capacities for vocalization.

Whether one accepts either or both Geschwind's and Gannon's conclusions, it is now clear that natural selection had neurological structures to work on, as language had fitness-enhancing value. Almost immediately after apes reached the African savanna there were pressures for enhanced communication—for a visually-based, rather than auditory, language—built around increased emotional capacities. Verbal language could not have fitness-enhancing effect until the brain had been further rewired to produce an animal capable of controlling emotions to some degree and, more significantly, of using them in visually based and solidarity-producing emotional communication. Verbal language thus could not evolve, I believe, until the cortical and subcortical emotion systems[5] of the brain had become better-integrated and used effectively in solidarity-producing communication. Once these changes in the brain were in place, selection could produce an ever more verbal primate. Yet true spoken language required additional adaptations in the neuroanatomy of hominids if it was to emerge in the hominid line.

THE VISUAL READING OF EMOTIONS

It would seem reasonable to assume that the first forms of primates' communication would come through their dominant sense modality (Napier and Napier 1985). True, all primates use audio calls to communicate intentions and dispositions, but among African apes it is clear that they also rely on very subtle facial and bodily gestures. In fact, recent findings on the auditory capacities of bonobo chimpanzees (*Pan panicus*) indicate that they are able to employ grammatical rules for perceiving speech sounds, suggesting that the placement of the vocal channel under cortical control for the *production* of voluntary sounds would not involve a major neurological overhaul, since the neocortex already houses much of the auditory modality (see Savage-Rumbaugh et al. 1993). Moreover, some Old World monkeys have shown a capacity for voluntary vocalizations that include encoded semantic qualities. For example, vervets (*Cercopithecus aethiops*) can vocally denote friend or foe and thus can warn conspecifics of danger. They have an alarm call for the approach of leopards, which seemingly means to flee to the top of the canopy; and an alarm call regarding snakes, which warns conspecifics to keep away from thickets (Cheney 1984). While these signals are clearly learned, the anterior cingulate gyrus within the limbic system retains control of most nonhuman primate vocalizations (see Snowdon 1990; Steklis 1985). Thus, there were in-place structures that selection could use to make primates speech-users, but my feeling is that these neurostructures were secondary to visually based communication. For among apes, lip smacking, movement of jaws, contraction of facial muscles, body countenance, hand gestures, and other nonauditory gestures are far more important than auditory cues for giving off information about self, dispositions, moods, feelings, and environmental conditions.

For selection to have enhanced communications among the ape ancestors of hominids on the open savanna, it would most likely have worked initially on these already-in-place visual modes of communication. Indeed, there might even have been selection against auditory modes, since emotionally charged and loud primates on the savanna were not likely to enhance their fitness. And so, given the necessary neurological wiring for use of signs, syntax, and sentence construction, and given that this ability came with visual dominance and its use for communication, then it is likely that selection began to change the brain further in order to increase the complexity and subtlety of communication with visual gestures.

In this way, a savanna-dwelling ape could send and receive information visually and, hence, quietly, under conditions where noise would increase risks of survival. The key to more effective visual communication was, of course, the signaling of emotions about feeling, mood, dispositions to act, reactions to acts of others, threats in the environment, and other necessary information that would, first of all, create stronger bonds among apes and, second, generate patterns of bonding that would enhance fitness. In order for this expanded capacity for communication to develop, however, it was necessary for the brain to be rewired so as to gain some degree of cortical control over the emotional responses being used in visual communication.

CORTICAL CONTROL OF EMOTIONS

Selection on the African savanna would favor a quiet primate who could control its emotional outbursts, or at least stifle their loudness. Selection for noise reduction would be particularly intense for primates who were not organized in terms of hierarchies of dominance and matrilines that could afford protection for noisy behaviors. *Cynocephalus* and anubis baboons (*Papio*), for example, are noisy but they organize large numbers of individuals in tight social structures and, hence, do not need to worry about being loud. In contrast, patas monkeys (*Erythrocebus*) are organized in smaller haremlike groupings of females with a dominant male who cannot provide the same protection as multiple males in a larger grouping; as a result, these groupings of patas monkeys move quietly across the savanna. Apes trying to survive on the savanna were probably not as well organized as patas monkeys, and it is for this reason that I believe selection would operate to create an animal with cortical control of loud emotional outbursts. Most apes do not have this kind of control, however, as a stimulus will often evoke a series of emotional and typically loud cries (Kaada 1951). Therefore, if emotions being signaled through the visual sense modality were to be the primary vehicle for enhanced communication and solidarity among apes, they would have to come under neocortical control in order to avoid noisy emotional outbursts along the auditory channel. The expansion of association areas of the neocortex in hominids probably reflects one path to gaining additional cortical control of emotions, as do various neuro-pathways to subcortical areas where emotions are generated. These pathways appear sufficient to generate control over most emotions, at least until they reach a high pitch.

It seems likely that, once selection had operated to give hominids control over emotional outbursts and this control had been wired into their neurology, it could then be subject to further selection for more complex and fine-grained emotional communication, promoting increased social solidarity among comparatively low-sociality primates. In other words, emotions had to come under cortical regulation in order to be used as a vehicle for solidarity-producing communications. With this control, emotions could be emitted volitionally and used to forge stronger bonds and ties as hominids communicated back and forth their moods, feelings, and dispositions in quiet and subtle ways. And once such communication facilitated adaptation by creating more cohesive patterns of social organization, selection would expand these capacities.

All of the changes discussed above had to exist, I believe, before the more advanced forms of language evident among humans could evolve. Natural selection had to have existing structures on which to select if language in the human measure was to evolve. Moreover, transition from the language abilities of the ancestors of present-day apes or the last common ancestors of apes and hominids to a fully-speaking primate had to be gradual because the kinds of mutations involved in such a transition would be harmful if they altered radically and rapidly the neuroanatomy of an animal (Fisher 1930). Much of the neurological wiring for language facilities thus would have to be in place, and this wiring would have to exceed, I believe, the current language facilities of contemporary apes for selection to generate language capacities of humans. How would such wiring evolve?

The answer is implied in the discussion above. Selection built on what it was given as apes left the arboreal habitat: a visual primate with a generalized body form that could be utilized in nonverbal communication and a primate with neurological wiring that, if pushed (as is revealed in language studies of apes), could produce the rudiments of language. Moreover, chimpanzees appear to use subtle visual signals for intended messages about the environment, for, as E. W. Menzel (1971: 220) once noted, "one chimpanzee can convey to others, who have no other source of information, the presence, direction, quality, and relative quantity or preference value of distant hidden objects." Thus, it would not take a dramatic evolutionary leap to expand this capacity into a system of emotional communication. The ability to control emotions would be a prerequisite for such a development, and with this ability, selection was free to continuously upgrade the visual communications among hominids, as long as these had fitness-enhancing value. And clearly they did increase fitness—so much so that the basis of survival of hominids became emotional bonds constantly renewed with each face-to-face encounter during which emotions were signaled back and forth.

Once evolution took this path, the cortical and subcortical connections in the brain allowing for the volitional use of emotions in communication would be continuously expanded in order to increase the fitness-enhancing properties of emotionally laden visual communication. At some point, auditory content was ever more a part of this communication, building upon capacities for vocalization that present-day apes possess; and over time a shift in relative proportions of body and spoken language began to occur. One critical preadaptation was upright stance, which freed the vocal track for fine-grained enunciation of sounds (Hill 1972). This development occurred very early in hominid evolution so that savanna-dwelling primates would be able to see above the grasses[6] (since they had a reduced olfaction and could not rely on this sense, as most mammals on the savanna do). Several million years of rewiring of the cortical and subcortical portions of the brain was *the other preadaptation necessary for* producing ever more sophisticated language, based on growing repertoires of arbitrary signs, abilities to organize these in terms of some form of grammar, and the capacity to emit them volitionally in order to signal meaning and emotion to conspecifics (Miller 1972). This shift was well under way, I believe, with *Homo erectus*, but it had been slowly evolving with *Homo habilis* as ever more verbal content was inserted into a visually based mode of communication (Fleagle 1988: 440).

A verbal language has many advantages over a visual one (Maryanski and Turner, 1992: 64, 74). First, it can be used when the hands and body are otherwise occupied; this would have great fitness-enhancing value for communication among animals involved in gathering, hunting, and defense activities, wielding tools or holding infants in their hands and arms. Second, auditory language can be used without having to expose the full face and body for visual reading of meanings; in fact, no visual contact whatsoever is necessary. This would mean that animals could communicate rapidly without having to mobilize their bodies and faces; and they could do so without seeing each other. Such abilities would have great value, of course, in defense and in coordinating gathering and hunting activities. Third, vocal language gives communication new dimensions when accompanied by body language; vocalizations can keep one track of communication going (typically more instrumental) while the body can reveal another track of meaning (usually affective and emotional). And, if vocalizations can also be used to impart affect (via pitch, inflection, intonations, rhythms, pauses, and the like), then very complex meanings can be communicated; and these, in turn, would allow for more flexible and sophisticated patterns of social organization.

So, it might be asked: why didn't hominids go immediately to a verbal language? After all, they were upright with *Australopithecus*, and hence the vocal track was sufficiently open for selection to create animals capable of enunciating diverse sounds; they had gained control over auditory sounds in order to reduce their noise on the savanna; and they were under intense selection to develop ever more effective means of communication that could enhance social organization. Many would argue that, indeed, the first real languages were verbal; and they have a most plausible point of view.

Still, I do not think that they are correct, for at least some of the reasons in Gordon Hewes's (1973) pioneering argument. Building on the work of other scholars (e.g., Tylor 1868, 1871; Morgan 1877; Wallace 1895; Wundt 1916) who had maintained early on that the first language was primarily gestural, Hewes argued that the ability of contemporary great apes to use sign language suggests that visual signaling would be the easiest route to language among australopithecines. Use of the auditory channel for language would have been difficult for several reasons: First, calls among primates are almost all emotional, being used primarily to broadcast danger and other highly charged affective states. Second, the auditory modality was not cross-linked among early australopithecines with the visual and haptic modalities, and this linkage is a precondition for spoken language (Geschwind 1970). As Hewes (1973: 7) emphasized, "early hominids may have found it very difficult to acquire proto-language depending on controlled vocal production, to say nothing of language requiring the precise articulations of modern speech." Third, the vocal track of early hominids up to *Homo erectus* was not yet organized in ways that would facilitate speech production (Lieberman 1984; Lieberman and Crelin 1971; Lieberman, Crelin, and Klatt 1972). Fourth, higher primates' reliance on nonverbal gestures to communicate suggests that the ability to orient to visual gestures was already in place in the hominid line and, hence, subject to selection for a nonverbal language. Indeed, as Hewes (1973: 11) stressed, "it may be that the ability to acquire proposition language based on gestures [as is the case in the sign language among the deaf] is not only an older innate character of man, but one which is shared in rudimentary form at least with *Pongidae*." Fifth, spoken language depends upon cerebral lateralization and integration of left-right brain functions; in Hewes's view, this could not occur until (a) hominids had begun to use tools in a precise way (tool use, in Hewes's view, is a precondition for not only integrated lateralization but also for muscular control of the entire vocal apparatus necessary for speech production), and (b) higher cognitive abilities, as indicated by a larger cerebral cortex, had evolved.

I do not fully agree with Hewes's argument, but it provides plausible reasons for doubting that the first language among hominids was verbal. I would add to Hewes's list several points of my own, drawing from the argument that I have developed thus far. First, for language to produce social bonds, it has to be emotional; and emotions are still best communicated visually, rather than verbally.[7] And to the degree that emotions were the key to overcoming the propensity for low sociality among apes, emotions would have to be the initial target of natural selection. Second, apes are visually dominant; selection, always tending to take the conservative route, would use the dominant sense modality of an animal as a means for expanding interpersonal communication. Third, language facility in the human measure could not emerge without the preadaptation provided by rewiring of the brain for visual language, with auditory signaling slowly becoming mixed with visual signals over several million years to produce the complex communication evident with humans (far earlier, I would add, than Hewes's argument suggests). And fourth, the areas for speech production (Broca's area) and comprehension (Wernicke's area) along the left hemisphere clearly look like rather late additions to human neuroanatomy (see Figure 4.1 on page 94). True, left asymmetry is evident with apes and, hence, was in place and subject to selection long ago, but the fact that language requires these two "translation boxes" for downloading the brain's way of thinking (which clearly is not verbal, unless we wish to slow it down and "talk to ourselves") and then uploading auditory signals back into the brain's mode of thinking suggests that the brain is organized more for visual than auditory processing. Indeed, I would even go so far as to suggest that "thinking" is constrained by the visual bias in the brain's wiring,[8] occurring in gestalts and configurations of images that have to be downloaded into slow, sequential auditory signals.

For these reasons, then, I believe that we are on the right track when viewing the most distinctive feature of early hominids as their emotional capacities. And, if we stop to think about it for a moment, these are still our most distinctive capacities—with all due respect to our language abilities. Indeed, people feel uncomfortable in face-to-face interactions where body and face language are absent, indicating that it is speech that supplements visual communication rather than the reverse.

Direct Selection Forces

If we assume that the big obstacle to the survival of apes on the African savanna was their lack of sociality and cohesive group structure, then selection forces were directed at reorganizing the hominid brain so as to increase sociality and bonding among hominids (Maryanski and Turner 1992: 65–67). As I have emphasized, the most direct way for selection to go was enhancement of the emotional capacities of hominids in ways that enabled them—like their human descendants—to forge social bonds and sustain social structures. In a very real sense, selection was constrained by sociological imperatives of organizing an animal in tighter-knit structures. These sociological imperatives can be viewed as the more direct selection pressures operating on hominids. What, then, were these pressures? I argue that selection operated along several fronts (see Turner 1996a, 1997a, 1997b): (1) mobilization and channeling of emotional energy, (2) attunement of interpersonal responses, (3) sanctioning, (4) moral coding, (5) valuing and exchanging resources, and (6) rational decision making. These six paths of evolution in hominids are what would be necessary to convert an animal with relatively low degrees of innate sociality into a more social and cohesively organized species, and they all depend upon elaboration of hominids' emotional capacities.

MOBILIZATION AND CHANNELING OF EMOTIONAL ENERGY

All primates can emote and reveal considerable emotional energy, and thus it is not so much the level of the emotional thermostat that is critical as the spectrum of emotional energy influencing patterns of sociality and social organization. The more diverse the emotions that can be mobilized during the course of interaction, the more varied are the forms of sociality and solidarity that can be created and sustained; and the more flexible are the social relations formed, the more fitness-enhancing are these relations. Thus, the subcortical areas of the brain that generate emotions, as well as their connections to the expanding neocortex, must have been rewired to produce an animal who could mobilize emotional energy in many directions and who could channel this energy into emotionally laden social bonds.

Apes could not rely on the female bonds that create matrilines among monkeys, nor could they build up male authority to monkeylike proportions (and even if selection went in this latter direction, male dominance alone could not sustain cohesive social structures[9]). What, then, could ape-like animals do? Most could do nothing and therefore died out; in fact, many species might have traveled along the path of enhancing male dominance, only to discover that this alone could not create sufficiently cohesive and flexible group structures. Somehow selection found another solution among hominids: it restructured the brain to produce higher levels of emotional energy channeled into a larger repertoire of emotional states. This change enabled hominids to mobilize emotional energy beyond mere power relations or mother-children bonds into more subtle and complex patterns of affect among all age and sex classes in a group. Yet, even after millions of years of evolution expanding the capacity of hominids to mobilize more varied emotional states, social interaction among humans still requires the use of emotion-arousing rituals (Goffman 1967; Collins 1987, 1988). Why should this be so?

Virtually all theories of interpersonal processes among humans recognize that interactions start with ritual openings and end with ritual closings, with additional rituals for tracking the flow of emotional energy, for repairing breaches to this flow, and for sustaining or shifting topics and other features of the interaction (Turner 1988). Thus, the mobilization and release of emotional energy in humans still needs a source of ignition for jump-starting an interaction and a monitoring system for tracking the flow of interaction. Even after millions of years of evolution along the hominid line, humans are still not able to spontaneously mobilize their interpersonal energies without rituals; they need rituals to get the process going, keep it going, and end it in ways that promote solidarity. Other animals use rituals, of course, but these tend to be neurologically hard-wired, and confined to very basic adaptive behaviors such as courtship, mating, sexual combat, defense of territories, and other critical activities. In contrast, humans need to use rituals at *each and every* episode of interaction and to employ them continuously during the course of an interaction in order to sustain focus, emotional moods, and solidarity. Herbert Spencer (1874–96) and Émile Durkheim (1912) recognized this fact of social life a long time ago, and most interpersonal theories build some model of ritual activity into their respective conceptualizations, but none seem to wonder *why* rituals would have to be so pervasive and prominent in human interaction.

The answer lies, I believe, in our ape ancestry's penchant for weak ties, mobility, autonomy, and low sociality. Although hominid brains were probably altered in order to increase the ability to mobilize a greater variety of emotions, selection did not wipe out more primal propensities for low sociality. Rather, evolutionary evidence suggests that the expanding capacity to mobilize emotional energy and to use rituals to assure that the requisite level of energy is generated was only laid over older propensities for lower levels of sociality and solidarity. Humans are thus of two minds, as it were, one pushing us to use rituals to mobilize emotional energy, the other asserting the tendencies of our ape ancestors.

This duality is reflected in human social arrangements and ideologies. On the one hand, we crave solidarity, closeness, community, and other associative relations, while on the other hand we rebel against authority, constraint, and control by others. We develop collectivistic ideologies, only to resent the constraint that they force upon our ape ancestry. We revel in freedom, autonomy, individualism, and egoism, only to feel that something is missing—the social bonds of solidarity. Since this duality and the constant dialectic that it sustains seem to be part of our neurology, we are doomed to live with it unless new selection pressures take the species in another direction.

My point in mentioning this duality is to emphasize how precarious the new ways of mobilizing energy were for hominids. Selection did not create a new being, but placed half of a new one over our ape legacy—a legacy that is still with us and not likely to go away. Thus, humans did not become solidarity-seeking junkies; they became animals capable of using rituals to mobilize bonds, *when they needed them.*

ATTUNEMENT OF INTERPERSONAL RESPONSES

As selection expanded the repertoire of emotions used in interpersonal relations among hominids, sociological imperatives for solidarities built from mutual interpretations of dispositions, moods, sentiments, and feelings channeled selection. For the kinds of social structures constructed by humans and, presumably, by humans' hominid ancestors required relatively fine attunement of responses, at least some of the time. Since chimpanzees appear able to communicate a great deal visually (Menzel 1971), this ability was probably evident in the last common ancestor to apes and humans and hence was subject to further selection. Thus, as selection expanded the

repertoire of emotions in hominids, it did so in order to create greatly enhanced attunement of responses. George Herbert Mead's (1934) concept of
role taking captures the essence of how selection was channeled: significant
symbols or gestures emitted by others are used by individuals to assume
their perspective in order to better coordinate their actions with these others. Ralph H. Turner's (1962) concept of *role making* captures the reciprocal of this process: gestures emitted by an individual consciously and un-
consciously signal to others a line of conduct, as well as the dispositions
and moods associated with this conduct. Role making is thus the stuff that
makes role taking possible. An increased ability to role-make and role-take
was the key for low-sociality animals in desperate need to get organized
with others and to reveal more permanent interpersonal attachments, for
only in this way could hominids become more attuned to each other.

As I have argued, this process of role making and taking was initially visual; that is, the significant symbols that signaled mood and dispositions to
act were primarily visual; only later in hominid evolution did they become
ever more associated with auditory cues. There are several reasons for this
conclusion, even if some are restatements of my earlier argument. First, vision is primates' dominant sense modality and, hence, the easiest to use for
the purposes of interpersonal attunement; if selection was operating rapidly, too much neurological work would have to be done to reshape the au-
ditory-speech modality for fine-grained attunement. Second, if my earlier
speculation on how the brain thinks in terms of visual gestalts is correct,
then visual images of others' moods and dispositions would automatically
plug into the brain's way of thinking. To use auditory modalities would require a major rewiring of the brain for specialized cortices like Broca's and
Wernicke's areas. Even with some left hemispheric asymmetry in place, selection could not work with enough speed to produce dedicated speech areas in early hominids who needed a quick route to attuning their responses
to each other in order to promote more intense social bonds and solidarities. Third, visual cues are gestalts of information; as such, they can impart
a great deal of information simultaneously. In contrast, auditory signals are
sequential and slow, signaling information over much longer periods of
time than visual gestalts. Hence, visual cues avoid the bottleneck of auditory sequencing and can impart information more rapidly. If hominids
needed to find new ways to read each other's more fine-tuned moods, the
visual modality, then, would be the fastest route to follow. This is especially

likely to have been the case because the auditory channel is not particularly efficient or robust in communicating feelings, moods, and dispositions, nor is the brain particularly well equipped for *temporal* pattern recognition outside of music melodies and speech rhythms (Warren and Warren 1976: 173; M. Jones 1976; Freides 1974). Considerable selection on the auditory system was necessary, no doubt, to rewire the brain so that speech could effectively communicate finer-grained states of affect. Thus, the auditory channel can add information about feeling and mood by virtue of inflection, rhythm, tone, amplitude, and other manipulations of sounds, but this information is never arrayed in as complete a pattern as visually based body language.

Thus, attunement was first a visual matter, only later to become increasingly supplemented by auditory cues. And even today in humans, people feel much more comfortable when they can see each other as they talk, especially for interactions involving high degrees of emotional attunement. It is questionable, in fact, if talk alone can generate much emotional attunement, unless each party is able to construct visual images, if only in their imaginations, about the body language that accompanies talk.[10]

SANCTIONING

Patterns of social organization that are socially constructed, as opposed to being innately driven, cannot emerge and persist without sanctions, both positive and negative. A negative sanction imposes punishments for behavior that does not conform to expectations, whereas a positive sanction communicates associative affect for meeting or exceeding expectations. Thus, if hominids were to construct more stable group structures, they needed to use sanctions, especially since such stable groupings were not part of their genetic makeup. For, as Maryanski's (1987) review of the data on apes shows, the genetic push for organization among apes appears to be toward the larger regional population or community,[11] with the groups within this community being very loosely structured and highly fluid. Such organizational patterns could be adapted to the savanna *only* if the local groups became more stable, cohesive, and orderly. And such changes could only occur through the mutual impositions of sanctions by animals who could use and read a larger repertoire of positive and negative emotions.

Indeed sanctions have no "teeth" or force unless they are part of emotional responses; if sanctions were to go beyond brute force, they had to be linked with a variety of positive and negative emotional states. Thus, in order for sanctions to sustain cohesive social structures among comparatively low-sociality animals, they needed to revolve around mixes of positive and negative sanctions associated with a much expanded emotional repertoire beyond simple assertion, aversion, and satisfaction. These kinds of primary emotions had to be combined, elaborated, and extended in order to promote solidarities among animals not genetically programmed to exhibit such solidarities.

Negative sanctions can be very effective because they rest upon the activation of mammals' most primal emotions: aversion-fear and assertion-aggression. These are most primal because an animal without fear is soon selected out, and one without the ability to mobilize defensive aggression is doomed to die at the hands of its predators when unable to flee and escape (Le Doux 1991, 1993a, 1993b, 1996). Thus, negative sanctions involve one party's anger (or some variant of this emotion) directed at another's failure to meet expectations; and the power of the sanction to effect behavioral changes resides in its ability to arouse fear (or some variant of this emotion) in the offending party. The problem with negative sanctions, however, is that they are based on the least associative of emotions—fear and anger. Moreover, the use of one individual's anger to sanction another individual will not only arouse fear, but will often generate counter-anger, with the result that negative sanctions can potentially initiate complex cycles of anger-fear-anger that do not promote solidarity (Turner 1995, 1996a).

To overcome these disassociative effects, more complicated emotions like shame and guilt evolved, such that negative sanctions did not initiate a rawly angry response. Rather, combinations of fear, anger, and sadness generate emotions like guilt and shame, which, as I will explore in the next chapter, are particularly effective emotions because they make the party who has not met expectations self-motivated to somehow make amends without excessive anger at those imposing a negative sanction (with much of the anger being directed at self). Thus, if negative sanctions were to produce associative bonds, it was necessary to wire the brain to produce varied and complex emotions that could take away the dissociative effects of negative sanctioning. This necessity became ever more critical as the neocortex of hominids expanded so that they could remember past sanctions that might evoke angry responses for past indignities in ways that would disrupt present efforts to maintain solidarity. Moreover, as hominids' emotional repertoire expanded, highly volatile emotions like rage, hate, fury, and disgust became possible; and these kinds of emotions would be highly disruptive to bonding, particularly if they could be readily revoked as the cognitive abilities of hominids for storing memories began to reach human proportions.

Thus, group solidarity cannot be built and sustained on negative emotions alone; social structures must also be constructed from positive sanctions that arouse more associative responses (Coleman 1988; Hechter 1987), it is possible that these kinds of positive emotions are not as hard-wired into mammals as fear and anger.[12] True, the mother-infant bond is universal among mammals, and even low-sociality apes can form some positive friendship bonds, as is the case among chimpanzee brothers. But compared to humans, apes are comparatively low on the emotional valences revolving around satisfaction-happiness; it is likely, then, that the brain of hominids was rewired so as to produce variants and combinations of satisfaction and happiness. New emotions like pride, love, joy, ecstasy, and delight became possible as limbic systems became rewired for emotions built from the primary affective state of satisfaction-happiness. Selection must have been intense to create limbic systems capable of generating the positive emotions on which solidarity and close social bonds are constructed. There was enough to work on—areas such as the anterior cingulate gyrus producing mother-infant bonds, areas like the brain stem releasing neurotransmitters, and areas such as the diencephalon and pituitary producing neuroactive peptides—to build up rapidly the ability to experience, emit, and read a wide variety of emotional variants of satisfaction-happiness.

Of particular importance for social bonding and solidarity is the emotion of pride, which consists mostly of happiness with self shadowed by fear that one might not be able to act in ways that make one proud. Charles Horton Cooley (1916) first recognized the importance of pride, and more recent work by Thomas Scheff (1988, 1990a, 1990b) continues to demonstrate its importance. Pride is especially significant because it is tied to an individual's feelings about self as an object; and pride comes when expectations imposed by self and others have been met or exceeded. Positive sanctions are essential to the production of pride, but once activated, pride has the capacity to push individuals to meet expectations in the future and to secure the positive sanctions that come with such efforts. Moreover, pride makes individuals act in ways that forge positive social bonds, since pride is basically happiness about self, an emotion that tends to be contagious. And so, as others role-take with those experiencing pride they too tend to experience positive affect. Thus, very early in hominid evolution, selection probably gave the ancestors of humans the capacity to experience pride. Pride would then give individuals a compass directing them to meet expectations and to encourage, through their emission of positive sanctions, the same behaviors in others. Out of such mutual pride would come much stronger social bonds and solidarities than could otherwise be the case without pride.

There is some debate as to whether or not disappointment-sadness is a primary emotion. A more Freudian view would have it as the product of repression which drains emotional energy and causes both diffuse anxiety and depression. There is some merit to this argument but for my purposes here, I want only to emphasize that sadness is a critical emotion if sanctioning is to have the complexity necessary for creating social solidarity. If neurotransmitter and neuroactive peptide systems originally generated only small or moderate amounts of substances that appear to cause sadness or, as is often the case, they simply failed to generate those that cause satisfaction, selection worked on these systems to expand the ability of humans to feel and recognize variants and combinations of sadness in others. Sadness adds dimensions to the emotional repertoire not possible with only anger, fear, and satisfaction; and moreover, it becomes an important part of both negative and positive sanctioning. As noted above, negative sanctions that produce emotions like guilt and shame, which in my view are predominantly characterized by sadness (see Chapter 3), reduce the volatility of anger-fear-anger cycles and, at the same time, motivate individuals to make amends. Sadness is also associated with the power of positive sanctions, since the sadness that we feel when we do not receive such sanctions motivates us to act in ways assuring the receipt of them. True, severe sadness and depression work against social bonding, and primates clearly have the capacity to experience such deep emotions. Yet more short-term episodes of sadness are highly associative because they mobilize primates to secure positive and reinforcing positive sanctions; and when such sanctions do indeed produce positive emotions like satisfaction-happiness, sadness becomes a marker to the individual and those in its environment that efforts need to be made to sanction positively those signaling sadness. In this way, sadness becomes a kind of trigger for the activation of more positive sanctioning processes that ultimately produce the most solidarity. Thus, without sadness and derivative emotions such as shame and guilt, both negative and positive sanctioning would have less force, subtlety, and power to build social bonds from emotions.

Once the brain could generate variants and combinations of such primary emotions as satisfaction-happiness, aversion-fear, assertion-anger, and disappointment-sadness, sanctioning took on entirely new dimensions among our hominid ancestors. Negative sanctions could now avoid disruptive anger-fear-anger cycles and, instead, rely on less volatile affective states like shame, guilt, sorrow, regret, and other emotions built from a base of sadness. Positive sanctions could be increasingly used to heighten cycles of associative affect, for social solidarity among humans cannot be produced without high levels of positive sanctioning. And sadness could be used to mobilize self to seek positive affect from others or to signal to others needs for more positive sanctions.

Imagine a social universe where the animals only had fear and anger as the emotions that could be used to sanction. It would be an unpleasant world, and one soon doomed to extinction, unless there were hard-wired drives in these animals to stay together, no matter what. Apes had no such hard-wired drives, and so if selection went the route of increasing aggression and dominance among apes, it would produce an inviable pattern of social organization. The power of negative sanctions to disrupt had to be mitigated if apes were to develop more local group solidarity, and the extension of sadness became the key to doing so. But even more importantly, selection had to take another route: elaborating those systems of the brain that make satisfaction-happiness a dominant emotion. Now, imagine a world where animals could only use positive sanctions tied to many variants of satisfaction-happiness. This, of course, would be a much more pleasant world, one that would generate very high levels of social solidarity (Coleman 1988, 1990; Turner 1992). Isolated cults perhaps come as close to this "heavenly" world of predominantly positive affect. For all its sense of sublime unreality, the positive-affect universe is more viable for an animal that has few strong bonding or herding tendencies in its genes. Thus it must have been for hominids with selection rapidly moving the species to the point where positive sanctions came to dominate virtually all interpersonal activity.

Out of such movement toward the disproportionate use of positive sanctions came a species that could use both positive and negative sanctions in very effective ways to secure conformity. Negative sanctions could be employed periodically to make individuals aware of the consequences of failing to meet expectations. Moreover, they could always remain in the background as an implicit threat supporting positive sanctions: that is, each individual could see that failure to respond to positive sanctions invites something much worse. Thus, hominid groupings became very complicated systems relying on mixes of positive and negative sanctions made effective by the elaboration of the emotional repertoire of those apelike ancestors who would evolve into humans.

MORAL CODING

Sanctions are directed at expectations which, in turn, are often part of moral codes of appropriate conduct. Conformity and nonconformity to moral codes rely on the arousal of emotions, since without these the rules of the social order have no power or force—they become mere guidelines in an instruction manual. Moral codes are, to a degree, the functional equivalent of genetic codes in many other animals, and they have a biological basis in the organization within and between the neocortex and subcortical limbic systems. Thus, the biological substrate that made moral coding possible in hominids was subject to selection, but unlike social insects and even other mammals, selection did not place bioprogrammers regulating the details of social relations into the neuroanatomy of hominids. Rather, it operated to give hominids the neurological ability to construct moral codes and to feel emotionally their power.

If we visualize a relatively low-sociality animal trying to get organized on the African savanna, what would selection have to do to the neuroanatomy of this animal? First, selection would have to enhance this neuroanatomy so that this animal would be alert and highly attuned to the expectations of others. Second, it would have to increase sensitivity to a fuller range of emotions emitted by others. Third, it would have to connect emotions and expectations together in some way so as to generate more general codes (i.e., norms, values) of conduct. The primary emotions of fear, anger, and satisfaction are sufficient to get this process started, and it can be hypothesized that selection expanded these primary emotions into variants in order to give moral codes, and the emotions on which they are built, more complexity and subtlety. Thus, when moral codes were violated, anger towards the violator could be aroused and used by others to demand conformity; and reciprocally, the fear aroused in the violator would mobilize efforts at conformity. When moral codes were obeyed, satisfaction-happiness toward the conformer would provide positive reinforcement for continued conformity.[13] As more subtle variants and combinations of these primary emotions evolved, the codes themselves and the sanctions could correspondingly become more complex, allowing for more flexible social arrangements in tune with hominids' ape ancestry.

One important selection was on disappointment-sadness, because it would allow for such critical emotions as pride, shame, and guilt to evolve. It appears that some higher mammals are already wired for the rudiments of these emotions—as anyone owning and sanctioning a dog can attest. Whether or not this is actually the case is less relevant than this point: a species organizing itself in terms of moral codes of its own construction, as opposed to internal bioprogrammers, requires that its members experience pride, shame, and guilt; and these can only be produced, I believe, with the ability to mobilize variants of disappointment-sadness (see the next chapter for the details of this argument). In this way, an organism can sanction itself, because it can feel sad and disappointed with self for not meeting the expectations of moral codes; it can mix sadness, fear, and anger together to produce shame at self and guilt about failures to meet expectations; and it can experience pride when it does not disappoint others or self. Once these kinds of emotional capacities exist, organisms can sanction themselves in relation to internalized moral codes; and the greater this capacity at self-monitoring and self-sanctioning, the closer moral codes can come to having the same power as innately programmed drives.

Another important selection was on satisfaction-happiness, since moral codes and the sanctions that sustain their power must be built on positive reinforcement if they are to increase social bonding and promote social solidarity. While all mammals display satisfaction, and most seem to reveal the ability to experience happiness or even joy, I believe that selection enhanced humans' capacity to experience variants and combinations of this primary emotion, if not in amplitude at least in diversity. If solidarity was to be built from moral codes, other emotions had to exist to counter the disruptive effects of more primal emotions like fear and, perhaps, defensive aggression. Sadness was one emotion that had this effect, happiness was another. For if social relations are to be constructed and symbolized in emotionally laden moral codes, then it is essential that happiness comes to have the same power as fear. As we will see in Chapter 4, there is some suggestive evidence that the neurological wiring of the human brain, when compared to our closest primate relatives, reveals changes in the limbic systems directed at expanding the human capacity to experience variations and combinations of happiness.

Elaboration of the emotional repertoire by expanding an animal's ability to generate emotions such as sadness and happiness also allows the codes themselves and individuals' relations to them to become more complex. Codes no longer have to be based on primary emotions like fear, satisfaction, or anger. They can be couched in terms of more subtle emotions and, thereby, can be constructed to handle more complex contingencies that would enable an animal to change codes as circumstances demanded. Moreover, sanctions applied to the codes can be more varied and complex and, as noted earlier, can avoid the problems in producing social relations based on primal anger and fear reactions. Thus, if selection took an animal in the direction of moral coding, fitness would be enhanced if these codes could be flexibly constructed, changed, and enforced in diverse ways. To try to use socially constructed codes to lock an animal into rigid behaviors would prove maladaptive and, in the case of apes, would require too much work to overcome their already built-in propensities for individual anatomy and fluid social relations. If selection is conservative, then it would be more efficient for the brain to be rewired for moral coding that was compatible with existing behavioral propensities. And it is for this reason, I believe, that ape propensities for autonomy, weak-tie formation, and fluid social relations were never selected out of hominids, including humans; instead, selection worked on the brain to give hominids the ability to use emotions to build flexible systems of moral codes and capacities for external and internal sanctioning that went way beyond primal and primary emotions.

Erving Goffman (1967) and Randall Collins (1987, 1988) have both stressed that interactions always involve the use of rituals, and that these rituals are directed at totems or objects (including individuals) symbolizing the underlying moral codes produced by face-to-face interactions. As I have already noted, the emotions backing up moral codes often need to be activated by the use of rituals; that is, rituals are the primary mechanisms in human interaction to keep the interaction focused and to sustain the morality that guides the parties to the interaction. Why should this be so? My answer is that rituals are needed to overcome the relatively low sociality contained in our ape ancestry and to maintain attention on moral codes and other sources of expectations. Moral codes thus do not overwhelm and engulf us; they exert their effects because humans use rituals to escalate the emotional energy to a point where the relevant moral codes are activated and begin to guide the flow of the interaction. Moral coding has not so much replaced humans' weak-tie propensities, as overcome them when it becomes necessary to sustain an interaction over time.

Moral codes can be either *pre*scriptive, indicating what should and can be done in a situation, or they can be *pro*scriptive, delineating what cannot or should not be done. The ratio of prescriptive to proscriptive content becomes important in generating a morality that produces increased social bonding and solidarity among relatively low-sociality primates. Proscriptive moral codes always hold the threat of negative sanctions and are heavily imbued with the emotion of fear among those who might engage in prohibited behavior. Such codes are often necessary, but alone they cannot produce solidarity, even when people's ability to avoid violations of prohibitions brings them positive sanctions. Most moral codes in a system of solidarity must be prescriptive, backed by positive sanctions for conformity and, of course, by negative sanctions for flagrant violations. But prescriptions are more likely to activate positive sanctions and emotions such as pride, whereas it is much more difficult to sustain a proscriptive system of codes with positive sanctions because there is always a threat of negative sanctioning implicit in prohibitions. Of course, prescriptive codes that only allow negative sanctioning would not be solidarity-producing, but in general prescriptive codes hold out the promise of positive sanctions.

Thus, systems of moral codes will generally reveal the following structure: some prohibitions as background conditions, indicating basic wrongs; many more prescriptive instructions, some of which are background conditions about basic rights but most of which are instructions about what can and should be done in a particular situation. Negative sanctions can be invoked in forcing conformity to all codes, but these cannot be used too frequently, because even the potential for negative sanctions generates emotions like anxiety, apprehensiveness, and worry, all of which contain varying amounts of the primary emotion of fear. Variations of fear (and anger) are not conducive to long-term solidarity because they are likely to generate anger-fear-anger cycles (Turner 1992). True, such sanctions can maintain conformity to moral codes, but not in ways that promote high solidarity. In contrast, the potential for positive sanctions activates emotions like joy, contentment, pride, love, affection, wonder, awe, delight, all based primarily on satisfaction-happiness, and, in so doing, these emotions give moral codes solidarity-producing effects. If negative sanctions and variants of fear and anger are to be used to sustain conformity to moral codes, mixing these negative emotions with sadness to produce shame and guilt are much more effective in promoting solidarity, because these emotions (a) mobilize individuals' internal energies to meet the expectations of moral codes and (b) avoid the dissociative effects of intense anger, fear, worry, and anxiety.

We can see the work of selection in humans today. We are far more likely to use prescriptive codes backed by positive sanctions than any other, for the simple reason that these are based on variants and combinations of happiness and, hence, are more likely to cause individuals to bond and form solidarities. Indeed, it could be argued that most codes among hominids were prescriptive, with relatively few negative sanctions; proscriptive codes and negative sanctions are more typical, I believe, of more complex patterns of social organization that emerge after hunting-gathering. Hunter-gatherers —the basic social form that sustained hominids—do not evidence large inventories of prohibitions or much use of negative sanctions; rather, these simple social structures are built primarily around allowing individuals considerable personal autonomy (in accordance with their ape ancestry) and, at the same time, pulling individuals together in sufficiently structured bands organized by prescriptions backed mostly by low-key positive sanctions or low-intensity negative sanctions such as sarcasm, pointed joking, and ridicule (Maryanski and Turner 1992; Turner 1996a, 1998). Apparently, along with the expansion of hominids' emotional repertoire, prescriptive moral codes were enough to overcome apes' weak-tie propensities and to organize hominids with sufficient solidarity to survive on the savanna.

VALUING AND EXCHANGING RESOURCES

For an object, thought, or behavior to possess *value* it must pull from various subcortical limbic systems emotional valences; and depending upon the particular emotions mobilized, its value will vary. This is true for all mammals, and probably for most other life forms with a nervous system. Thus, feeding mobilizes satisfaction, and this satisfaction is what leads to satisfaction-seeking behavior; or danger activates fear, and this fear causes aversive behaviors. This process of generating values is, therefore, ancient and widespread in the history of life; and selection began to expand upon it when a low-sociality primate sought to survive on the savanna. Selection had to make valuable the responses of others, if stronger bonds were to be forged among hominids. This is, of course, another way of stating that the more the emotional repertoire of hominids could be expanded, the more potential sources of value there would be to pull together primates accustomed to weak ties and individual autonomy.

It was critical, as all exchange theories would emphasize, for responses of others to take on value that, in turn, would lead hominids to behave in ways promoting solidarity. In fact, emotions were not only the yardstick by which value was determined, but also became the very resource exchanged. And the more hominids could exchange states of affect revolving around satisfaction-happiness, the more associative would be their relations. They would actively seek social relations producing such value, just as they would seek food and other positively reinforcing objects. Even negative emotions, such as anger, fear, and sadness, could promote solidarity *if their avoidance* was achieved through the positive value of associative relations. And the more others could be seen as sources of value, positive in their own right and positive to the degree that they allowed an organism to avoid negative emotions, the more emotions moved beyond their use as a measure of value and became the actual objects of value in interpersonal exchanges.

Indeed, all human exchange operates this way, even exchanges in large and complex market systems. As Randall Collins (1993) has emphasized, emotions are "the common denominator of exchange" because they establish criteria for determining value and for making choices in what resources individuals will seek in exchanges. Those options that are seen by actors to bring value will be sought, while those that bring less value or negative values will be avoided. Moreover, as Marcel Mauss (1925) recognized, exchanges also generate a new "utility": the social relations that mediate exchange of value. With exchanges of objects comes another, perhaps more fundamental: the exchange of affect. Indeed, most face-to-face ex-

changes are highly ritualized not only in order to structure the flow of ne-
gotiations, but also to assure that emotions are aroused to the point where
this more emotional sense of solidarity is also *the* utility exchanged.

If this is true of more impersonal market exchanges, it certainly was the
case with hominids. Exchanges of goods, favors, or anything will occur because they promote value, but more fundamentally, exchange relations per
se became a reality in their own right offering even greater value to the actors involved. In the case of an animal that needed to forge stronger bonds
more than it needed to share food or other objects, this emergent property
of exchange would be more critical to survival; and on the basis of this enhanced solidarity came the trust and bonds that would facilitate more extrinsic exchanges of material objects, which, reciprocally, would enhance
the intrinsic emotions inhering in the exchange process itself. In addition,
as the capacities for storing memories increased among hominids, exchange
relations could be remembered and, even when not active, could nonetheless generate the emotions associated with the exchange relation—thereby
sustaining social attachments and solidarity. Recent experimental studies
document that, even when the exchange is less personal and face-to-face,
the commitment and solidarity-producing effects of the exchange relation
per se are still activated (Lawler and Yoon 1993, 1996)—suggesting, perhaps, that elements of exchange and reciprocity are probably hard-wired
into humans' neuroanatomy.[14] The use of rituals would only heighten further the emotions involved, making the process of exchange intrinsically
valuable, irrespective of whatever extrinsic sources of value were involved.

As many diverse scholars have advocated (e.g., Gouldner 1960; Alexander 1974; Cosmides 1989), it might well be true that "the principle of reciprocity" is hard-wired into human neuroanatomy. If selection was working
toward increasing emotions and forging stronger social bonds, the brain
might well have been rewired so that animals would feel obligated to reciprocate the receipt of resources from others. The need to reciprocate would
push members of a species into exchanges, thereby activating the solidarity-
producing effects of exchange relations. And as the resources exchanged
were themselves emotions, these effects would become that much stronger,
since the emotions, if positive, would bestow value in their own right and
the exchange itself would add another layer of positive reinforcement.

Moreover, these effects would become more sustaining if satiation or
marginal utility could be avoided by increasing the range of emotions that

actors could use in exchange relations. And it might be argued that the increasingly large repertoire of emotions revealed by hominids was one strategy for getting around what Michael Hammond (1990) has termed *habituation*, where further increments of a given source of value become progressively less valuable. But if new reinforcers, or new sources of value built from ever expanding emotional repertoires, could be added to the exchanges, some of the effects of habituation could be mitigated. Indeed, for an animal that needed to get more organized at the group level, expanding the emotional repertoire was about the only option for avoiding habituation—at least until more complex types of social structures could be developed as humans began to abandon hunting-gathering to pursue horticulture and, later, agriculture.[15]

RATIONAL DECISION MAKING

To select among alternatives requires some way to assess the relative value of these alternatives, and this ability to assess alternatives is tied to emotions. Emotions give each alternative a value and, thereby, provide a yardstick to judge and to select among alternatives. This process need not be conscious; and indeed, for all animals including humans, it rarely is. Thus to be rational means also to be emotional; and any line that we draw separating cognition and emotion fails to understand the neurology of cognitions. One cannot sustain cognitions beyond working memory without tagging them with emotion; and as Damasio has emphasized, memory and thinking also depend upon tagging experiences with emotion (Damasio 1994).

Humans' ability to engage in complex decision-making processes does not, therefore, eclipse emotionality; sophisticated decision making *depends upon* the ability of humans to produce large arrays of emotional valences. Expanding the neocortex would have little effect for the complexity of rational thought *until* the ability to generate a wide variety of emotional states was in place. I would go so far as to argue that hominids' expanding emotional abilities represented a preadaptation for higher forms of rationality—a preadaptation that had little to do with decision making per se, and much more to do with creating as many affective hooks as possible for forming relations among low-sociality primates.

Once the ability to emote was in place, selection could rewire the brain so that these emotions could be used to enhance memory and decision making. Selection would have first produced closer social bonds among low-sociality primates through expanded emotional abilities; then selection would use emotional abilities to increase the capacity for thought and memory. With expanded capacities for memory and thinking, new hooks to social bonds could come into play and new options for building social structures could be pursued. Selection could not take apes back to monkeylike matrilines and male-dominance hierarchies, especially given the punctuated nature of the forces at work, and so it operated to produce abilities that are far more consistent with hominids' ape ancestral tendencies for fluid social ties and individual autonomy. An animal that can use a wide variety of emotions to tag cognitions, memories, and behavioral options reveals the ability to retain some autonomy and individualism in social relations.

These selection processes became interwoven: as the fitness-enhancing value of decision-making abilities played themselves out, selection would then expand emotional abilities in order to increase the rationality and complexity of decision making. The subcortical limbic systems were rewired, and new and seemingly unique structures in the neocortex, especially the subgenual regions of the prefrontal cortex (Drevets et al. 1997), emerged to integrate cognitions, memories, and emotions that produced an ever more rational animal. But the process could not get started without already expanded emotional abilities; and I would argue that the initial increases in the size of hominid brains from australopithecines to *Homo habilis* were the result of expanding the emotional abilities of hominids, with decision-making capacities through expansion of the prefrontal cortex gradually being mixed into the emotional system. Auditory language facilities might also have begun to be integrated into these mutually reinforcing processes, but my belief is that language was mostly visual, being driven by the rewiring of the brain for emotions and new decision-making abilities. Later, and certainly by the time of *Homo erectus*, selection created new forms of precise communication through the auditory channel as a supplement to the visual modality.

Thus, let me repeat again my view that what are often seen as humans' most distinctive characteristics—rational thought and language—were built on another of our most unique characteristics: our ability to be so emotional. Again, my point is that memory and thought cannot take place without the capacity to tag thoughts, experiences, and emotions with affect. And the more the affective variety possible, the more complex and subtle the cognitive abilities.

Not all memories guiding thoughts and action are conscious, however. It appears that the brain can store emotional memories subcortically[16]— that is, outside of the neocortex where conscious thought and deliberation occur (Le Doux 1996). This makes sense, once we consider how selection would have enhanced the fitness of primitive mammals. To respond rapidly to dangers, it is useful to bypass the loop through the neocortex (especially if it is not large) to store in the subcortical limbic systems experiences that could, if repeated, fire off the appropriate emotional response very rapidly. To loop all experiences through the neocortex takes time[17] and delays activation of emotion centers that will push bodily responses; and under conditions of danger, to lose precious time is to reduce fitness. This kind of subcortical memory system was not replaced by hominids' expanding cognitive abilities; rather, the more primal, subcortical emotional memory system was supplemented by one controlled from the neocortex. The result is that humans often make decisions and behave in ways driven not so much by conscious memories stored in their neocortex or by the subcortical hippocampus and transition cortices that are integrated with the neocortex to store intermediate memories (of up to a few years); rather, decisions are also made under the influence of bodily responses pushed by other subcortical limbic systems that store emotional memories outside the direct preview of the neocortex. Indeed, individuals often are at a loss, cognitively, to understand why they make certain decisions or behave in certain ways; the answer is that subcortical, emotional memory systems are mixed in with cortically controlled ones. Thus, rationality is often a mix of emotional valences, some capable of being articulated to self if need be and others remaining outside of full self-awareness.

Sigmund Freud (1936) was correct in his belief that much thought and behavior are driven by subconscious impulses; he may have been wrong, however, in his emphasis on repression as the central mechanism for these impulses (Le Doux 1996). I have no doubt that repression and other defense mechanisms of self are involved in rational calculations, but perhaps more prevalent are emotional memories that never have made it to consciousness (to be subsequently repressed); these emotional memories are stored subcortically and hence are not readily reached by conscious reflection.

Whatever precise mechanisms are involved the power of Antonio Damasio's (1994) argument remains: memory, cognitions, thinking, and rationality are all dependent upon the ability to generate emotions; and the greater the emotional repertoire of an animal, the more complex, varied, and subtle can be its memories, cognitions, thoughts, and decisions. As Damasio has emphasized, Descartes' "error" was that he saw the mind and body as separate realities, whereas in fact they are inseparable. And as Joseph Le Doux (1996) has also emphasized, rationality and emotion are not separate dimensions of behavior, but in fact part of the same connection between mind and body systems.

Conclusions

In this chapter, I have reviewed the indirect and direct selection pressures that made humans ever more emotional. This emotionality set the stage for selection to create what are typically viewed as humans' most unique characteristics, language and rational thought (and, from these, "culture"). But as has been emphasized, these human achievements were not possible without preadaptations that came from rewiring of the brain for visually based communication of affect among hominids. In a sense, I have conducted a thought experiment in this chapter by asking what would be necessary for group structures that would increase solidarity and coherence while not working too hard against humans' ape legacy for weaker ties and individual autonomy. In answering this question, the more direct selection pressures exerted by sociocultural forces can be isolated: mobilization and channeling of emotional energy, interpersonal attunement, sanctioning, moral coding, exchange of value, and decision making. Unless a weak-tie ape could evolve along these lines, then more cohesive and, yet, flexible social structures could not be constructed. Since most savanna-dwelling apes did not take this path in the distant past, they apparently were doomed to extinction. And the four genera of apes that survive today are not savanna-dwelling; they live in the tops of trees, woodlands, or secondary forests. If forced to survive exclusively on the savanna, present-day apes would, no doubt, go the way of their ancestral cousins.

I have emphasized that selection worked first to expand hominids' emotional repertoire, but I have not examined this repertoire in any detail. In the next chapter, then, I will discuss the range of human emotions as elaborations of more primary emotions. I also have not offered any details yet about the rewiring of the human brain; in Chapter 4, the neurological basis of emotions will be explored in order to fill in the details[18] of the general line of argument made in these first two chapters.

1. I might also add that, without "the early warning system" provided by the sense of smell so prominent among most mammals, group organization would be even more critical in dealing with potential predators.

2. Putting apes in cages and restricted enclosures, or even caging them by forcing proximity to food sources, as Jane Goodall did at Gombe, increases competition, fighting, and hostility among individuals and between subgroups. These outcomes would not be fitness-enhancing in open-country savanna. Moreover, these outcomes show how *un*natural caging an individualistic primate is. As De Waal (1996 and other works) and as Glendon Schubert and Roger Masters (1991) have so well documented, chimpanzees are very capable of becoming political, playing very serious games of domination and coalition formation. De Waal's and Masters' work thus reveals that dominance can emerge among chimpanzees, who do not display much hierarchy in truly natural settings, and that selection may have taken this route for many—perhaps, most—apes. But it is an evolutionary dead end for individualistic apes, and those species that sought to organize on the savanna through accentuation of dominance were selected out. I believe that accentuating dominance would not promote fitness of apes trying to become better organized because (1) without matrilines organizing female networks, dominance cannot produce monkey-like groups; (2) with efforts at dominance, without matrilines, comes constant competition and fighting, which would not promote fitness on open-country savanna; (3) with dominance, males would spend a great deal of their time trying to horde females who do not naturally bond; and (4) with dominance, individualistic apes would leave the group in order to escape forced cooperation.

3. A preadaptation is the evolution of a trait in the past for reasons having little or nothing to do with the subsequent adaptation that it provides for a species, as is argued in the next section for language.

4. There are data that indicate that the auditory cortex decomposes an auditory scene into parts using a feature-processing system reminiscent of one used for cortical decomposition of visual images (deCharms, Blake, and Merzenich 1998). This similarity may also be an integrating process.

5. These subcortical portions of the brain generating emotions are often termed "the limbic system," but it is now clear that this system is not as coherent as once

thought (MacLean, 1990), and some (e.g., Le Doux, 1996, 1991, 1987) have argued
for the abandonment of the notion of a limbic system. I will continue to use this
label, but I refer to limbic system*s* rather than to a unified system, and what I mean
with this label is that there is a variety of systems in the brain for generating emotions. Most of these are subcortical, but they are integrated in ways explored in
Chapter 4 with neocortical systems.

6. Australopithecines by the time of *afarensis* were clearly upright, and this
adaptation occurred long before there was growth in the size of the brain significantly beyond the measure of present-day apes.

7. Moreover, for subtle and complex emotions to be communicated verbally,
it would be necessary to have considerable voluntary control of speech production; like Hewes, I do not see this level of control as likely in early hominids. For
it is one thing to vocalize greetings and warnings, but quite another to communicate diverse types of nuanced emotions vocally. Even humans today, possessing
evolved brains and control of the speech apparatus, cannot do so with great clar-
ity. Australopithecines and their ancestors certainly could not do so.

8. I have no data for this assumption, but it is clear that most thinking is not an
"internalized conversation," as George Herbert Mead (1934) had argued. Thinking
is fast, involving patterns and configurations of information brought together with
a kind of simultaneity as a gestalt. Only when the process is slowed down in "talking to oneself" is thinking verbal, but even here "brain thinking" is being downloaded into a slow, sequential mode of representation. Most thinking is far too
rapid to be sequential speech. In fact, humans would appear ponderous and dim-
witted if thinking was internalized talk.

9. Try to visualize, for example, a dominant "alpha male" attempting to organize a bunch of mobile and individualistic apes. This male would exhaust himself
monitoring and sanctioning, while at the same time generating conflict, tension,
and out-migration of resentful members at the earliest opportunity. For without
the matrilines evident in monkeys, there would be no force to keep members of
the group together; and as a result, the male would be in a constant state of frenzy
to keep his "followers" together. Attachment to a group for an ape, then, must be
voluntary; and the best mechanism for voluntary attachment is stronger affect.

10. For example, imagine a telephone conversation that is highly emotional.
For each party to appreciate fully the emotions involved, and to respond appropriately, each must imagine what the other "looks like" from the auditory cues
that trigger mental images.

11. At least this appears to be the case for chimpanzees. I suspect that this
propensity is also evident among all *Pongidae* (that is, gorillas and orangutans as
well), but the data are not so clear on the matter, especially since the habitats of
these other Pongidae have been so disrupted.

12. At the very least, I would argue that they are not as ancient, at least in their higher intensity states. On the other hand, research by Joak Panksepp (1998) suggests that joy and other high-intensity states of happiness are found among mammals such as mice and rats.

13. The power of this "positive" emotion would be greatly enhanced as rituals became an ever more prominent feature of communication. Rituals would increase the valences, while focusing attention on the "moral good" performed by an individual.

14. I am not trying to push this point, which indeed is not necessary for my general argument. Still, there is some indirect evidence, or at least informed argument, that reciprocity is innate in humans. See, for example, Axelrod and Dion (1988), Cosmides (1989), Fiske (1991), Trivers (1971).

15. Once there was a larger variety of material goods, humans could get around habituation by varying the mix of extrinsic goods exchanged. Hammond argues that this is the motive behind inequality, as elites usurped wealth to avoid habituation at the expense of those they exploited. One could also interpret postmodernist theories of constant and ubiquitous commodification as our anti-habituation strategy made possible by world-level capitalism.

16. The hippocampus is probably the central subcortical structure, as it adds context to emotional experiences. See Chapter 4 for more details.

17. In milliseconds and, perhaps in a second; but more than this is an eternity in neurological time.

18. At least as much as a sociologist who is not trained in neurology can.

CHAPTER 3

The Emotional Repertoire of Humans

In 1872, Charles Darwin published *The Expression of Emotions in Man and Animals*, arguing that many of the expressive actions of humans and other animals are innate and, hence, inherited rather than learned. Using mostly anecdotal evidence, Darwin reasoned that since bodily expressions of emotions, particularly those of the face, are similar among humans around the world, they must be innate, existing today because they have promoted survival. Darwin devoted considerable attention to primates, both monkeys and apes, and here too he noted similarities in the expressions of humans and other primates. In particular, emotions such as pleasure, affection, joy, pain, anger, astonishment, and terror are expressed in similar ways by all primates, including humans. And Darwin gave voice to the argument that I am developing: facial as well as vocal expressions of emotions are critical to a group-living animal because they attract animals to one another, regulate their interactions, keep them together, and enable them to reproduce successfully.

What Emotions Are Primary?

What is remarkable about this great work is how it slipped into obscurity. Given Darwin's reputation, *The Expression of Emotions in Man and Animals* was launched with great fanfare and enjoyed large sales upon publication.

And still, the theoretical and empirical leads in it were not followed until well into the twentieth century; among social scientists, these leads were not picked up until the 1960s. Work by Paul Ekman (1973a, 1982, 1992a, 1992b) and his associates (Ekman and Friesen 1975; Ekman, Friesen, and Ellsworth 1972) is perhaps the best known and follows Darwin's lead in examining facial expressions to determine the biologically based or primary emotions of humans. More generally, researchers from many disciplines, using a wide variety of approaches, have produced over the last four decades lists of what they see as the primary emotions of humans. Table 3.1 summarizes the arguments of some of the more prominent works. I have deliberately mixed different approaches together and ignored variations in methodology in order to highlight the commonality of findings. The names across the top of the table are representatives of such diverse fields as psychology, sociology, biology, psychiatry, physiology, and neurology; and they have employed many varied approaches, ranging from stimulation of emotions in rats through asking people questions about emotions, to experiments and cross-cultural research of facial expressions. What is remarkable is the convergence of findings, despite the disparate disciplinary orientations and methodologies of researchers.

There is complete consensus among researchers that fear is a primary emotion; virtually all agree that anger is also primary; some variant of happiness is seen in almost all schemes to be primary; sadness or something close to this emotion is prominent in most schemes; surprise appears in some, as does disgust, shame, guilt, interest, anticipation, and expectancy. Thus, if we just tally the "votes," then happiness, fear, anger, and sadness are viewed by most researchers to be primal emotions. Disgust and surprise are considered by many to be primary, and a somewhat smaller group considers interest, anticipation, expectancy, and similar emotions as primary; the same is true for guilt.

A number of years ago, Beverly Fehr and James Russell (1984) asked two hundred subjects to list as many emotions as came to mind, stopping after one minute or after having listed twenty emotions. Table 3.2 summarizes their results, eliminating some 187 emotions that were mentioned only by one person. Obviously, this is a verbal exercise and one in which subjects were simply asked to list emotions, but what came to the subjects' minds, as it were, were emotions very similar to the more theoretically informed research conclusions listed in Table 3.1. Happiness was the most mentioned

TABLE 3.1

Representative Examples of Statements on Primary Emotions

Johnson-Laird/Oatley (1992)	Emde (1980)	Panksepp (1982)	Sroufe (1979)	Turner (1996a)	Trevarthen (1984)	Arnold (1960)	Osgood (1966)	Darwin (1872)	Izard (1977, 1992b)
happiness	joy		pleasure	happiness	happiness		joy quiet pleasure	pleasure joy affection	enjoyment
fear	fear	fear panic	fear	fear	fear	fight	fear anxiety	terror	fear
anger	anger	rage	anger	anger	anger	fight defensive aggression	anger	anger	anger contempt
sadness	sadness	sorrow loneliness grief		sadness surprise	sadness		sorrow		
	surprise						amazement	astonishment	surprise
disgust	disgust						disgust		disgust
	shame shyness								shame shyness
	distress								distress
guilt	guilt								guilt
	interest	expectancy			approach		interest expectancy		interest
					inhibition		boredom	pain	

TABLE 3.1

Representative Examples of Statements on Primary Emotions, *continued*

Ekman (1984)	Epstein (1984)	Arieti (1970)	Fromme/ O'Brien (1982)	Plutchik (1980)	Scott (1980)	Fehr/ Russell (1984)	Gray (1982)	Kemper (1987)	Malatesta/ Haviland (1982)
happiness	joy love	satisfaction	joy elation satisfaction	joy	pleasure love	happiness love	hope	satisfaction	joy
fear	fear	fear tension	fear	fear	fear anxiety	fear	anxiety	fear	fear
anger	anger	rage	anger	anger	anger	anger	anger	anger	anger
sadness	sadness	unpleasure	grief resignation	sadness	loneliness	sadness	sadness	depression	sadness
surprise			shock	surprise					
disgust				disgust					
					anticipation curiosity				interest
		appetite		acceptance					
									pain
									brownflash knitbrow

emotion, anger was the second, sadness was the third, fear was the fifth, and depression was the tenth most mentioned emotion. If we take what I see as variants of happiness (joy, love), anger (hate), and sadness (depression), then the rank order is happiness, anger, sadness, and fear—which corresponds to the emotions seen as primary by scholars working out of a number of different traditions. Fehr and Russell's findings were similar to those reported earlier by Hunt and Hodge (1971), who had also asked subjects to list emotions.

As we will see in the next chapter, fear is probably the most primal emotion in all animals, since it is essential to avoid danger and predation. Anger is often tied to fear in defensive aggression; indeed, the two emotions are activated in different portions of the amygdala, one of the most ancient subcortical limbic systems in mammals. Happiness and its variants are somewhat more elusive emotions, not being clearly located in any one limbic system. There appear to be enlargements for pleasure in the amygdala and in the septum (the center for sexual drives and activity). These two limbic systems—the septum and amygdala—are among the most primal and ancient structures in the brains of mammals. The cingulate gyrus, especially its anterior portions, appears to be the source for mother-infant bonding (involving love and attachment), typical of all mammals. And various neurotransmitters (e.g., serotonin) and neuroactive peptides (e.g., opioids) also seem to be involved in producing happiness and satisfaction. The fourth primary emotion—sadness—seems to be the result of neurotransmitter and neuroactive peptide releases, or, as is often the case, the failure to release substances promoting variants of satisfaction and happiness.

Thus, if selection favored the expansion of emotions in hominids, it initially had to work on those limbic systems generating fear, anger, happiness, and sadness. The first requirement, I believe, was to expand the capacity for happiness, since this is the emotion that generates solidarity and is so essential to the positive sanctions and prescriptive moral codes that individualistic apes must have used to form social bonds. It is for this reason, I speculate, that satisfaction-happiness is produced by more limbic systems than other primary emotions: there was great pressure to generate this emotion, any possible way. Fear and anger were already hard-wired and located in a very discrete place (various segments of the amygdala); and indeed, selection may have added areas for pleasure onto the amygdala because unmitigated fear and anger responses had disrupted associative bonds and solidarity.

TABLE 3.2

Free Listing of Exemplars of Emotion

Happiness (152)	Hurt (16)	Lust (8)	Dislike (5)	Stress (4)	Thinking (3)	Insecurity (2)
Anger (149)	Liking (16)	Tenderness (8)	Exuberance (5)	Thrilled (4)	Wonder (3)	Malicious (2)
Sadness (136)	Lonely (16)	Annoyed (7)	Panic (5)	Tranquility (4)	Admiration (2)	Meditating (2)
Love (124)	Sympathy (16)	Arousal (7)	Satisfaction (5)	Unhappy (4)	Alert (2)	Mixed (2)
Fear (96)	Compassion (14)	Cheerful (7)	Touching (5)	Violence (4)	Amazement (2)	Outgoingness (2)
Hate (89)	Ecstasy (14)	Disappointment (7)	Aggression (4)	Vulnerability (4)	Appreciation (2)	Protective (2)
Joy (82)	Envy (14)	Distress (7)	Amused (4)	Ambivalence (3)	Anguish (2)	Rapture (2)
Excitement (53)	Grief (14)	Frightened (7)	Apprehension (4)	Attraction (3)	Belonging (2)	Relaxed (2)
Anxiety (50)	Mad (14)	Hopelessness (7)	Awe (4)	Bliss (3)	Boisterous (2)	Repulsion (2)
Depression (42)	Sorrow (14)	Irritation (7)	Deep (4)	Confidence (3)	Closeness (2)	Responsibility (2)
Frustration (39)	Warmth (14)	Kindness (7)	Desire (4)	Conflict (3)	Communication (2)	Responsiveness (2)
Crying (36)	Nervous (13)	Longing (7)	Dismay (4)	Defeat (3)	Complacent (2)	Self-concept (2)
Feelings (35)	Pain (13)	Melancholy (7)	Enjoyment (4)	Dejection (3)	Contempt (2)	Self-esteem (2)
Jealousy (29)	Tense (13)	Pleased (7)	Enthusiasm (4)	Expectation (3)	Criticism (2)	Sentimental (2)
Disgust (27)	Moody (12)	Rage (7)	Exhilaration (4)	Expressive (3)	Cynical (2)	Softness (2)
Laughter (27)	Pride (12)	Relief (7)	Gay (4)	Giving (3)	Devotion (2)	State (2)
Elation (26)	Smiling (12)	Respect (7)	Hostility (4)	Helping (3)	Distrust (2)	Stubbornness (2)
Caring (24)	Trust (12)	Scared (7)	Humor (4)	Helplessness (3)	Disturbed (2)	Successful (2)
Guilt (22)	Passion (11)	Sensitive (7)	Loyalty (4)	High (3)	Dread (2)	Tiredness (2)
Embarrassment (20)	Tears (11)	Sex (6)	Miserable (4)	Humility (3)	Edgy (2)	Turbulent (2)
Contentment (19)	Pleasure (10)	Shyness (6)	Mournful (4)	Jubilation (3)	Expression (2)	Uncertainty (2)
Peace (19)	Calmness (9)	Sincerity (6)	Needs (4)	Negative (3)	Euphoria (2)	Uncontrollable (2)
Upset (19)	Glad (9)	Strong (6)	Pensive (4)	Passivity (3)	Frown (2)	Understanding (2)
Worry (19)	Affection (8)	Afraid (5)	Rejection (4)	Positive (3)	Gentleness (2)	Unstable (2)
Empathy (18)	Boredom (8)	Anticipation (5)	Remorse (4)	Quiet (3)	Hardness (2)	Uptight (2)
Boredom (18)	Delight (8)	Bitterness (5)	Serenity (4)	Reaction (3)	Heart (2)	Wanting (2)
Confusion (17)	Greed (8)	Concern (5)	Shame (4)	Resentment (3)	Hyperactive (2)	Weak (2)
Delight (17)	Hope (8)	Control (5)	Sharing (4)	Terror (3)	Impulse (2)	Withdrawn (2)
Surprise (17)						
Despair (16)						

SOURCE: Data from Fehr and Russell 1984

NOTE: The number in parentheses is the number of subjects, out of 200, who listed each item or some syntactic variant of it. Items listed by only one subject were omitted.

The neurological details, such as they are known, will be pursued in the next chapter. For the present, I simply want to focus on what the limbic systems in humans are able to generate: a wide range and variety of emotions. The written lists of Fehr and Russell's (1984) subjects provide some information about this range and diversity, but we need to be a bit more systematic in conceptualizing these and other emotions.

Emotional Arousal in Humans

VARIANTS OF PRIMARY EMOTIONS

Many of the emotions listed in Tables 3.1 and 3.2 are variants of, as well as combinatory elaborations among, four primary emotions: satisfaction-happiness, aversion-fear, assertion-anger, and disappointment-sadness.[1] We can say with some confidence that these are primary, particularly the low-intensity poles of each emotion—satisfaction, aversion, assertion, and disappointment. Most mammals probably reveal variants toward the higher-intensity ends as well, and certainly humans, who appear to have the largest emotional repertoire of any animal, experience many variants at the low, intermediate, and intense level of satisfaction-happiness, aversion-fear, assertion-anger, and disappointment-sadness. It may well be that other emotions are hard-wired and primary, as I will explore shortly, but we can be confident that these four are indeed part of the responses generated by our limbic systems.

In Table 3.3, I have listed examples of the low-, moderate-, and high-intensity variants of the four primary emotions of satisfaction-happiness, aversion-fear, assertion-anger, and disappointment-sadness (Turner 1999). Only humans and other higher mammals can, I believe, produce the emotions listed in the high-intensity column, although this is certainly a debatable conclusion.[2] For humans, satisfaction can move from contentment, through cheerfulness, to joyfulness and, as I will examine shortly, to more complex emotional states, like pride. Aversion can move from hesitancy, through anxiety and trepidation, to terror, and to many other elaborations that are listed in Table 3.3. Similarly, assertiveness can move from low-intensity states, like irritation, to such moderate states as animosity, and from there to high-voltage emotions like hate, disgust, and loathing. Finally, disappointment can shift from low-intensity states like discourage-

TABLE 3.3

Variants of Primary Emotions

	Low intensity	Moderate intensity	High intensity
Satisfaction-happiness	content sanguine serenity gratified	cheerful buoyant friendly amiable enjoyment	joy bliss rapture jubilant gaiety elation delight thrilled exhilarated
Aversion-fear	concern hesitant reluctance shyness	misgivings trepidation anxiety scared alarmed unnerved panic	terror horror high anxiety
Assertion-anger	annoyed agitated irritated vexed perturbed nettled rankled piqued	displeased frustrated belligerent contentious hostility ire animosity offended consternation	dislike loathing disgust hate despise detest hatred seething wrath furious inflamed incensed outrage
Disappointment-sadness	discouraged downcast dispirited	dismayed disheartened glum resigned gloomy	sorrow heartsick despondent anguished crestfallen woeful pained dejected

SOURCE: Data from Turner 1999a, 1999b

ment, through dismay, to high-intensity states such as sorrow, anguish, and despondency.

I do not know, of course, if I have analyzed these variants exactly right; indeed, any such list is subject to debate. But I do believe that it is useful to view one source of the diversity in human emotions in terms of the capacity to generate variants of the primary emotions. This process alone gives humans many subtle and complex ways to role-make and role-take through emission of gestures communicating emotional hues and tones. The emotions listed in the columns in Table 3.3 are, I think, best communicated and interpreted through the visual sense modality, although voice inflections, amplitudes, and other dimensions of the auditory channel make them that much more meaningful. Still, if I am correct in my belief that the visual modality was the first to be used to enhance emotional communication, then it might be argued that the first step in this process was to expand the variants of primary emotions. This would be the easiest way for selection to work, neurologically; and from this base, limbic systems and their connections to neocortical areas could be reorganized by selection so as to produce more complicated combinatory elaborations among primary emotions—although the notion of mixing primary emotions like primary colors is problematic, I think, once the neurology of what is involved is examined. Just counting the number of variants listed in Table 3.3 reveals around fifty emotional states, and even if we consider that some of the terms listed denote the same emotions, we are still left with a repertoire of twenty-five to thirty-five affective states that can be sent and received via the visual sense modality.

My hypothesis, then, is that the early expansion of the limbic systems of hominids started along this path, and that initially their emotional repertoire was probably not much greater than a chimpanzee's today. But there was, I suspect, one important difference between apes and the chimplike ape that evolved into the hominid line: emotions in the latter were probably under more volitional control; moreover, higher degrees of sensitivity to these emotional states were emerging as hominids began to use elaborations of the primary emotions to forge social bonds.

ELABORATIONS OF PRIMARY EMOTIONS

First-Order Elaborations. How would selection proceed, once the expanded emotional repertoire of an animal had produced greater fitness for survival?

It is reasonable to hypothesize that the first change would be an increase in the animal's capacities for variants of primary emotions. But if emotional diversity and variety were the key to survival, then it is likely that selection would work on limbic systems producing primary emotions and their variants to expand the emotional repertoire. One way to enhance hominids' emotional repertoire would be to generate new emotional states through simultaneity of limbic responses that would, in essence, combine variants of primary emotions. Robert Plutchik (1962, 1980) has developed the most complete scheme of what might have been involved. Figure 3.1 presents Plutchik's eight basic emotions on a wheel, much like a color wheel. A primary dyad is a mix of adjacent emotions, such as a combination of joy and acceptance to produce "friendliness." A secondary dyad mixes emotions once removed from each other on the wheel, as is the case when sadness and anger are mixed to generate "sullenness." A tertiary dyad is where emotions twice removed are mixed, as can be seen when joy and surprise are combined to create "delight." This scheme is fascinating—and it does seem that there is something to the idea of a wheel of emotion analogous to the color wheel, since most emotions seem to be blends of primary emotions, but I suspect that the scheme is a bit too mechanical. When the nature of the limbic systems involved is better understood (see Chapter 4), I am not sure that this notion of an emotion wheel holds up. But there is something to the argument, because it does appear that emotions get combined in some way, or at least, the limbic systems involved fire off variants of primary emotions to create a greatly expanded array of emotional states.

An alternative to the idea of mixing at the neurological level is social construction of emotions at the sociocultural level, an approach that Theodore Kemper (1987) has pursued. Here, many of the combinations among primary emotions are seen as socially constructed and, then, socialized into succeeding generations. For social constructionists, the only neurological substrate is the capacity to expand the emotional repertoire in this way. It is probably a weakness in the theories of social constructivists—although Kemper is unusually conscientious in this regard—that they barely consider the neurology underlying social phenomena.[3] For if natural selection led to a rewiring of the hominid brain in order that it could generate a larger repertoire of emotions for use in social bonding, this happened before the neocortex had increased to the current human capacity. Thus, much of the "mixing" of emotions, if this is even the right way to refer to

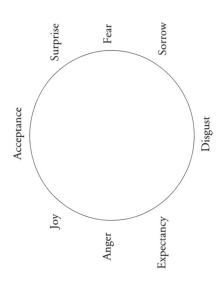

Surprise

Acceptance

Fear

Joy

Sorrow

Anger

Disgust

Expectancy

Examples of dyads

Primary

anger + joy = pride
joy + acceptance = love, friendliness
acceptance + surprise = curiosity
surprise + fear = alarm, awe
sorrow + disgust = misery, remorse
disgust + expectancy = cynicism
expectancy + anger = vengeance

Secondary

anger + acceptance = dominance
joy + surprise = delight
acceptance + fear = submission
surprise + sorrow = disappointment
fear + disgust = shame, prudishness
sorrow + expectancy = pessimism
disgust + anger = scorn, loathing
expectancy + joy = optimism

Tertiary

anger + surprise = outrage, hate
joy + fear = guilt
acceptance + sorrow = resignation
fear + expectancy = anxiety, dread
sorrow + anger = envy, sullenness
disgust + joy = morbidness
expectancy + acceptance = fatalism

Figure 3.1. Plutchik's (1962, 1980) conceptualization of emotions

what happens neurologically, was probably hard-wired; and perhaps as subcortical limbic areas were rewired in new ways to interact with the expansion of the neocortex, the ability to construct socially and to pass these emotions on through socialization began to shift the ratio of hard-wired to socially constructed emotions. But complex emotions like guilt, shame, grief, delight, regret, depression, dread, and nostalgia are, I suspect, more hard-wired than constructed, or, at the very least, human brains are wired to learn these emotions with very little coaching. A good example would be humans' language capacities, where the brain's wiring is set up to learn language as soon as infants are exposed to natural language.[4] True, the way that emotions are displayed is subject to socialization (just like different languages are), but even here, there are limits to the plasticity of displays because these emotions are universal and, it seems, part of human neurology. The social construction of emotions requires a large neocortex in the human measure, and I think that natural selection had hard-wired as much as was possible, right through *Homo habilis*, and perhaps up to *Homo erectus*. At some point, the only neurology involved for socially constructed emotions was the generalized capacity to generate new emotions through the activation of diverse limbic systems. Just when this shift from wired propensities for emotions to socially constructed emotions occurred can never be known, but I doubt if it was during the first jump in the size of the brain from australopithecines to *Homo habilis*.

To some extent, this issue is not very important sociologically. What is clear is that humans possess the neurological capacity to use many diverse emotions and that many of these look like combinations of primary emotions. In some sense, it is clear, the emotional mixing happens on the neurological level, but just what force is doing the mixing—past natural selection or social selection—is unknown and perhaps always will be. In Figure 3.2, I present my views on what I term *first-order elaborations*, taking this idea from Kemper (1987) and following the logic of Plutchik's primary dyads. The idea here is that the mixing of emotions involves dominance of one primary emotion and its variants, with lesser amounts of another primary emotion. That is, one primary emotion is combined (to use a mixing-bowl metaphor) with smaller portions of another primary emotion, and this lesser amount can be just a smidgen or a cupful. For example, the emotions of wonder, hope, relief, gratitude, pride, and reverence are mostly comprised of happiness with varying amounts of aversion-fear. Or, to take

Satisfaction-Happiness

Satisfaction-happiness + *aversion-fear*	*produces* →	wonder, hopeful, relief, gratitude, pride, reverence
Satisfaction-happiness + *assertion-anger*	*produces* →	vengeance, appeased, calmed, soothed, relish, triumphant, bemused
Satisfaction-happiness + *disappointment-sadness*	*produces* →	nostalgia, yearning, hope

Aversion-fear

Aversion-fear + *satisfaction-happiness*	*produces* →	awe, reverence, veneration
Aversion-fear + *assertion-anger*	*produces* →	revulsed, repulsed, antagonism, dislike, envy
Aversion-fear + *disappointment-sadness*	*produces* →	dread, wariness

Assertion-anger

Assertion-anger + *satisfaction-happiness*	*produces* →	condescension, mollified, rudeness, placated, righteousness
Assertion-anger + *aversion-fear*	*produces* →	abhorrence, jealousy, suspiciousness
Assertion-anger + *disappointment-sadness*	*produces* →	bitterness, depression, betrayed

Disappointment-Sadness

Disappointment-sadness + *satisfaction-happiness*	*produces* →	acceptance, moroseness, solace, melancholy
Disappointment-sadness + *aversion-fear*	*produces* →	regret, forlornness, remorseful, misery
Disappointment-sadness + *assertion-anger*	*produces* →	aggrieved, dicontent, dissatisfied, unfulfilled, boredom, grief, envy, sullenness

Figure 3.2. First-order elaborations of primary emotions. Adapted from J. H. Turner 1999a, 1999b.

emotions like awe, reverence, and veneration, these are mostly fear combined with substantial but lesser amounts of satisfaction-happiness.

Just how this combining process works at the neurological level is unclear. If we want to make some speculations about which of these kinds of first-order elaborations might be hard-wired, a useful way to approach the question is to ask which first-order combinations would best accommodate the direct selection pressures examined in the last chapter. Which, in other words, would best achieve mobilization of associative emotions, interpersonal attunement, positive sanctioning, prescriptive moral codes, exchanges of emotional values, and rational decision making? I will develop the argument more fully in Chapter 5, but here I will illustrate this procedure by selecting one or two emotions from each row on the right side of Figure 3.2. Looking at the first block of combinations under satisfaction-happiness, we can see that *pride* would be critical because it pulls in emotions about self into group processes; *appeased* and perhaps *calmed* help mitigate the effects of raw fear generated by negative sanctions; and *hopefulness* would also mitigate against excessive sadness and keep actors oriented to future relations that are positive. Turning to the second block, where aversion-fear is the dominant emotion, *veneration* of others and moral codes would translate fear into a more associative emotion; *antagonism* would at least alert others to a failure to achieve solidarity, although most combinations of fear and anger are disruptive to social bonds; *dismay* and perhaps *dejection* would alert others that another party requires interpersonal attention and positive sanctioning or exchanges of positive emotions. Turning to the assertion-anger block, *mollified* would be a way to turn anger into a more associative emotion; again, fear-anger combinations do not promote solidarity, but if any of the emotions listed in this row would be associative, perhaps *abhorrence* would be used as an effective sanctioning device in relation to moral codes; and *depression* would act, much like dejection and dismay, as a signal to others and maybe to self as well to attend to more positive sanctions and exchanges. Finally, looking at the disappointment-sadness block, *acceptance* takes the sting out of disappointment and sadness in ways promoting continued bonds; *remorse* is a good way to make self mobilize sadness and fear to make amends and thereby promote solidarity; *aggrieved* or maybe *dissatisfied* would be a lower-key way to reveal anger and alert others to breaks in social bonds that need to be attended.

The above is, of course, wild-eyed speculation;[5] and I have no idea whether any of the statements offered are accurate. But my intention is to posit an appropriate way to examine first-order combinations: which ones would promote sociality and enhance solidarity, even when more negative affective states like fear, anger, and sadness are activated? Answers to this question might provide one criterion for guessing—and indeed, this is what is involved—which emotions are hard-wired. Conversely, we can turn the question around: which emotional combinations are most likely to disrupt social relations and social bonds? These might be emotions that were socially constructed, using the general emotion-generating capacities of diverse limbic systems. I would guess that these emotions were constructed when more complex social orders began to generate high rates of internal conflict—certainly by the time of horticulture and probably in more settled hunter-gatherer populations, especially those relying on "Big Men" leadership patterns (where a charismatic leader dominates activities among settled hunter-gatherer populations). Admittedly, the foregoing compounds the wild-eyed speculation; the point I want to stress here is that sociologists need to at least consider such questions. Too often, we simply view everything as socially constructed; and yet this approach is not adequate for such primal forces as human emotions. It is clear that biology is an essential factor in emotion; just how much and what kind is not so easy to say, but we need to ask the questions because it may well be that the rapid advances in neurology may soon be able to provide some answers. And it makes a great deal of difference for understanding the flow of interaction as to whether an emotional elaboration is innate or socially constructed.

Second-Order Elaborations. A quick look at Table 3.1 indicates that guilt and shame are seen by some researchers as primary, in that they are essential to the social order. In my view, however, they are not primal in the same way as fear, anger, happiness, and sadness. In fact, guilt and shame are very complicated emotions, because they are composed of the mix, again assuming this is an adequate metaphor, of three primary emotions in varying combinations. I term these *second-order elaborations*, and there may be more of these than guilt and shame but these are the most critical. Some researchers, such as Helen Lewis (1971) and her associates, and Thomas Scheff (1988, 1990a, 1990b), view shame and guilt as essentially the same emotion, with guilt being a variant of shame. In my view, these emotions are similar because they are constructed by activation of limbic systems

TABLE 3.4

The Structure of Shame and Guilt

RANK ORDER OF PRIMARY EMOTIONS	SECOND-ORDER EMOTIONS	
	Shame	*Guilt*
1	Disappointment-sadness (at self)	Disappointment-sadness (at self)
2	Assertion-anger (at self)	Aversion-fear (about consequences to self)
3	Aversion-fear (about consequences to self)	Assertion-anger (at self)

SOURCE: Data from Turner 1999a, 1999b

generating disappointment-sadness, assertion-anger, and aversion-fear, but the proportionate activations among these three primary emotions differ when generating shame and guilt.

In Table 3.4, I list the rank orders of primary emotions—that is, their relative proportions—in generating either shame or guilt. Shame is an emotion that arises when individuals have not demonstrated competence in a situation; and it is predominately composed of (a) disappointment and sadness directed at self for having displayed inappropriate behaviors that reveal incompetence, (b) anger at self for having done so, and (c) fear to self about the consequences of what has transpired. Guilt is the emotion generated when individuals have not met expectations of others and of moral codes; it is mostly composed of (a) disappointment at self for having failed and sadness about this failure, (b) fear about the consequences to self of this failure, and (c) anger at self for having so failed. The difference between shame and guilt is thus the reversal in the rank order of aversion-fear and assertion-anger; and while this may not seem like much, it produces very different emotions and feelings.

It is significant, I believe, that disappointment-sadness is the dominant emotion of both shame and guilt. A more psychoanalytic theory might propose that clinical depression is the result of repressed shame and guilt. Such may be the case at times, but often what is seen as the result of repression is simply built into the structure of shame and guilt. Extreme shame and guilt fire off the limbic systems generating sadness and its high-intensity variants listed in Table 3.2; the result is a depressed individual, but not necessarily a repressed individual.

Even though shame and guilt are complex second-order emotions, they are, I believe, hard-wired in the sense that humans are predisposed to develop the neurological capacity to fire off those limbic systems creating these emotions. I suspect that they are much like language abilities: we are predisposed by our neurological wiring to experience these emotions, given some exposure to sanctions that generate them; and moreover, there may be a window in early childhood when these emotions must be laid into our neurology if they are to become part of a person's emotional repertoire. The basis for this conclusion is that social order among individualistically inclined hominids would not have been possible unless individuals could experience shame at failure to behave appropriately and competently in interactions with others and guilt over having failed to meet expectations of others and moral codes. Without shame and guilt, morality has no internal footing within individuals' cognitive frames and feelings about themselves; in the absence of shame and guilt, then, social control would depend upon constant monitoring and external sanctioning of individuals by others. In contrast, emotions like guilt and shame, especially when they operate in conjunction with pride for having behaved competently and for meeting expectations, locate morality inside the individual and make the individual self-monitoring and self-sanctioning in ways that promote social solidarity—while avoiding the dissociative costs to the group of negative sanctioning.

If an animal has other bases for bonding hard-wired into the neurology generating behavioral propensities and routines, then shame, guilt, and pride would not be as necessary in this sense. Quick negative sanctions can bring the animal back into line with what it is already predisposed to do. But if animal is not predisposed to bond at the group level and is, rather, semi-autonomous and mobile within a larger regional population, then it is more difficult for that animal to create stable bonds at the local group level. Even if the animal can generate moral codes, monitor conformity or nonconformity, and then sanction those who do not meet expectations or who behave aberrantly, these sanctions have no force, beyond the here and now of the immediate situation. To carry force outside the purview of monitors and to assure that individuals remain motivated to behave competently as group members and to stay alert to moral codes and expectations of others, even when these others are not actively monitoring individual behavior, requires neurological wiring for new kinds of emotions—like shame, guilt, and pride—that do what bioprogrammers provide for many other mammals.

Thus, once emotions became the key to enhanced social bonding among hominids, selection began to expand the repertoire of emotions in ways that gave individuals new and flexible affective responses to each other. This enhanced emotional repertoire, in turn, enabled individuals to form and sustain close-tie social relations at the local group level through enhanced attunement, moral coding, responsiveness to sanctioning, exchange of affect, and decision making oriented to others and group expectations. These and other processes so necessary for groups must be sustained by active role taking and role making; thus selection would eventually wire the brain for emotions that drive an individual from inside. This may not have occurred initially, because the neocortex would have to expand so as to enable an individual to hold and remember codes and expectations in its memory and to apply these in appropriate contexts, but at some point in hominid evolution the expanded neocortex and alterations in subcortical limbic systems enabled hominids to experience shame, guilt, and pride. And once this capacity began to emerge, it would dramatically enhance fitness and, as a result, would be subject to further selection. The result is humans who display all kinds of behavioral pathologies associated with shame and guilt, but these are only pathologies in the complex societies that developed after hunting and gathering—societies to which humans can adapt but that are not natural to us as a species that evolved in a hunter-gatherer mode of social organization.

NOTES

1. In earlier work, I have included *surprise* as a primary emotion, as have many others. But now I believe this emotion has a different nature; following Carol Izard (1992a) and others, I see it as a kind of clearing emotion, one that alerts an organism and forces it to drop other emotional states and to mobilize the appropriate primary emotion toward the source of surprise.

2. Panksepp's (1998) data and analysis of emotions in mammals would clearly challenge the point.

3. However, Theodore Kemper (1984, 1990) has sought to examine the underlying neurology of emotions, but he is the exception rather than the rule.

4. I would not go so far as Noam Chomsky, but I would say that there is a period—from a few months of age to perhaps ten years—during which children learn language. Once the brain of infants receives language cues, the hard-wire potential for language is, so to speak, activated. Moreover, children do not learn via socialization every single noun, adjective, and verb, as well as the means to vary them and to construct sentences; rather, the combinatory capacity exists as a hard-wired potentiality in the brain—if this capacity is activated during early childhood. Emotional production probably involves a similar process; there may be innate capacities to elaborate emotions in combinations, but like language, there must be sufficient emotional prompting in a child's environment to release these capacities. For it would seem impossible for a child to learn via conditioning, or even modeling, every combination of human emotions and the precise contexts in which these are appropriate. Much of this work is probably done by the brain as it is for language, which is, I believe, built from the neurological substrate generating not just cross-modal associations under visual dominance, but also the production of emotions.

5. And yet, "just so" stories can be useful, if speculative, because they lead us to ask how and through what mechanisms a capacity evolved and now operates. In Chapter 5, I will attempt a more systematic analysis, but this too will read like a "just so" story.

CHAPTER 4

The Neurology of Human Emotions

The evolution of humans' emotional capacities occurred through changes in the ape brain. Not only did selection produce an animal capable of controlling emotions and using them to communicate meaning; selection also worked to create an animal able to generate a wide array of emotional states. The complexity of human thought, interaction, organization, and culture are not possible without this ability; in fact, as I have been arguing, it is possible that humans' emotional abilities are more unique than their language facilities. In any case, the ancestors of humans survived, I believe, by using their expanded emotional abilities to forge strong bonds of solidarity among animals that did not have powerful genetic propensities to do so. My goal in this chapter is to further delineate some of the neurological underpinnings of human emotions; in so doing, we can gain some appreciation for the neurological changes produced by natural selection over the past few million years of hominid evolution.

Some Qualifications and Concerns

When I first began to think about how human emotions were generated, I used a "mixing" model—somewhat along the lines of Robert Plutchik's (1980) theory. I began with Kemper's (1987) suggestion for examining combinations of emotions, summarized in Tables 3.3 and 3.4, and Figure 3.2,

85

TABLE 4.1

The Mixing of Primary Emotions

PRIMARY EMOTION	VARIATIONS IN INTENSITY			FIRST-ORDER EMOTIONS	SECOND-ORDER EMOTIONS
	Low intensity	*Moderate intensity*	*High intensity*		
Satisfaction-happiness	content sanguine serenity gratitude	cheerful buoyant friendly amiable enjoyment	joy bliss rapture jubilant gaiety	+fear: wonder, hopeful, gratitude, prided +anger: vengeance, appeased, calmed, soothed, relish, triumphant, bemused +sadness: nostalgia, yearning, hopefulness	
Aversion-fear	concern hesitant reluctance	misgivings trepidation anxiety	terror horror high anxiety	+happiness: awe, reverence, veneration +anger: revulsed, repulsed, dislike, envy, antagonism +sadness: dread, wariness	
Assertion-anger	annoyed agitated irritated vexed perturbed nettled rankled	displeased frustrated belligerent contentious hostility ire animosity	dislike loathing disgust hate despise detest hatred seething wrath	+happiness: snubbing, mollified, rudeness, placated, righteousness +fear: abhorrence, jealousy, suspicion +sadness: bitterness, depression, betrayed	

TABLE 4.I

The Mixing of Primary Emotions, *continued*

PRIMARY EMOTION	VARIATIONS IN INTENSITY			FIRST-ORDER EMOTIONS	SECOND-ORDER EMOTIONS
	Low intensity	*Moderate intensity*	*High intensity*		
Disappointment-sadness	discouraged downcast dispirited	dismayed disheartened glum resigned gloomy woeful pained	sorrow heartsick despondent anguish	+happiness: acceptance, moroseness, solace, melancholy +fear: forlornness, remorseful, misery +anger: aggrieved, discontent, dissatisfied, unfulfilled boredom, grief, envy, sullenness	+fear, anger: guilt +anger, fear: shame

presented in the last chapter. For convenience of reference, Table 4.1 re-produces this argument in one table. Thus, I set out to discover the neuro-logical mechanisms, not only expanding the number of variants of primary emotions, but also "mixing" primary emotions into an even larger emo-tional repertoire. I soon realized that the mixing metaphor may be over-stated. Perhaps we need not give up on this metaphor completely, but the neurology of emotions is more complex than my work and the work of others have implied. Let me enumerate some of the reservations that I now have about a view of human emotions as the product of "mixing."

A cursory understanding of the mechanisms behind the production of emotions leads to following conclusion: there are many neurological sys-tems involved in emotions; assuming all emotional potentials in these sys-tems were activated and then mixed into every combination and permuta-tion, many thousands of emotional variants and combinations could be generated. This is not what happens, however; in fact, humans signal and interpret less than a hundred emotional states during the course of most interactions. If the mixing of emotions is the proper analogy for what hap-pens, then humans do not utilize the full range of their neurological ca-pacity to generate variants and combinations of emotions. This might be expected, because people can interact in very subtle and highly complex ways utilizing just a few dozen emotions; and to add too many shades of emotional texture to the process would make interaction overly complex and, probably, exhausting.

Another feature of human neurology that gave me pause about using the mixing metaphor is the fact that emotions are not simply based in dis-crete nuclei in the brain, but in systems of nuclei located in various regions of the brain. This systemic quality of the structures producing emotions— what is sometimes loosely termed the "limbic system" (MacLean 1990), or what I see as limbic system*s*—is not one system but a series of systems in-volving neocortical, subcortical, and brain-stem structures (Le Doux, 1991, 1993a, 1993b, 1996). Each of these systems can generate, to a degree, a large range of emotions, but they do not operate separately; they are intercon-nected to each other and they are involved in relations with body systems that make their effects on each other and, hence, on humans' emotional states that much more complex.

What did emerge from these initial glimpses into the neurology of emotions was the growing awareness that body systems operate to create the emotions that are used in signaling and interpreting (Damasio 1994; Le Doux, 1996). Moreover, signaling and reading emotions are mostly nonverbal and visual, while often being subcortical and unconscious (Le Doux 1996). To "have a feeling" is only a special case of being cognizant of how your body or that of another person has been mobilized, but conscious feelings are only those emotions that penetrate neocortical functioning from the much greater number of emotions that we send and receive subcortically, or subconsciously. Indeed, the flow of interaction on an emotional level is typically a subcortical process involving the mobilization of body systems by participants to an interaction. Subcortical responses to the emotions revealed by the body thus circumscribe the flow of interaction.

An additional complication arose during my early foray into neurology: humans possess an emotional memory system residing outside of the neocortex; and while this system can be attached to memories stored in the neocortex, such need not be the case (Le Doux 1996). Hence, human responses to each other's emotions may not only be conducted subcortically, they may also involve stocks of emotional memories that are not, or cannot, be retrieved consciously.[1] In fact, a good portion of humans' emotional responses to each other may involve invoking subcortical emotional memories about which they remain unaware. Humans thus respond emotionally to stimuli, and they are often unaware that they have seen and responded to emotional cues. This conclusion is supported by recent studies (e.g., Whalen et al. 1998), indicating that the human emotional system is activated outside conscious awareness when exposed to split-second glimpses of faces revealing emotions.

It also appears that the experience of intense emotions at critical junctures in early life can generate physical-chemical alterations in the brain (Mlot 1998). Patterns of brain activity are altered, with the result that these early experiences bias responses later in life. Often the source of these responses is mysterious to individuals; for example, an infant or young child subjected to fear responses will potentially have its brain altered in ways biasing emotional responses toward fear, although the adult may not be conscious of the fear's origin.

These kinds of initial insights come from the literature on the neurology of emotions, and they indicate to me that sociologists need to learn something about the emotion systems of the brain in order to develop more accurate and robust theories of emotion. Furthermore, notions of mixing of emotions may gloss over what are complicated interactions among, or perhaps simultaneous activations of, diverse cortical and sub-cortical systems that need to be re-examined in light of the rapid advances in the neurological sciences. Where, then, do we begin to learn about the biology of these emotion systems? My answer to this question in the preceding chapters has been to construct hypothetical evolutionary scenarios regarding why humans needed to become emotional in the first place; in this chapter, I seek to explore the alterations in the brain that were involved in transforming hominids into such emotional creatures.

Neurological Changes During the Evolution of Emotions

If one compares the human brain to our closest living relatives—the great apes (i.e., gorillas, chimpanzees, and orangutans)—several differences are evident. First, humans reveal more asymmetries in significant portions of the neocortex, indicating that the left and right sides of the brain probably have somewhat more differentiated functions than in pongids (Bradshaw and Nettleton 1983; Needham 1982; Sperry 1982). Associated with this "split" of certain brain functions is the greatly expanded connectivity through the corpus callosum between the right and left sides (Bogen and Bogen 1969; Eccles 1989). Asymmetry allowed portions of the neocortex to have increased cognitive capacities without increasing the size of the neocortex to the point that the newborn would not easily pass through the female's cervix. Much of the specialization involved areas dedicated to language production (Broca's area) and comprehension (Wernicke's area) as well as to pattern recognition (right side) integrated with temporal recognition (left side).

Second, much of the increase in size of the human brain is in the frontal lobe, where thought, long-term memories, and other cognitive functions are carried out. Yet, more recent data suggest that across apes and humans, there has not been as dramatic an increase in the relative size of the frontal lobe as once thought, although the issue remains unsolved (Semendeferi et al. 1997; see also, Ruff, Trinkaus, and Holliday 1997). At a minimum, it is clear that humans' prefrontal cortex (lower anterior portion of the frontal lobe) is developed considerably beyond that in any other primate; and it is

TABLE 4.2

Relative Size of Brain Components of Apes and Humans,
Compared to *Tenrecinae*

Brain component	Apes (Pongids)	Humans (Homo)
Neocortex	61.88	196.41
Diencephalon thalamus hypothalamus	8.57	14.76
Amygdala	1.85	4.48
centromedial	1.06	2.52
basolateral	2.45	6.02
Septum	2.16	5.45
Hippocampus	2.99	4.87
Transition cortices	2.38	4.43

SOURCE: Data from Stephan 1983, Stephan and Andy 1969, 1977, and
Eccles 1989.
NOTE: Numbers represent how many times larger than *Tenrecinae* each
area of the brain is, with *Tenrecinae* representing a base of 1.

this structure that is particularly important to emotional responses, thinking, planning, and decision making (Damasio 1994).

Third, and most relevant to my argument in this chapter, there was significant growth in ancient limbic systems in the symmetrical subcortical
regions of the brain. Controlling for relative body size, the septum, amygdala, hypothalamus, cingulate gyrus (which is the distinctive-looking neocortical tissue sitting on top of subcortical limbic systems), and diencephalon (thalamus and hypothalamus) are all significantly larger than their
counterparts in apes. Thus, humans' capacity to emit emotions increased,
and dramatically so during the course of hominid evolution.

Some of this enhanced emotional facility came with selection on emotion systems existing in all primates and, indeed, most mammals. This
can be seen in Table 4.2, which compares apes and humans relative to a
primitive mammal, *Tenrecinae*. In Table 4.2, I selectively report data from
Stephan (1983), Stephan and Andy (1969, 1977), and Eccles (1989) who re-
ports on his personal communications with Stephan. What these data

show is an index of growth in the size of various brain systems, controlling for body size[2] (which correlates positively with brain size in mammals) and using *Tenrecinae* as a base of 1.0 (this is the most primitive mammal form, probably very much like the one from which all mammals evolved). I have included only apes and humans, but the original data report on prosimians, insectivores, and monkeys. The numbers give us a way to compare relative sizes of brain components; and so the indices in Table 4.2 can be used to make comparisons.

As can be seen from this table, the neocortex has the greatest increase in relative size. But most subcortical areas encompassing humans' emotional systems are also substantially larger: (1) the diencephalon, which is situated on top of the brain stem and stimulates or mediates a good portion of emotional responses; (2) the amygdala, which in most mammals is the center for aversion and aggression, especially its basolateral components, which are an evolutionary addition to older centers for fear and anger with some new nuclei apparently devoted to pleasure; (3) the septum, which is the center for sexuality in mammals, with most of the growth in *Homo* coming from an addition concerned with pleasure with sexual overtones (in its older, more primal areas the septum increased much less); (4) the hippocampus, which is central to tagging cognitions with emotion and which may also store emotional memories that work subcortically; and (5) the transition cortices consisting of the perirhinal, parahippocampus, and entorhinal areas, which initially order sensory inputs for the hippocampus.

Thus, while not nearly as dramatic as neocortical development, the limbic systems involved in generating human emotions also expanded, indicating that natural selection worked on what it was given: limbic systems that probably approximated those of apes, especially the chimpanzee (our closest living relative with whom we share over 98 percent of our genetic material). Selection layered over older nuclei in the septum and amygdala areas for generating pleasure that, perhaps, could serve as the basis for human altruism, reciprocity, positive sanctioning, and other associative responses. Moreover, I argue that these centers grew much earlier in hominid evolution than did the neocortex. These centers could work in concert with the neurotransmitters, neuroactive peptides, and hormonal systems to augment more positive and associative emotions listed in Table 4.1 under satisfaction-happiness.

Human Systems of Emotions

To appreciate what these changes represent in the evolution of emotions, we need to place them in the context of the entire set of limbic systems in the human brain responsible for the production of emotions. In the middle and bottom sections of Figure 4.1, a medial cross section of the brain is drawn so as to expose the subcortical systems, plus the cingulate gyrus, which appears to be a special kind of neocortical system, and the forebrain, which is clearly neocortical (Vogt 1993a, 1993b; Jackson and Duncan 1996). Not all structures of the brain are drawn, but only those that appear most crucial to the production of emotions. It is important to recognize in this medial view that the diencephalon portrayed on the bottom penetrates into the core of the subcortical regions of the brain and is, therefore, encapsulated by both the remaining subcortical systems and the neocortex. Similarly, the midbrain portion of the brain stem penetrates into the core of the neocortex. The diagram can give the impression that these areas are stacked on top of each other, which, in terms of their successive evolution (MacLean 1990) may be an appropriate metaphor, but it does not take into account the fact that they are also enveloped by newer centers of the brain, and, indeed, that they penetrate into the middle of the brain. The top portion of Figure 4.1 represents the neocortex, as one would look at it from the outside. Along this left hemisphere are language centers (Broca's and Wernicke's areas), the sensory lobes (parietal for haptic, occipital for vision, and temporal for auditory) that receive inputs from the specialized sensory areas of the thalamus, the olfactory bulb that projects directly into subcortical areas, and the frontal and prefrontal lobes.

The bottom portion of the figure highlights the top of the brain stem and diencephalon, as well as the pituitary gland that is activated by the thalamus and hypothalamus. Also highlighted is the midbrain, which is largely responsible for the production of neurotransmitters (Kandel, Schwartz, and Jessell 1995). The diencephalon, composed of the thalamus and hypothalamus, along with the pituitary gland, are mediators of emotionally charged sensory inputs (Le Doux 1996), while being critical to the production of hormones and peptides involved in emotional responses (Shepherd, 1994: 603).

The middle portion of Figure 4.1 represents those limbic systems surrounding the diencephalon. The amygdala is the center for fear (Le Doux 1987, 1996), anger (MacLean 1990), and as noted in connection with its

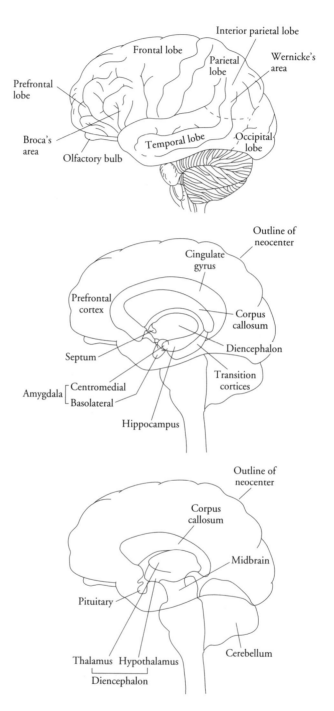

Figure 4.1. The human brain and emotions. Adapted from
J. H. Turner 1996a, 1999b.

basolateral portions, apparently for pleasure as well (Eccles 1989), while being a major center for integrating emotional responses between subcortical and cortical areas (Le Doux 1996; Aggleton 1992). The septum is the center for instinctual sex drives (MacLean 1990) and in humans has additional nuclei that generate pleasure and satisfaction (Eccles 1989). The hippocampus and related transition cortices are involved in integrating emotional memories, both those that become part of long-term memory and, perhaps, those that remain subcortical (Le Doux 1996; Eichenbaum and Otto 1992; Eichenbaum, Otto, and Cohen 1994; Schacter 1998; Clark and Squire 1998; Cohen 1993). The basal forebrain or prefrontal cortex is involved in integrating emotional responses to thought, planning, and calculation by receiving inputs from all other limbic systems—hippocampus, transition cortices, diencephalon, amygdala, and septum—and using these to construct lines and courses of action for self (Damasio 1994). In particular, layer four of the prefrontal cortex—often termed the granulofrontal cortex—is especially critical for (a) anticipation and planning; (b) empathic and altruistic feelings; (c) concern for welfare of self and others; (d) visual reading of gestures via connections to vision cortices; (e) touch, as this reveals emotional content via connections to motor areas; and (f) via connections to the cingulate gyrus, crying and laughing. The cingulate gyrus, particularly the anterior portion, is also involved in integrating other emotion systems and the forebrain (Devinski and Luciano 1993; Vogt 1993a, 1993b; MacLean 1993), while being the locus of unique mammalian behaviors like mother-infant bonding, audio-vocal communication such as the "separation cry," and playfulness (MacLean 1990).

These areas of the brain are critical to most theoretical questions that microsociologists pursue: the nature of self, the dynamics of decision making and choice, the processes involved in consciousness and feelings, the use of memory and stocks of knowledge, and the dynamics of role making and role taking. While language and related features of linguistic abilities like pacing and intonation are important, these processes are not as fundamental to microlevel interactions as nonverbal emotional dynamics. How, then, do we begin to get a handle on these emotional brain systems? I do not have a complete answer to this question, only some tentative suggestions regarding what to examine. Let me begin with what I will term, in deference to Damasio's (1994) "somatic marker hypothesis," the nature of emotional body systems.

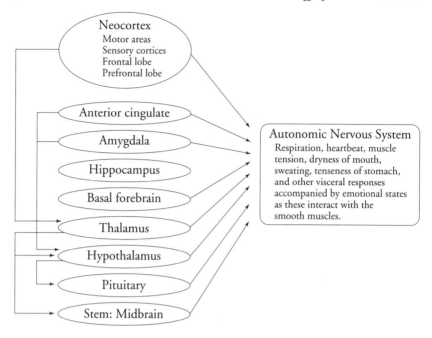

Figure 4.2. Body system number 1: ANS responses. This and all the remaining figures in this chapter are adapted from J. H. Turner 1999b.

EMOTIONAL BODY SYSTEM NUMBER 1:
THE AUTONOMIC NERVOUS SYSTEM

The autonomic nervous system (ANS) is composed of the smooth muscles that control visceral responses accompanying emotional arousal. These responses include respiration, heartbeat, muscle tension, dryness of mouth, sweating, and tenseness of stomach (Shepherd 1994: 395). Figure 4.2 presents a very rough diagram of some of the important brain systems involved in ANS responses. By far the most important is the hypothalamus, which receives inputs from other areas of the brain and converts neural information into hormonal information by targeting areas of the pituitary gland that secrete hormones into the bloodstream. Once activated, the ANS operates as a feedback system, working primarily through the thalamus, which takes inputs and projects them to other emotion systems and to the cerebral cortex (Le Doux 1996). As Damasio (1994) and Le Doux (1996) have argued, these kinds of feedback processes are crucial in emotional arousal; initial arousal in response to some stimulus mobilizes a body system in ways that sustain, change, or enhance the original arousal, while activating other emotional body systems. And as I argue, it is the mobilization of these body systems that is so important in presentations of self (including unconscious emission of gestures) or role making (R. H. Turner 1962) and in the responses of others to these presentations, or role taking (Mead 1934). Moreover, individuals are often unaware of their body mobilization until they role-take with others and see the responses of these others to their unconscious emission of gestures. Thus, the feedback from the arousal of an emotion system is not only internal to the individual; it often depends upon role taking with others who are responding to the visible sights of body-system mobilization. What is true of the ANS system is, as we will see, true of the other three body systems as well.

EMOTIONAL BODY SYSTEM NUMBER 2:
NEUROTRANSMITTERS AND NEUROACTIVE PEPTIDES

This body system concerns the release of neurotransmitters; the most important are listed in Table 4.3 and Figure 4.3. Most of the neurotransmitters involved in emotional states are released by the midbrain portions of the brain stem, usually under stimulation from other emotion systems and, as recent work by Drevets et al. (1997) underscores, under the influence of the subgenual prefrontal cortex. The basal forebrain also appears to release one neurotransmitter, acetylcholine (ACh); and it may be that the thalamus is also directly involved (Bentivoglio, Kultas-Ilinsky, and Ilinsky 1993). Indeed, emerging research appears to indicate that neurotransmitters are released in more areas outside the brain stem than was once thought to be the case. It is tempting in discussing neurotransmitters to list the mood-enhancing effects of each, as is implied in Table 4.3. For example, we might view serotonin as involved in creating a sense of well-being, relaxation, and sleep, or we might see dopamine as a stimulus to attention, arousal, and feeding. Yet the effects of these and other neurotransmitters probably vary for each individual, and their interaction effects are not well understood. As Kety (1972: 120) noted more than twenty-five years ago, "It seems quite futile to attempt to account for a particular emotional state in terms of the activity of one or more biogenic amines. It seems more likely that these amines may function separately or in concert as crucial nodes of the complex neuronal networks . . . (but these) are probably derived from the . . . experience of the individual."

TABLE 4.3

Effects of Neurotransmitters and Neuroactive Peptides

	Effects on Brain
Neurotransmitters	
Acetylcholine (ACh)	Cortical arousal, learning, and memory as these stimulate body systems; some evidence that ACh is related to mild satisfaction
Monoamines	
Dopamine	Regulates motor and hypothalamic functions and stimulates most limbic systems
Noradrenaline (norepinephrine)	Enhances ability of neurons to respond to inputs and stimulates arousal
Adrenaline (epinephrine)	Same as noradrenaline
Serotonin	Regulates sleep-wake cycles and generates relaxation and pleasure
Histamine	Not completely understood, but appears to be involved in autonomic neuroendocrine functions
Amino acids	
y-Aminobutyric acid (GABA)	Inhibitory action controls outputs of neurons
Glycine	Unclear, but may modulate effects of glutamate
Glutamate	Causes excitatory action in neurons, including those in the limbic system
Neuroactive peptides	Of the several dozen known peptides, many are produced in the brain and act like neurotransmitters because of their small size and ability to travel in the brain's vascular system. These appear to affect a wide range of emotions stimulated by various limbic systems. The opioids appear to be particularly important in emotional responses. Larger peptides are more likely to work through the endocrine system and more inclusive circulatory system of the body. Recent data indicate that Substance *P* may be critically important in emotional responses (Wahlestedt 1998; Kramer et al. 1998), especially in relation to monoamines.

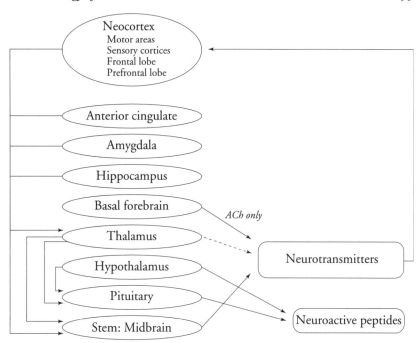

Figure 4.3. Body system number 2: Neurotransmitters and neuroactive peptides.

There are two properties of neurotransmitters that are interesting to note. First, they can work very rapidly to generate an "as if" effect—as if, in the sense that the release of the neurotransmitter within the brain fools the individual into sensing that other body systems have been fully mobilized. This is why, I suspect, that individuals on antidepressant drugs that activate neurotransmitters without also mobilizing the full body system will sometimes experience emotions in a very "shallow" way, or at least individuals who role-take with them perceive the emotion as less than real because other body systems are not mobilized in ways corresponding to the emotional mood described by an individual. Second, Figure 4.3 also emphasizes that portions of the endocrine system operate as neuro-modulators. These are termed neuroactive peptides in Figure 4.3; they modulate the connections between axons and dendrites. These neuroactive peptides are produced in the cell body, packaged in secretory granules, and transported from the cell body to terminals. They are released by the hypothalamus, pituitary, and closely associated areas (Heimer 1995: 388–93; Kandel,

Schwartz, and Jessell 1995: 298–301), and as they travel to target areas, they modulate the connections among neurons. In so doing, they act very much like neurotransmitters, except that they are hormones. Peptides are released all over the body, and it is becoming clear that there are many more of these than previously believed—so far, at least fifty, but perhaps several hundred peptides in all. It is only recently that the effects of peptides on the brain have become fully recognized; and further research will, no doubt, reveal their involvement in neurotransmission. They may also be generated by structures less directly involved in hypothalamic activity.

Neuroactive peptides are seen as part of the neurotransmitter body system because they are produced in and operate within the brain's vascular system. Other hormones and peptides operate through the more general endocrine system, at times coming back to the brain to exert their effects. Peptides generally work with less speed than neurotransmitters, which can be activated very rapidly (especially those, like ACh, involved in modulating muscle movements). Thus, the effect of neuroactive peptides on emotions will in general take longer to be evident to the individual and others in his or her environment; moreover, the effects on mood will tend to be longer lasting than those of other body systems. Much of the current research on peptides has focused on their role in various addiction problems, but they are clearly an important system in the production of emotions. For example, the opioids are much involved in creating emotions on the pleasurable side of the scale and in suppressing activation of other body systems (Smith and Stevens 1997a, 1997b). Yet a great deal needs to be learned about how they operate; for the present, we can only recognize that they have important, though not fully understood, effects on human emotions.

EMOTIONAL BODY SYSTEM NUMBER 3:
THE ENDOCRINE SYSTEM

This system is comprised of the endocrine system, which is composed of the flow of neuroactive peptides through the bloodstream of the brain and the flow of hormones through the inclusive vascular system of the body. The hypothalamus receives inputs from other limbic systems, and either directly or, more typically, through the pituitary gland and closely related areas, causes the release of hormones and peptides into the bloodstream. As these circulate they activate the body, and as they work through and come back to the blood system of the brain, they have important feedforward and feed-

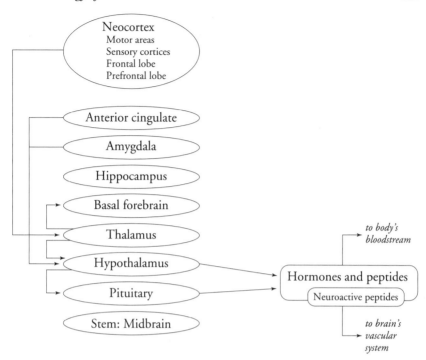

Figure 4.4. Body system number 3: Endocrine responses.

back effects on other limbic systems (Le Doux 1996). These effects take time, of course, because hormones must often circulate through the body.

EMOTIONAL BODY SYSTEM NUMBER 4:
THE MUSCULOSKELETAL SYSTEM

The musculoskeletal system involves stimulation of the striated muscles controlling skeletal structures that dictate body movements. The basic processes operating in this system are roughly outlined in Figure 4.5. Again, the hypothalamus is crucial in channeling inputs from other limbic systems into contractions of striated muscles; and because striated muscles react more rapidly than the smooth muscles of the ANS, the emotional arousal associated with their stimulation and the feedbacks from their contraction are rapid (Le Doux 1996). In fact, it could be hypothesized that the initial role taking of individuals (and role making, whether inadvertent or intentional) relies upon cues from the musculoskeletal system, especially the muscles of the face.[3] As Ekman (1982, 1992b) and various associates have

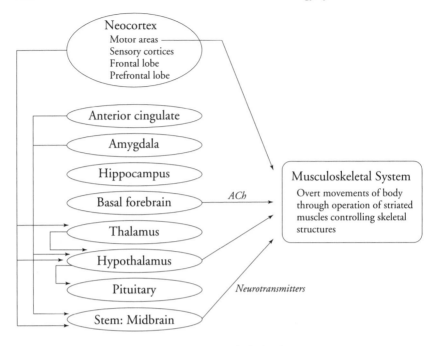

Figure 4.5.   Body system number 4: Musculoskeletal responses.

clearly documented, primary emotional responses of the face do not vary dramatically cross culturally because humans all have the same muscular set up on their faces, and the stimulation of the striated muscles works so rapidly (in milliseconds). Moreover, since neurotransmitters are involved in muscle contractions, the reading of facial gestures will reflect both musculoskeletal and neurotransmitter body systems.

THE BODY FEEDBACK SYSTEM

Figures 4.2–4.5 imply that these four body systems are discrete, which in a way they are; but these systems are also very much interconnected. For example, musculoskeletal and ANS responses are facilitated by neurotransmitters; neurotransmitters are augmented by neuroactive peptides; and endocrine processes are activated by the other body systems, and vice versa. Thus, the systems involved in mobilizing the body emotionally play off each other in complex ways that are not fully understood. Moreover, as *systems*, they are also involved in iterations of responses; and thus their interconnections are further complicated by the way they play off each other

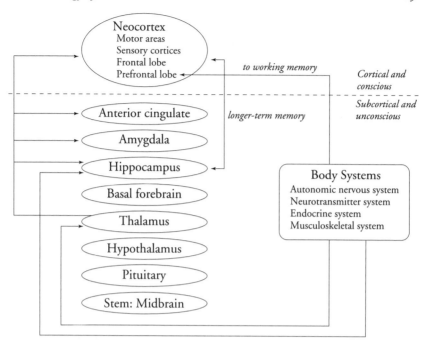

Figure 4.6.   Body feedback systems.

over time during the course of successive waves of activation and deactivation. This interconnectedness points to the importance of feedback processes in these body systems so important to human emotions.

As is emphasized in Figure 4.6, these four systems feed back to the rest of the limbic system, primarily via the thalamus, which in turn can stimulate other limbic structures and make emotional responses available to the neocortex (Le Doux 1996). Short-term or working memory, lasting just a few seconds, can also pick up body mobilizations, but these do not become full-blown feelings unless other limbic systems are activated, particularly the hippocampus. It should be emphasized that this feedback system can remain unconscious; individuals can literally be unaware of the emotions being aroused by their four interconnected body systems (Le Doux 1996). Others will usually be aware of the operation of these body systems and, in fact, they will use the signals that these body systems provide as their primary bases for role taking. Indeed, conscious awareness of emotional body systems is more a special case of the much older and primary (in an evolutionary sense) subcortical feedbacks from all four body systems.[4]

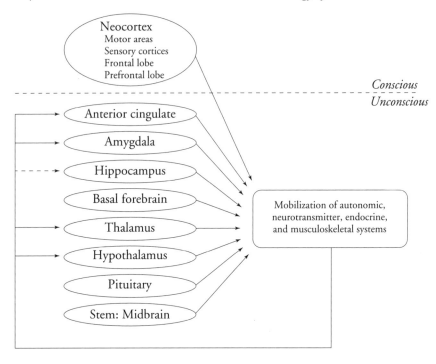

Figure 4.7.   The unconscious emotional memory system.

As Le Doux (1993a, 1993b, 1996) has emphasized for the amygdala and as is probably the case for other limbic systems, animals have an emotional memory system that is often unconscious. Just how and where such emotional responses to various stimuli are stored is unclear,[5] but it appears that humans can maintain repertoires of emotional memories and responses outside of the neocortex. Figure 4.7 offers a rough approximation of the processes involved. The existence of an emotional memory system assures that many of the emotional signals emitted by a person, and read by others, will remain removed from the person's conscious thought (Bowers and Meichenbaum 1984). They will be emotions but not feelings; and again, it can be hypothesized that these unconscious emotional memories are in many respects more fundamental to role taking than conscious ones. Indeed, if others communicate to a person that they are picking up certain emotional responses, or if bodily feedbacks are strong enough to penetrate consciousness as emotional feelings, the person can still be surprised that they are giving off or experiencing certain emotions—and not only surprised, but also unsure as to the source of their emotional responses. As a further implication of this unconscious memory system, it may be that humans engage in less repression of emotional responses than psychiatric theory would suggest; rather, they are simply unaware of emotional responses that are stored subcortically.

CONSCIOUSNESS AND FEELING

There is considerable debate over whether or not other animals possess consciousness in the human measure: awareness of internal and external stimuli, seeing self as an object, and reflection on self and sources of stimulation in an environment (see, e.g., Heyes 1995, 1998; Dewey 1922; Block 1995). We need not enter this debate for the purposes of this chapter, although apes and perhaps other higher mammals appear to possess the rudiments of these cognitive capacities (Savage-Rumbaugh et al. 1993). The key brain structure in consciousness is the prefrontal cortex,[6] which has connections to virtually all parts of the brain: the neocortex, the limbic systems, and other subcortical systems (MacLean 1990; and Damasio 1994).[7] Consciousness of a stimulus involves receipt of an input via the sense modalities—vision, auditory, olfaction, and haptic—which then goes to a specialized sensory area of the thalamus; and from there, the sensory input travels to both subcortical limbic systems and the appropriate lobe of the neocortex (Le Doux 1996): occipital for vision, temporal for auditory, parietal for haptic, and olfactory bulb for smell (the latter, it should be noted, projects directly into subcortical areas housing the various limbic systems, especially the amygdala; for this reason, smells can often excite emotions very rapidly). The association cortices, which comprise a good part of the neocortex and which are involved in integrating sensory inputs, generate an image that is temporarily stored in buffers (Geschwind 1965a, 1965b). The transition cortices consisting of the parahippocampal, perirhinal, and entorhinal cortices then pool the images and send them to the hippocampus, which, in turn, creates a representation that is sent to the transition cortices for intermediate storage as a memory (Heimer 1995; Gloor 1997). Recent studies indicate that the parahippocampal cortex, in interaction with the dorsolateral prefrontal cortex, is particularly important in determining if memories endure (Rugg 1998; Brewer et al. 1998). After a few years, if the images are reactivated through experience or thought, the assembled im-

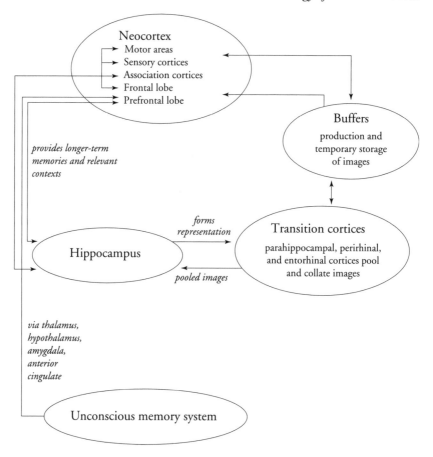

Figure 4.8. The conscious memory system.

ages will be shipped to the neocortex, most particularly the frontal lobe, for storage as long-term memory (Damasio 1994; Eichenbaum 1997; Vargha-Khadem et al. 1997).

The subcortical memory system is very much involved in this process, sending via the thalamus, hypothalamus, amygdala, and anterior cingulate information to the hippocampus and to the prefrontal cortex, which then places this information into temporary buffers to be pooled by the transition cortices and represented by the hippocampus. Thus, consciousness almost always involves inputs from the limbic systems, either directly from limbic memories or indirectly via intermediate and long-term memories that have been previously tagged by the hippocampus with emotional in-

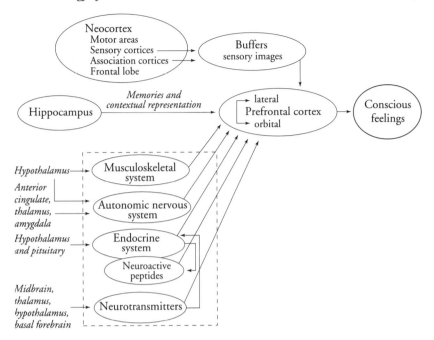

Figure 4.9. Body system arousal and the production of consciousness.

puts from the limbic body systems. Figure 4.8 delineates some of the key processes.

Conscious sensations of emotion, or feelings, are simply an extension of these processes, as is outlined in Figure 4.9. What makes consciousness emotional is the arousal provided by the four body systems outlined earlier (Damasio 1994; Le Doux 1996). The prefrontal cortex is the central structure because it receives inputs from the four body systems, the limbic structures, the hippocampus, the sensory cortices, the association cortices, and the motor areas (Damasio 1994). Without inputs from one or more of the emotional body systems outlined in Figures 4.2–4.5, however, consciousness will reveal little real affect, only abstracted and emotionally flat cognitions *about* feelings.

Memories involve pulling from the transition cortices and frontal lobe, via the hippocampus, coded instructions that then fire off the relevant sensory cortices. Thus, memory recall does not involve pulling ready-made and fully developed pictures or images stored in the neocortex; rather, it involves activation of shorthand, coded instructions stored in the neocortex, or more intermediately in the transition cortices, that *re*activate the sensory cortices and the relevant body systems in order to reproduce in rough form the experience that was coded in memory (Damasio 1994). If this experience had heavy emotional content, then reproduction of this memory will set into motion the four body systems that then give the memory much of the same emotional flavor as the original experience.

Why should sociologists care about these dynamics producing feelings? My answer is that it makes a big difference in how we conceptualize feelings in analyzing social interaction. When a person feels shame, guilt, happiness, anger, or any emotion, these feelings involve mobilization of the four body systems—from direct stimulation of the thalamus in the present and from refiring of sensory cortices so as to re-stimulate the relevant body systems that were activated in the past. The character of the feeling is thus a complex mixture of present stimulation of limbic systems via the thalamus at subcortical and cortical levels, coupled with re-stimulation of memories that have been tagged and represented in the past by the hippocampus as coded sets of instructions which reactivate the relevant sensory cortices and body systems. But often, long before a person recognizes an emotion in himself or herself, others in this person's environment can see the underlying emotions that are expressed subcortically through the body systems and that only sometimes penetrate consciousness as a feeling. We can do so because of the work of natural selection on our hominid ancestors to produce an animal capable of forming emotionally laden bonds via the visual sense modality. Thus, a sociology of feelings is only a special, and perhaps the less important, case of a more general and, in evolutionary terms, more primal mobilization of emotional body systems.

Thought and Thinking

Sociologists and cognitive scientists tend to have a poor model of humans as organic calculators, in which we (a) weigh options in light of the present situation and past memories, (b) assess alternatives, and (c) select lines of conduct to maximize utilities. This process is, of course, an important part of thinking; and like so much in the brain, the prefrontal cortex is critical in this process. Damasio's (1994) review of cases reveals that damage to the prefrontal cortex appears to disrupt the capacity to plan and make rational decisions. As Damasio has also emphasized, the reason for this failing of subjects to think and behave rationally is that the prefrontal cortex is linked to both the neocortex and subcortical regions of the brain; it is only because emotional valences are brought to bear on alternatives from various limbic systems that individuals can make "rational" decisions. Collins's (1993) emphasis on emotion as the "common denominator of rational choice" is well supported by the neurology of the brain, and this neurology revolves around the connection between cortical and subcortical emotion systems.

Another problem with sociological conceptions of thought and thinking is their verbal bias. The view that thought is internalized conversation is widespread, but a moment of reflection would reveal this to be impossible. If thinking were merely covert talk, we would seem very dim-witted, since talk is a sequential modality and hence very slow. Moreover, we have Broca's and Wernicke's areas on the left hemisphere of the neocortex to translate auditory signals back and forth into the "brain's way of thinking," which, as I noted in Chapters 2 and 3, is in patterns and gestalts.[8] Thinking occurs in a "brain language" that, I would argue, relies heavily on the right hemisphere to produce patterns among images that can be manipulated with incredible speed and converted, when needed, into auditory or written speech. Moreover, although we can often slow the process of thinking down by "talking to ourselves," this kind of thinking is the exception rather than the rule.

A further speculation on why thinking occurs in patterns and configurations stems from the fact that humans, unlike most mammals who are olfactory dominant, are a primate and hence are visually dominant (Forbes and King 1982); and the association cortices at the point where the temporal, occipital, and parietal lobes meet—areas such as the inferior parietal lobe—involve integration of sensory information under vision (Geschwind 1965a, 1965b). I believe that this subordination of other sensory inputs under vision shapes the way humans actually think: in blurs of images, many of which do not penetrate our consciousness.

Emotions are very much a part of these images, above and beyond the values that they may give various options that might be considered when individuals try to make decisions. Whether from the transition cortices and hippocampus or pulled up from the subcortical emotional memory system, thought involves a constant tagging of images with emotional valences. But these emotional tags are not always accessed by consciousness; indeed, I would guess that the vast majority of thought does not occur in ways we are conscious of, and to the extent that emotions are part of "the brain's way of thinking," we do not have easy access to the emotions that structure in unknown ways human thinking. Only when we become consciously aware of feelings that we represent to ourselves in words do we become self-aware of how emotions are implicated in thinking. It is often the case, however, that others can "read our thoughts" in ways that we cannot, since if the emotional valences are high, mobilization of body systems can tip others off as to what emotions are behind our thinking, long before we become aware of our own emotional responses.

Thus, to the extent that sociologists are concerned with thinking as it influences the flow of interpersonal behavior and, ultimately, the kinds of cultural and social systems that are built from interactions, it is essential to know something about how the process occurs at a more neurological level. If my above speculations are plausible, then the way we study interaction could shift away from a verbal bias to a nonverbal, emotional emphasis.

Let me illustrate this conclusion with an argument about how to reconceptualize self. We see ourselves as objects in situations primarily via the right brain, which generates pattern recognition in space; and our image of ourselves in situations is heavily biased toward spatial representations of where we are. As to *who* we are in a situation, this involves role taking with others and bringing forth more enduring concepts of self. Like any cognition that comes from memory, self-cognitions have been tagged with emotions and, at the same time, they may re-stimulate sensory cortices, especially the visual one, and remobilize limbically stimulated body systems. Thus, humans see themselves not only in Cooley's looking glass and thereby derive a "self-feeling"; they also invoke their memory and emotion systems to enhance this self-feeling. Much of the emotion invoked, however, will not be conscious if it remains subcortical and therefore only perceived by others who tune into the mobilization of others' body systems in their role taking.

The difficulty in measuring self is related to our verbally biased measuring instruments, which are too crude given the complexity of the processes involved. Moreover, the problem of measurement also resides in the unavailability of measuring instruments for gaining access to subcortical emotional states and to the emotionally laden thoughts of individuals as they think in the visually biased "brain's way of thinking." Self is not so much a cognitive construct as an activation of the emotion systems implicated in storing memories in the frontal lobe, in thought processes couched in the brain's way of thinking, in subcortical emotional memories, and in the re-activation of the emotional body systems. Given the complexity of these dynamics, it is not surprising that people oftentimes do not know who they are or where they stand; or to state the matter less dramatically, they have difficulty giving verbal expression to cortical and subcortical processes that are occurring outside of their working memory.

Implications for Studying Interpersonal Processes

Role making and role taking are, on the one hand, conscious processes of responding to situational cues and bodily signals through the use of work-ing and longer-term memory systems. On the other hand, role making and role taking are subcortical and unconscious processes of responding to cues and signals through activation of the emotional body systems outlined in Figures 4.2–4.5. The dimensions of role taking and role making are not op-posed; in fact, they often become intermingled when limbic processes pen-etrate the working memory as feelings, or when limbic processes are given conscious interpretations through vocabularies of motives and emotions. Understanding something of the neurology of the brain and bodily systems adds some useful insights for theorizing about interpersonal processes.

Much of what occurs during the course of interaction is subcortical, re-volving around mutual emissions of signals via the body systems and, recip-rocally, responding to these signals limbically. I would go so far as to argue that most of the emotional dynamics of interaction operate subcortically, and only under relatively high degrees of emotional mobilization do limbic processes become part of conscious feelings. Moreover, in terms of sustain-ing a sense of interpersonal contact, focus, tracking, and rhythm, I suggest that role taking and role making subcortically are more important than talk, rhythmic conversational turn taking, and conscious reflection. Even if soci-ology does not accept this extreme conclusion, it needs a more neurologi-cally informed conceptualization of nonverbal, "body language" processes.

At a neurological level, our most hard-wired and ancient emotion system is the amygdala, especially those older portions activating fear responses. For a species that does not possess fear would soon be killed off by predators; and since aggression is also part of the amygdala and, indeed, part of the fear response as defensive aggression, fear and aggression are humans' most fundamental emotions (Le Doux 1996). Indeed, separate nuclei in the amygdala appear to be involved in different types of fear conditioning (Kill-cross, Robbins, and Everitt 1997). One implication of this fact is that humans are especially attuned both cortically and subcortically to signals of fear and aggression. Among hominids, these amygdala-generated emotions were, no doubt, used to overcome weak-tie propensities and, thereby, to build social structures based on fears of negative sanctions. Thus, negative sanctions have the most power to affect us emotionally. If a low-sociality primate had to build conformity to moral codes, keep individuals in line, force them to stay alert to others and the rules of the community, and pay attention to breaches of codes and interpersonal cues, then negative sanctions that activate fear responses would be an especially effective means of doing so—especially, as I have been emphasizing, among hominids who were biologically disposed to individualism and loose group structures.

On the other hand, activation of fear and use of negative sanctions are very costly: these emotions can consume physical and emotional energy as body systems are mobilized; they can heighten anger-aggression to danger-ous levels when those who receive negative sanctions become angry, while those seeking to sanction become even more angry over the aggression from those whom they have attempted to sanction; they can eventually activate depression, whether through use of defense mechanisms or alterations in the release of neurotransmitters and neuroactive peptides; and they can cause maladaptive and antisocial behaviors. Thus, as emphasized in Chapter 3, solidarity and cohesion cannot be built on fear and aggression alone.

Once it is recognized that selection worked to create more associative or positive emotions to build sociality and solidarity, some of the rewiring of the amygdala and the septum for pleasure makes sense. Moreover, the expansion of the anterior cingulate gyrus, as the center for playfulness and mother-infant bonding, may also have been rewired to produce a more generalized source for happiness and propensities for bonding, altruism, and reciprocity beyond the mother-infant dyad. Add to these the possible reconfiguration of neurotransmitters, hormones, and neuroactive peptides to generate more pleasurable emotional responses, and we can safely hypothesize that much of the rewiring of the human brain is the result of natural selection creating centers for positive and associative emotions. Such emotions are the basis for positive sanctions that activate pleasure, satisfaction, happiness and other variants and combinations of the satisfaction-happiness emotions listed in Table 4.1. Since these propensities may be late evolutionary additions to the more primal emotions of fear and anger,[9] it is my opinion that more positive emotions are layered over potentially negative ones; thus positive sanctions always contain the implicit threat that if these do not work more negative ones will follow.

Moreover, to the extent that positive emotions come from neuroactive peptides and hormonal circulation in the bloodstream, they will tend to work less rapidly, even if only seconds slower than those stimuli activating musculoskeletal and neurotransmitter responses for fear. While such a difference in response time may not seem like much, it is an eternity in neurological time, and even in interpersonal real time where individuals read and respond to gestures in milliseconds. Fear and anger, in other words, will immediately activate the musculoskeletal body systems long before happiness will have done so: a smile takes a bit longer to form than a frown, since the latter is activated by the amygdala whereas the former is the product of several neurological systems, some of which are slower.

As implied in the above remarks, the four body systems work at different speeds, and this fact has implications for how people role-make and role-take. The musculoskeletal system is the fastest, although neurotransmitters like acetylcholine must be released to contract muscles. In milliseconds, the striated muscles can contract under stimulus, move an organism and, in the case of humans and higher primates, become an emotional response—and, perhaps in humans alone, a conscious feeling. Thus the first and fastest signals that individuals mutually send out and receive are musculoskeletal, particularly involving the muscles of the face. We first seek, if only subcortically, information about the operation of the musculoskeletal system, and the effects of neurotransmitters on that system. The other emotion systems take longer, again sometimes less than a second but often several seconds or longer. Aside from the neurotransmitters facilitating motor responses, they can also have mood-enhancing effects in "as if" feeling, but these must often become involved in iterations of bodily feedback to exert their full effect. The hormone-peptide system can also work fairly rapidly, especially under stimulation of fear by the amygdala, but the opioid hormones producing pleasure appear to take longer to generate their effects. The ANS system is primarily a fear system, working as rapidly as smooth muscles can under stimulation by the amygdala and release of neurotransmitters affecting stimulation of muscles—although more pleasurable states of the ANS take longer, especially when other body systems must also be activated. Moreover, ANS activation for more associative emotions often involves conscious interpretation of what is occurring and, as a consequence, this process takes a considerable amount of time (again, on a neurological scale). Thus, besides "as if" neurotransmitter effects, contentment and happiness require longer to form in humans; we all implicitly recognize this fact in our role taking, where we initially scan, usually subcortically, for aggression-anger, while waiting a bit for more associative responses to form (if the situation dictates that they should). Augmenting Collins's (1988) theory, I would also venture the speculation that rituals are often necessary to initiate positive emotional energy because the human emotion system is still trying to work around the more ancient fear-aggression systems.

Sadness is the last of the primary emotions listed in Table 4.1. In many ways, this emotion is the most complicated, since no clear center for this emotion exists in the human brain, although recent evidence indicates the amygdala in its integration functions and the subgenual area of the prefrontal cortex appear to bring on clinical depression when damaged (Drevets et al. 1997; Damasio 1997). Even taking into consideration the recent findings of hard-wired centers, it may be that sadness is an emotion that originates with configurations of neurotransmitters, neuroactive peptides, and other hormones; or, more typically, with a lack of such activity in neurotransmitters like serotonin, dopamine, norepinephrine, and with endocrine processes that work through the circulatory system. Thus sadness takes longer to form, especially if it also involves stress hormones or the suppression of hormones involved in the production of more positive emotional states. Also, defense mechanisms are often implicated as individuals consume emotional and physical energy through repression or by otherwise dealing with highly unpleasant emotions such as anger, fear, guilt, and shame. Thus, while sudden disappointment may operate very rapidly on the musculoskeletal system, as facilitated by neurotransmitters like acetylcholine responding to stimulation by the amygdala, the "mood" of being sad takes considerably more time to form—anywhere from a few seconds to hours—as neurotransmitter release is suppressed and as hormones/peptides operate through the bloodstream to dampen emotional energy.

We might ask a further question: why would there be selection for sadness beyond mild disappointment? One answer is that sadness is simply a by-product of depression of neurotransmitters, neuroactive peptides, and, as recent imaging studies reveal, underactivation of the subgenual prefrontal cortex (Drevets et al. 1997). Another answer is that sadness is a very effective mechanism of social control. For example, guilt and shame are often the outcome when a person senses that they have made others unhappy or sad by not meeting expectations; and so moral codes and conformity to them are built, not just on positive and negative sanctions, but also upon more complex sanctioning practices that avoid the full mobilization of anger. Sadness is a very effective negative sanction because, as emphasized in Chapter 3, it does not contain the volatility of anger-based negative sanctions; and it is effective as a direct sanctioning technique by others, while at the same time it often evokes sadness in the person who feels that they have failed to meet others' or their own expectations (recall from Table 4.1 or 3.4 that sadness is the dominant emotion in both guilt and shame). Thus, guilt, shame, and other emotions in which sadness is a dominant component are probably more than a by-product of suspension of other emotional responses; sadness is a key to social control revolving around negative sanctioning that avoids the volatility of anger and fear, although these latter emotions are part of complex second-order emotions like shame and guilt. Moreover, sadness is also a signal to others that the individual is in need of social support. By reading signals of sadness, others become aware that a person requires attention and positive emotions. In fact, sadness is a good example of how humans read emotions nonverbally, because we respond most actively to body signals that a person is unhappy. There was probably selection for this kind of response, since, if a group-living animal without strong bioprogrammers for such living is to sustain solidarity, it must be able to read and respond to cues that individuals are not mobilized to put energy into solidarity-maintaining rituals.

Conclusions

The neurology of emotions is obviously more complex than the cursory outline presented in this chapter. Yet, my goal has not been to outline a model of neurology, but to communicate two major points. First, sociological analyses of interaction in general, and emotions in particular, cannot ignore the neurology of emotional responses. The way people role-take and role-make is intimately connected to the four body systems as they interact with each other in complex feedback and "feedforward" relations and as they influence conscious and subconscious reactions of individuals. Second, the analysis of the neurology of emotions as it influences face-to-face encounters is best performed from an evolutionary framework. By understanding that humans are a primate, that they evolved from an ancestor similar to contemporary chimpanzees, and that their hominid ancestors survived by virtue of overcoming apes' propensity for weak ties through the production of an expanding repertoire of emotions, we gain considerably more insight into human interaction.

Indeed, it could be argued that sociologists' understanding of interaction and the emotional undertones of all interaction have been terribly biased and distorted by our failure to engage in both biological and evolutionary analysis. Some of the obvious shortcomings of our current models of interaction that stem from the failure to be evolutionary sociologists are: the widespread view that thinking is covert speech; the overemphasis on speech as the paramount process during the course of interaction; the view of self as a verbal and cognitive construct; the failure to ask why humans need to use rituals in the first place; the view that human interaction is guided by just a few master emotions; the overemphasis on feeling as the conscious experience of emotion over the subcortical; unconscious dynamics of emotion; and the view that the human actor is rational and instrumental over its affective and emotional dimensions. I could carry this list on for several pages, but my point should be clear: we cannot study face-to-face human interaction by placing the evolutionary history of *Homo* and the neurology that this history changed into a black box. We cannot simply cede this area over to other disciplines; these kinds of evolutionary questions are central to microsociology.

NOTES

1. When Alfred Schutz (1932) used the provocative phrase "stocks of knowledge at hand" to describe memories of stored information used to organize individuals' responses in situations, he had no way of knowing about unconscious memories, although he did emphasize that individuals have difficulty articulating

their knowledgeability. Human "knowledgeability" is thus a vast repertoire of information stored neocortically and subcortically, often making full awareness of this knowledge problematic, even as we use and respond to it.

2. There has been a number of techniques for establishing controls for body size or weight. The technique used to array the data in Table 4.2 is explained in Stephan (1983), Stephan et al. (1988) and, briefly, in Eccles (1989: 42).

3. Connected to the skin of the face are vast numbers of striated muscles that control expressions. For an animal relying so heavily on nonverbal role taking, it is perhaps not surprising that the human face is so controlled by fast-acting striated muscles. The face is also heavily laced with blood vesicles that expose blood flows and other ANS responses that can be read and interpreted by others. Similarly, the hormonal system outputs can also be read directly in the face, or indirectly, through their feedback effects on other body systems.

4. The existence of an emotional memory system makes human self-awareness often rather indirect. As a person responds emotionally by activating body systems, others in the individual's environment read gestures produced by body system mobilizations about which the person may remain unaware because these body system responses are linked to unconscious memories. The individual may become aware of the activation of body systems, if the experience is sufficiently intense, and through this route a person can begin to achieve self-awareness of how he or she is responding. Yet it is often through role taking "in the looking glass" of others' responses that the individual becomes more fully aware of how their responses are affecting others. As such self-awareness emerges, additional emotional responses may be activated as the individual evaluates how he or she is seen in the eyes of others. Again, some of these responses may be tied to unconscious memories, forcing the individual to interpret body-system responses and the reactions of others to this person's body-system activations. Thus, the existence of an unconscious memory system explains the processes described by George Herbert Mead as the "I" and the "Me"; our behaviors (the "I") can only be known in experience (the "Me") because we cannot know how our body systems will be mobilized and interpreted by others until we have responded through conscious manipulation of gestures and through unconscious activation of body systems.

5. The hippocampus is probably the key structure, since it is already devoted to providing context to memories.

6. There is increasing evidence that the thalamus is a critical routing structure, pulling images from working memory and then moving them to cortical and subcortical areas where memories are stored (Glanz 1998).

7. The superior frontal sulcus now appears to be the area for spatial working memories (Courtney et al. 1998). In fact, it is now clear that "the prefrontal

cortex is functionally compartmentalized with respect to the nature of its inputs" (O Scalaidhe, 1997: 1, 35).

8. There is some evidence that the brain synchronically fires neurons to code and uncode information. See Baringaga (1998) for a brief summary of findings.

9. Again, Panksepp's (1998) data on "joy" in small mammals may make this argument incorrect.

CHAPTER 5

What Kind of Emotional Animal?

Every facet of human endeavor is emotional. Without emotions, humans could not choose among behavioral alternatives, see themselves as objects, engage in face-to-face interpersonal behavior, organize groups, and construct the large-scale institutional systems cutting across entire societies and, today, a global network of societies. As much as language and the complex cultural systems that are made possible by language, humans' emotional capacities are what make patterns of human organization viable. Given the significance of emotions to human behavior, interaction, and organization, it is important, I believe, to understand where they come from and how they now operate. This has been the goal of this book, and in this closing chapter, I would like to summarize the argument briefly and, in one last burst of speculation, draw out some of the implications of this argument.

A Brief Overview

Humans are apes, at least at their genetic core. True, we call ourselves *Homo* to make the distinction between us and our close primate cousins, but we still carry with us the genetic legacy of our ancestors' adaptation to marginal arboreal niches. Our anatomical closeness to *Pongidae* is clearly evident, once you take the fur off of our cousins and stand them upright, as was shown on Figure 1.2 (page 22). More significantly, we still retain the behavioral tendencies for individualism, autonomy, freedom, and mobility of *Pongidae* and the last common ancestor to humans and our ape cousins. The behavioral and organizational changes required of our ancestors were probably greater than many of the alterations to the basic ape anatomy. Somehow and some way our hominid ancestors needed to become more tightly socially organized. Selection had some inherent tendencies to work on toward this end: perhaps the strong bonds between mothers and infants; maybe the often strong ties among some male siblings (as is the case among chimpanzees); possibly the ritual greetings, occasional grooming behaviors of males (as evident among chimpanzees); and in many cases, the modest tendencies for male leadership among some species of apes (as can be seen with gorillas). But these alone, I believe, could not be utilized by natural selection to produce the necessary level of social organization; and it is for this reason that apes continued to decline as the retreat of the forests decreased arboreal niches and opened up new ones on the African savanna. Our ancestors hit upon an additional solution: to expand the emotional repertoire to produce bonds sustained by visual contact among groupings of hominids wandering the savanna in search of food under conditions of high predation.

This conclusion is obviously speculative, but it is difficult to see how else a low-sociality primate whose more natural structure is the regional population would become better organized at the local group level. Could selection extend the mother-infant bond to include males, thereby creating cohesive groups? Could selection build up male dominance in ways that would create social solidarity among individualistic primates? Could selection build upon greeting rituals among some males to organize unrelated females, who do not use rituals in their interactions, into more committed group members? Could selection take limited patterns of males grooming each other and females (as part of courtship) to include more day-to-day grooming among all age and sex classes? Could selection suddenly reverse twenty to thirty million years of evolution away from female matrilines and overcome patterns of female transfer from natal groups when there was probably nothing for selection to work on? Even if we could answer modestly in the affirmative to all these questions, we still would have do ask whether movement in these directions would be enough to create flexible and yet sufficiently cohesive and stable group structures that did not do violence to apes' propensities for autonomy, individualism, and mobility, and for fluid organization at the community level. I do not think so, although admittedly one could make a plausible argument.

It was far easier, I believe, for selection to rework the hominid neuro-anatomy to produce a more emotional animal who could use already developed tendencies for visual readings of gestures still evident among our closest relative, the chimpanzee,[1] to forge new kinds of bonds. Other behavioral tendencies, such as mother-infant bonding, ritualized greetings among males, occasional grooming among males, and male attachments and friendships, could all operate as modalities for using finer-grained emotions to create social bonds, but without the expanded emotional content and the ability to role-take and role-make in terms of emotional dispositions, I do not think that the requisite level of flexible social organization at the local group level could have been achieved. Moreover, without emotional communication, how were the tendencies of ape females to avoid each other or, at best, tolerate each other (typically, in order to encourage their respective offspring to play together) to be overcome,[2] since they do not enact rituals or groom each other? How could increased solidarity and longer-term relations among females and between males and females be achieved without a new emotional attachment? Most species of apes did not change, and they died out. Among hominids, selection changed the brain in subtle but significant ways to create a new way to overcome the relatively low sociality of apes. For males, especially if they were like present-day chimpanzees, selection had to do less, because males form bonds, use rituals, groom, and perform other associative behaviors. But more was needed to build even stronger ties among males and, more significantly, to create stronger and more enduring ties among females, between females and males, and between males and their offspring. The brain was, I believe, the easiest route for natural selection to build these new patterns of tie-formation that would produce more stable, enduring, and cohesive groups.

At the neurological level, we can see some of what selection did to the brain: expansion of limbic systems and greater neocortical control over emotional presentations. At the behavioral level, the evidence is clear each and every time humans interact: ritualized openings, repairs, and closings of encounters; extensive use of body positioning and countenance to communicate meanings; and heavy reliance upon facial gestures and voice intonations to communicate emotional states. When any of these signals is missing or is produced in an inappropriate way, interaction becomes strained, even if a constant flow of instrumental verbal chatter continues. For language alone, without an accompanying array of nonverbal, emotional cues first used by our hominid ancestors to strengthen social bonds, cannot sustain the flow of an interaction. Without the more primal, visually based language of emotions, interaction becomes problematic along several fronts: individuals are not sure how to frame the encounter in terms of what is to be included and excluded (Goffman 1974; Turner 1995, 1997a); they are not sure of the relevant norms and other cultural systems to be employed; they are not sure of what resources, especially the intrinsic ones so essential to interaction, are to be exchanged; they are not sure if they are really a part of the ongoing flow of interaction; they are not sure if they can trust others to do what they are supposed to do; they are not sure if they can predict the responses of others; and they are not sure if they can even presume that they subjectively experience the situation with others in similar ways. Harold Garfinkel's (1966) early "breaching experiments" demonstrate how fragile face-to-face interaction is; and how easily it can be disrupted. It is fragile because propensities for high levels of social solidarity are not in our genes as bioprogrammers and because, as a consequence, we must use rather subtle and complex emotional communication to keep the interaction from feeling awkward and strained.

Some Highly Speculative Implications

THE VOCABULARY AND GRAMMAR OF EMOTIONS

While the specific neurological centers and body systems involved in the production of emotions are known, at least in rough approximation, one of the more intriguing issues is how the human brain is organized for what might be called "the emotion facility." Much like language, humans' ability to read and use emotions seems to involve more than just learning from operant conditioning or exposure to models of appropriate emotional production in a given context. Of course, during socialization and experience in diverse encounters, humans do learn a great deal of contextual knowledge, tagged and stored in the hippocampus, and then shipped off to the frontal lobe of the neocortex. Still, it would be impossible for individuals to learn every single emotional response appropriate to every potential interaction situation. At times, we are indeed at a loss as to how to respond in new contexts seemingly requiring unfamiliar emotional responses. Yet these are exceptional cases; far more typical are situations, even novel ones, where we seem to know implicitly how to respond and how to interpret nonverbal cues of others.

For example, a very young child who has never experienced a funeral, or even seen one on television, can engage rather effective orchestration of ritualized sadness. True, there is some parental coaching and observation of others, but what is remarkable about the child's demeanor and internal feelings is how well they are configured to the situation. This kind of ability to configure the experience and expression of emotions in situations has, I am convinced, a neurological basis, above and beyond the mere activation of the emotions. Emotions are too easily organized as a kind of emotional syntax to be just the products of operant conditioning, modeling, imitation, or attention to rules of feeling. There is, perhaps, a hard-wired template that structures the emotional experiences and expressions of emotions. How, then, does this template work to allow humans to respond appropriately in most situations, even those about which they know little?

It may be that there is something like a language facility for emotions that is hard-wired in the brain.[3] Selection may have produced neurological templates[4] that generate and organize emotional production in diverse contexts. To some extent, the modes of expressing emotions are culture-specific—as is the case for language, where particular sets of phonemes are selected and used to construct morphemes that are organized by culturally defined syntax or grammars—but the facility to employ emotional grammars to construct emotional sequences of gestures is, I suspect, more universal. We might even see primary emotions and certain first- and second-order elaborations as the hard-wired equivalent of phonemes in language; and as is the case when phonemes are selected to produce morphemes and, eventually, syntax, these hard-wired emotions are strung together to produce configurations of emotional responses in situations. For example, Thomas Scheff and Suzanne Retzinger's (1991: 44) analysis of nonverbal "hiding behavior" on the television show *Candid Camera* reveals stereotypical "surprise responses," followed by sequences of gestures for embarrassment and, occasionally, variants and first-order combinations of anger. Averting of eyes, head down, hands over eyes or face, and other bodily movements occurred in most cases of embarrassment, and in a sequence and configuration that suggests an innate tendency to order and orchestrate emotional responses in certain ways, beyond feeling rules and other norms. If we examined most emotional production this way cross-culturally, I believe that we could get some sense of the underlying syntax of emotions lodged in the neurology of the brain. During this construction of emotional syntax there is interaction between the neurological templates generating emotional phonemes and syntax, to carry the analogy further, and the cultural scripts and rules about when these are to be used in diverse contexts and how the expressive equipment of the body is to present emotional cues to others.

This facility may be activated via socialization during a window of opportunity that approximates those years where language is either learned or never fully acquired. Case studies of feral children demonstrate that this window is relatively narrow, and I believe that these studies suggest that the same children are deficient in their more primal "language of emotions" and, as a result, cannot role-take and role-make very effectively (e.g., Davis 1940, 1947). Too often, the deficiencies of these children are seen as the result of their lack of exposure to language, which is certainly true, but equally significant is their lack of experience in dealing with normal emotional signs emitted through body systems; and in fact, it might be argued that they are even more deficient in this latter sense than in language per se.

I would speculate, then, that there are universal, pan-human structures in the brain that give humans emotional abilities analogous to those for language. In fact, if the hypothesis that the first languages were emotional is plausible, then we could conclude that the generative rules of spoken language evolved from those for emotional languages. They might even use the same underlying brain systems, especially if the evolution of language selected on those areas of the brain generating nonverbal emotion languages. Like sequences of speech, we can interpret and use configurations of emotional cues in rather remarkable ways, even with people and situations to which we have never been fully exposed, and this fact suggests that there is a generative capacity in the human brain to organize the emotions portrayed in Tables 3.3, 3.4, and 4.1 (pp. 73, 81, and 86). We could not learn through conditioning each and every one of these emotions and how they are to be used and interpreted in each and every context; this would require far more exposure than the average child has between the ages of two and twelve. Moreover, to require the brain to learn everything through conditioning would be inefficient, perhaps overloading the cognitive development of children. Thus, natural selection probably created generative capacities to develop cultural grammars for emotions; just where in the brain generative capacities are located is unknown, to the best of my knowledge. But it seems like something well worth looking for, as we seek to understand more fully how language abilities are acquired. Geschwind's (1965a, 1965b) original hypothesis that the rewiring of the brain for cross-modal associations under visual dominance may be the key evolutionary event. As he and, later, Damasio (Geschwind and Damasio 1984) have argued, the association cortices integrating the lobes of the neocortex provided the ability to use language, *if* subsequent selection favored language use. We can, perhaps, push their argument back and hypothesize that these association cortices provided the neurology for generative rules of emotion use via the dominant sense modality—vision. Thus, rather than view these association areas as a preadaptation "waiting" to be selected on for spoken language or for hand-based sign language, we might consider the view that these cortices were used immediately to enhance emotional and visual communication. Chimpanzees not only have the generative capacity to understand and use language (see, e.g., Savage-Rumbaugh, Rumbaugh, and McDonald 1985; Rumbaugh et al. 1993), but also the ability to communicate visually what appear to be complex directions to each other via the visual channel (e.g., Menzel 1971). It is the latter ability of the last common ancestors to hominids and chimpanzees that may have been selected on to produce a visually based emotional language.

If this line of argument is correct, then it suggests that the brain provides templates for ordering and organizing the presentation and interpretation of emotional cues, both conscious and unconscious, that humans use to attune their responses to each other. Such generative capacities would make the use of emotions for creating and sustaining social bonds more efficient, coherent, and powerful. Thus, in trying to understand how emotions are used in face-to-face interaction, we might do well to search for underlying "emotional grammars" typical of a culture, and then see how these grammars are generated by the neurology of the brain. At the very least, we should begin to explore the possibilities of "emotion grammars" above and beyond the normative feeling rules that apply to situations (Hochschild 1979). How do such grammars, for example, guide the flow of affect during role making and taking? What are the templates and generative capacities for emotions that might be the equivalent of how sounds become phonemes and, subsequently, how phonemes become morphemes and syntax? Perhaps there is no answer to these questions, but they are certainly worth pursuing if we are to understand more fully how natural selection created humans' amazing emotional abilities and how these abilities are used today in face-to-face interactions.

There is of course a major difference between emotions and spoken language: emotional displays represent more robust configurations and patterns of information than language production, which always involves a translation of gestalt "brain thinking" into auditory sequences. Thus, there is a neurology behind emotional grammars; this neurology probably orders emotions, not just sequentially as a line of behavior as interaction proceeds over time, but also configurationally as a pattern of cues emitted simultaneously. For the body systems generating emotions interact in complex ways to present arrays of emotional cues that are exhibited in more robust and complex configurations than is possible with spoken language.[5] This is so because emotions are read visually, with individuals seeing multiple body systems at work at any moment in time.

THE CONSTRUCTION OF EMOTIONAL CONFIGURATIONS

All emotions ultimately have a biological basis because they are built from body systems activating one or more primary emotions. True, humans can attach linguistic labels to a wide variety of emotions, thereby giving them a constructed character, but there are limits to how far one can go in such an exercise. There are constraints imposed by the neurological and body systems activating different emotions, and while it is possible to be delusional, defensive, and deceitful (to oneself and others), it is difficult to call anger another emotion; likewise, happiness or sadness cannot be easily labeled anger, and so on. Our body systems thus constrain how we label emotions. But is there some definitive line between emotions that are built into our neuroanatomy and emotions that are socially and culturally constructed?

Are there, in other words, first- and second-order emotions hard-wired into the human neuroanatomy or, at the very least, wired in such a way that we are predisposed to experience these emotions if, in the past, we have been given relevant cues during the formative years when "emotional languages" are learned? It might be argued, as I will shortly, that humans are predisposed to experience complicated emotions like shame and guilt.

These emotions, unlike primary emotions, cannot be experienced unless activated by socialization and experience, but humans do seem to acquire them easily, if they have been exposed to and have experienced the sanctions that stimulate them. They appear to have a kind of "activation potential" that is perhaps lodged in the neurology of the brain. How, then, can we speculate about which emotions summarized in Figure 3.2 and Tables 3.3, 3.4, and 4.1 might have this seeming sensitivity to activation?

One way to address this issue is to ask the same question posed in Chapter 3: what emotions would be critical to creating and sustaining increased group solidarity among individualistic primates trying to get organized? Or: what emotions do gatherer-hunter groupings require in order to sustain themselves. For it is reasonable to assume that hominids were gatherers and scavengers, later becoming hunters as well, resulting in groupings that resembled those hunting-gathering populations who survived until the modern era.

We can begin speculating with the assumption that natural selection is a conservative force, doing what is minimally necessary to promote fitness. From this assumption, we can conclude that, if selection was to create hard-wired templates for converting emotional responses into emotional syntaxes, independently of culturally-generated feeling rules about how to express emotions in particular contexts, it would provide neurological programs for variations of primary emotions and for first- and second-order elaborations of primary emotions necessary to produce bonds among individualistic primates. What, then, would be minimally necessary to generate enough social solidarity and persistence of social structures for our ancestors to be viable in the savanna habitat?[6] In Chapter 2, I reviewed the selection forces that operated to create group structures among hominids, and it is from this discussion that we can make some inferences about what emotions might be a part of "deep structures" or what I have termed templates that organize basic emotional responses.[7] We can begin to use the discussion in Chapter 2 by asking what emotions are most essential to mobilizing and channeling emotional energy, interpersonal attunement, sanctioning, moral coding, exchanging, and decision making. The discussion in Chapter 2 and perhaps the illustrative comments in Chapter 3, may be sufficient to answer this question in general terms, but here I want to develop more specific but highly speculative hypotheses.

For the mobilization and channeling of emotional energy, for the attunement of responses, and for effective sanctioning, the key would be to make individuals responsive to each other when co-present and willing to use and accept sanctions that sustain cooperative relations. With respect to variants of primary emotions, at least moderate levels of satisfaction-happiness would be essential for satisfaction-happiness to produce social bonds. Thus, emotions along the moderate column of intensity for satisfaction-happiness in Tables 3.3 and 4.1 (pages 73 and 86) are most likely to mobilize emotional energy at a sufficient threshold for individuals to channel energies into creating and sustaining social bonds, to facilitate interpersonal attunement, and to make positive sanctions effective. Emotions such as friendliness and amiability would be minimally necessary to make individuals mutually receptive to bond-producing interactions, whereas the lower-intensity emotions along the satisfaction-happiness spectrum are insufficient, I believe, to mobilize and channel sufficient associative affect to achieve either enough initial interpersonal attunement or to put adequate amounts of reinforcement in positive sanctions. In contrast, the high-intensity end of the spectrum produces emotions that are perhaps overly intense because they mobilize too much energy to sustain longer-term relations, because they attune in such unsustainable emotional "highs" as to disrupt longer-term but lower-key attunements that maintain emotional bonds, and because they force positive sanctioning to extremes that tax others' willingness to deliver them in a consistent fashion. Thus, I would offer the hypothesis that if there are neurological templates generating configurations for an emotional language, then these revolve around the production of low- to moderate-intensity forms of satisfaction-happiness. The higher-intensity end obviously involves high degrees of activation of neurological and body systems, but I would venture to say that these are not structured by our neurology but rather by the emotional ideologies and feeling rules of culture.

For assertion-anger, the low-intensity end of the spectrum is sufficient to mobilize energy and channel it into sanctioning activities and into efforts at interpersonal attunement. More moderate and intense releases of anger will increasingly be counterproductive to mobilizing and channeling associative emotional energy, to sustaining subtle and associative interpersonal attunements, and to sanctioning that does not invite counteranger and countersanctioning from those receiving the sanctions. Thus, it might be hypothesized that the lower-intensity end of assertion-anger is all that was minimally necessary to sustain social ties; if there are neurological templates organizing emotional languages of anger, they must be dedicated to fine-grained management of the lower-intensity end of the aversion-anger spectrum, especially since these would be the most effective in negative sanctioning. Yet anger is a powerful emotion, and its release in very intense forms is highly disruptive to the normal flow of interaction. Initial neo-cortical control of vocalized emotions among hominids may well have been directed primarily at anger (and perhaps at fear as well) activated in the amygdala so as not to disrupt mobilizing and channeling emotions into finer-grained attunement and lower-key sanctioning. Yet humans do emit high-intensity anger, and unlike happiness, where there is less imperative to control it, intense anger may need to be regulated by neurological templates. Even when individuals "lose it" and emit very high-voltage anger, there is a stereotypical configuration of responses that, I hypothesize, are universal. Such anger has exceeded the feeling rules of a culture, and it might be worth examining cross-culturally the visual cues emitted by extreme anger. I suspect that, once beyond the reach of rules of feeling, the emission of anger is very similar across cultures. It would be interesting to pursue this hypothesis more systematically.

For aversion-fear, mobilization of moderate-intensity emotions would be essential to sustaining social order. If sanctions for violations of expectations, moral codes, and exchange agreements could not arouse at least moderate levels of fear, then these sanctions would have no real force. Hence, I hypothesize that there are neurological templates that organize fear responses so as to assure that individuals are sufficiently motivated to mobilize and channel their energies into meeting individual and group expectations. Like anger, the high-intensity end of fear is disruptive to social relations, although not in the same way. Extreme anger invites counter-anger or fear, and avoidance of those who are angry—neither of which are associative reactions. Extreme fear often renders individuals incapable of functioning, but does not invite extreme counteranger. Thus, while high levels of fear disrupt ongoing social relations, they can also lead to associative efforts at helping others overcome fear or seeking the source of the fear. Fear can serve to signal to others that sanctioning has gone too far, or that there is a need to attend to breaches. Anger may do the same thing, except that it generally arouses such counteranger or fear that it is difficult to repair the breached interaction. Indeed, it is the shame and guilt that a person experiences after an episode of high-intensity anger that is most likely to repair the breach. For fear, however, it is difficult to know if its high-intensity end is like anger and regulated by neurological templates in the brain. It would be interesting to see if high levels of fear, like, perhaps, high levels of anger, eventually push past the control of feeling rules and reveal a universal character in the configurations of cues emitted. The pictures of fear used by Ekman and associates (1972) in their cross-cultural studies, like those used in studies of anger, would indicate that such might be the case, since the pictures display rather extreme states of these two emotions that would rarely be expressed when feeling rules are operative.

For disappointment-sadness, selection would favor the low- and moderate-intensity ends of the spectrum. These emotions would alert others to an individual's need for attention, without making the task seem so hopeless as to not be worth the effort—as is often the case with highly depressed individuals. Individuals burdened with having to respond to such highly depressed persons generally lose their ability to sustain positive sanctions and to mobilize positive affect, whereas individuals experiencing high levels of depression become ever less able to stay attuned, to respond to sanctions, and to mobilize energy for associative relations. Thus, there would be no reason for high-intensity forms of disappointment and sadness to be structured by the neurology of the brain. Yet there may have been some neurological structuring of short-term, high-intensity emotions for particular situations, such as the death of another to whom one was attached, but these emotions cannot be sustained for long because they deplete energy of individuals to maintain associative bonds, while burdening others with having to respond with too much emotional energy. Thus, it could be hypothesized that there may be emotional grammars across the whole spectrum of disappointment-sadness, but that these neurologically generated grammars work to limit how long the high-intensity end of the spectrum can be sustained; this end of the emotional continuum may be highly regulated by culture-specific ritual responses that regulate behaviors so as to reinforce group solidarity rather than wear it down through the expenditure of too much emotional energy.

First-order elaborations of these primary emotions or the "combining" of two primary emotions—whether this be a mixing, simultaneous activation, or iterated feedforward-feedback relations—are controlled by neurological templates. These are the emotions that selection created to mobilize and channel emotional energies for sustaining social bonds, for sanctioning, for being responsive to sanctions, and for signaling needs for attentive responses, for moral coding, and for decision making; I would hypothesize that it is these first-order elaborations that are the emotions most regulated by neurological templates. With minimal exposure to these emotions, children soon can activate them in rather complex configurations tailored to specific situations without necessarily having been exposed to situations where these emotions are expressed. Humans are predisposed, it would seem, to use these emotions; their use arises so rapidly in children, well beyond what could be learned through conditioning or modeling, that it seems likely that their mobilization and channeling are organized by neurological templates.

For second-order elaborations, individuals who cannot mobilize and channel shame and guilt have difficulty participating in social relations. They are sociopaths, in a sense, even if they do not seek to engage in devious activities. Natural selection thus organized the human brain to orient sanctioning so as to make others feel ashamed and guilty, to perceive in interpersonal attunements if others are feeling ashamed or guilty, and to make decisions so as to avoid feeling shameful and guilty. It is reasonable, then, to hypothesize that the activation of shame and guilt are hard-wired in the human neuroanatomy, for with just a little exposure to situations of shame and guilt, children begin to experience these emotions in complex ways; and by middle childhood (Piaget 1932; Kohlberg 1976), they are so highly attuned to the broader issues of morality that shame and guilt are very effective in maintaining social control.

It will probably never be possible to draw a sharp line between, on the one hand, emotions whose manifestation is organized by generative templates in the human brain and, on the other, emotions whose arousal by neurological and body systems is regulated by socially constructed rules. This line will always be fuzzy, because culture-specific rules of emotion *always* interact with emotional production and interpretation (Kemper 1981); thus, perhaps it is ill-advised to make the kinds of speculations offered here. Yet to understand human emotions, it is desirable to assess the ratio or relative amounts of neurological to cultural programming behind emotional syntax or grammars organizing humans' emotional repertoire. True, there is a fuzzy line between neurological templates and cultural feeling rules, but we should engage ourselves in sharpening our understanding of this line. To assume that emotions are socially constructed is, I believe, to limit our knowledge of how emotions operate in human affairs. For I would argue that biologically organized emotional responses are *the most important* for sustaining interpersonal relations because they were so essential long ago to the survival of hominids, well before their brains were sufficiently large to house vast stores of cultural coding. Extreme social constructionists would emphasize cultural codes, whereas I think that social theory needs to question this conventional line of emphasis. There can be no doubt that specific demeanors of individuals in their use of emotions are culture-specific, just as language is, but the very fact that cross-cultural studies by Ekman and associates (1972) indicate that at least facial expressions of emotions are pan-cultural, it may be that the underlying, "deep structures" of the brain, to use what was once faddish structuralist terminology, guide the way in which culture-specific emotional grammars are constructed.[8] For it seems that humans learn emotional languages too easily for these to be the product of learning alone, and humans' ability to generalize their emotional responses to new classes of situations never actually encountered suggests that more than socialization and experience are involved in shaping how emotional signaling and interpreting among humans transpire. At the very least, social scientists should consider the question of neurologically based templates for the production of emotional syntax.

One way to phrase the question of whether or not there is emotional syntax in the nonverbal gestures of individuals is to turn research on the synchrony between verbal and nonverbal gestures around: instead of seeing the nonverbal as a supplement to speech, what if we view speech as a supplement to configurations and sequences of nonverbal gestures? At first glance, this seems like a preposterous idea, but there are at least some data that lend credence to the notion that nonverbal, and particularly emotionally laden nonverbal syntax communicated via the face, is more primary than vocal syntax. Studies by Kendon (1972, 1980, and 1988) and Birdwhistell (1966) clearly indicate that there is considerable synchrony between body movements and speech; and in Kendon's studies, the larger the body movement, the more pronounced are the speech units uttered. Moreover, many body movements preceding speech indicate something about, and perhaps set the context for, subsequent speech. It may be argued, therefore, that the more basic and primal "speech" here is the nonverbal syntax and the emotions that such syntax communicates, and that the subsequent speech simply adds to these nonverbal cues. Of course, there can be no doubt that the speech communicates a great deal, especially with respect to instrumental activities, but a wide spectrum of data indicates that individuals feel more comfortable when the body language is visible and synchronous with speech. Moreover, Argyle (1988) has argued that when nonverbal and verbal cues are inconsistent people rely more upon the nonverbal, looking for information about another's feelings and emotions. In one study, for example, facial gestures were relied upon over half of the time, whereas vocal cues were drawn upon less than 40 percent of the time (Mehrabian and Ferris 1967). In this same study, the authors concluded that voice is better suited to convey dominance and potency, while face has a greater impact on people's judgments of positive emotions, which makes a lot of sense in light of my earlier emphasis on how critical positive emotions are to sociality and solidarity.

Another source of data comes from Kendon's (1988) review of studies showing that children use more innate nonverbal gestures in infancy and early childhood—which would be expected since speech capacity takes two years to develop—but that children continue to rely upon nonverbal gestures instead of speech, often in rather elaborate pantomimes. Later, these elaborate nonverbal enactments begin to recede as verbal fluency increases. Of course, data indicate that when individuals have trouble communicating ideas verbally (Knapp and Hall 1992: 205–6), they utilize the nonverbal channel that much more. Infant studies clearly show that neonates can imitate and use adult facial gestures (Meltzoff and Moore 1983a, 1983b) long before any ability to utter adult vocal sounds. Indeed, to the degree that we see biological development as a rough indicator of the evolutionary development of the species, the very fact that the use of emotional syntax precedes the later development of language suggests that facial and other nonverbal syntaxes are more primary, with vocal syntax being layered over emotional syntax in much the same way as they were during the evolutionary history of hominids. At any rate, it is an idea that might reorient studies on synchrony of verbal and nonverbal syntax.

EMOTIONS, SELF-AWARENESS, AND SELF-CONCEPTIONS

There is some debate as to whether the great apes can recognize themselves in mirrors and, by implication, see themselves as objects in their environments.[9] Yet it is likely that chimpanzees, at least, can recognize themselves as objects and respond to perceptions of themselves as distinct entities. Chimpanzees therefore can be seen as possessing the rudiments, not only of self-awareness, but of a conception of themselves in relation to others. What our closest relative can do at a rudimentary level, humans do with great acuity; and indeed, one of the most unique features of humans is their ability not only to see themselves as objects in situations, but also to carry within them more permanent conceptions or identities of themselves as beings of a certain kind. The capacity of humans to engage in such self-referential behaviors adds new dimensions to their interaction, and this ability would not be possible without humans' emotional facilities. True, a certain level of neocortical development is essential to hold long-term memories of self, but these cognitions about self are only possible by virtue of the emotional tags and valences that have been attached to them by ancient subcortical limbic processes.[10] Once we recognize that, without emotions, humans could not maintain self-images beyond the few seconds allowed in working memory or sustain a more stable and coherent identity, we can see that the evolution of hominids' emotional abilities and their capacity for self were interwoven, each feeding off the other. As more emotions could be used to evaluate self, the importance of self for organizing behavioral responses increased; and the more self was essential to interaction, the more the evolution of emotions was constrained by self-mediated interpersonal relations.

If the elaboration of emotions was to be the basis of increasing group solidarity among low-sociality apes, then these emotions would need to be directed at self-aware individuals. Among more emotionally attuned animals, mobilizing and channeling emotions toward moral codes, use of positive and negative sanctions, cooperative exchanges, and decision making cannot occur without the ability to see and evaluate oneself and others with emotional valences. Social control and the coordination that such control makes possible are best achieved through self-control by individuals who see themselves as objects and who make decisions about their lines of conduct through self-evaluations corresponding to moral codes and expectations of others. A self-controlled animal is one that does not need to be constantly monitored and sanctioned, because this animal engages in self-monitoring and self-sanctioning. Such self-monitoring and self-sanctioning are only possible with the ability to mobilize particular kinds of emotions toward self.

One of these emotions is pride, which provides emotional reinforcement for meeting moral obligations toward others. With pride, individuals are motivated to do what is appropriate in order to cooperate in groups, because pride provides a positive evaluation of self. Since pride is coupled with fear attached to a much greater amount of happiness (see Figure 3.2 and Tables 3.4 and 4.1), the fear that one cannot meet obligations or that others will not approve of one's behavior makes success in cooperative behaviors even more rewarding. One has not only done what was right and expected, one has also avoided potential negative sanctions for failure to act appropriately. Thus, pride focuses attention on self and becomes a source of reinforcement that pushes individuals to do what is expected. Natural selection, therefore, would elaborate the ability to experience pride because it helps organize an individual's responses to others and to self in ways promoting social solidarity.

Another of the emotions critical to self-monitoring and self-sanctioning is shame about not having behaved adequately or competently. Shame is a composite of sadness, anger, and fear, and is therefore an unpleasant emotion, with the result that individuals seek to avoid its activation toward self. Shame provides motivation to meet obligations and to act competently in relations with others and with respect to moral codes, because individuals generally do not want to see themselves as incompetent and to evaluate themselves as such (Shott 1979). Shame is often repressed in an effort to protect self from experiencing it, and while such repression leads to behavioral pathologies and potentially disassociative behavior, shame more typically motivates individuals to behave appropriately and competently. It is for this reason that shame probably evolved very early in hominids' trying to use emotions as a way to increase social solidarity and to assure that each individual behaved competently and cooperatively. Without the prospect of shame, there is no emotional force beyond here-and-now monitoring and sanctioning by others; with shame, individuals become self-motivated to behave competently, even if others are not around to monitor and sanction. In addition, with the prospect of potentially experiencing shame, competent behavior makes the sensation of pride that much more rewarding.

Another of the emotions essential to self-monitoring and self-sanctioning is guilt over having violated moral codes or the expectations of others. Like shame, guilt is a blend of sadness, anger, and fear and, as such, it is an unpleasant emotion; as a consequence, it too is often repressed. But guilt is not simply an unpleasant way to view self; it also motivates individuals to rectify wrongs committed and to unburden themselves of their guilt by behaving in appropriate ways that repair breaches in the moral order. Moreover, it motivates individuals to make decisions so as to avoid the unpleasant experience of guilt in the first place; and these decisions will typically assure that individuals act to meet expectations. Thus, guilt would become ever more a part of the emotional repertoire of animals using emotions to forge social bonds, since like shame, it becomes a part of individuals' self-appraisals and thus pushes them to behave in cooperative ways.

While other emotions may also be involved in self-awareness, as was discussed in Chapter 3, it is pride, shame, and guilt that are essential to a self-awareness that directs individuals to engage in appropriate, competent, and cooperative responses. Without these emotions, self-control would not be possible in the absence of bioprogrammers pushing individuals to act in cooperative ways. For individualistic primates, trying to become better organized on the African savanna, there would be heavy selection to increase the ability for self-awareness so that this awareness could be used to increase self-control; and if self-control were to be critical to enhancing solidarity, then selection would work to elaborate hominids' emotional repertoire to include pride, shame, and guilt as the keystones for translating self-awareness into self-control.

Understanding the nature of self among humans can add further insight into how emotions enhance cooperative self-control. As Charles Horton Cooley (1916) recognized long ago, an individuals see themselves as an object as a result of the "looking glass" or mirror provided by the responses of others to their behavior. The gestures of others become a mirror or looking glass in which we see ourselves, and as Cooley argued, we evaluate ourselves in terms of what we see reflected from this looking glass. If we see incompetent behavior, we experience shame; if we see violation of expectations and moral codes, we experience guilt; and if we see competence and appropriateness, we experience pride. The looking glass is thus one way that reactions of others become internalized as part of a person's self-evaluation and, if this evaluation is negative, as a motivation to see a more positive self in the looking glass.

The biography of an individual is ultimately a life-long series of such looking-glass reflections, with the first images one sees no doubt having a more powerful effect on the substance of a person's self-conception. Neurologically, the images that we see reflected of ourselves are passed through the transition cortices to the hippocampus (see Figure 4.8 on page 106), where they are contextualized and stored for a couple of years. If these images remain in the hippocampus, they are seen as tied to specific contexts, as something that one did and evaluated at a particular time and place. I would argue, however, that as these memories are moved to the neocortex for longer-term storage as memories, they may lose some of their context-specific content and become more global memories of how competent and moral one is. Thus, the emotional tags that are placed upon a memory of self in a specific situation by the subcortical hippocampus (as it collates subcortical emotions about self in the situation) become more general evaluations of self as a certain type of being as they move to the neocortex for longer-term storage as memories. Out of this movement and decontextualization comes a person's more stable and enduring self-conception; and once this conception of self exists, it filters and sorts perceptions of responses of others to one's actions as they become memories stored in the hippocampus and as they move to the neocortex for longer-term storage. Thus, at some point a person's perceptions of self become somewhat reflexive as a result of selective attention and selective perception. Still, such reflexivity can have highly associative effects because the individual's behaviors become predictable to others, thereby facilitating cooperation.

The dynamics of self and the emotions surrounding self-evaluations have an additional layer of self-awareness, above and beyond Cooley's notion of deriving a self-evaluation from the reactions of others as seen in the looking glass. Not only do we evaluate ourselves in light of the responses of others to our behavior, but we also evaluate our evaluation. For example, if the reactions of others, as we perceive them in the looking glass, say that we did not do what we were supposed to do in the face of danger, these images may force an evaluation of ourselves as "cowardly." But the evaluation does not end here; we will evaluate, in turn, this sense of being cowardly in light of moral codes and our conception of ourselves as a particular kind of person. There is, then, a double evaluation when we become self-aware of the responses of others. It is this second level of evaluation that is important for social control because we will feel shame, guilt, or pride as we evaluate our initial evaluation of ourselves. And it is these emotions that move self to make amends or to behave competently—all of which increase social solidarity.

With a larger neocortex, these processes of seeing oneself in the looking glass can become entirely covert and hypothetical as an individual weighs alternatives before making a decision. As Dewey (1910) argued with his concept of "mind," thinking is a process whereby individuals "imaginatively rehearse" alternative lines of conduct, see the potential outcomes of each line of conduct, and select that line of behavior most appropriate to the situation. Such decision making is conducted, as I have emphasized, in terms of the emotional valences attached to each alternative that one is considering, but the most important emotions are those directed at self. Thus, one can rehearse alternatives, see the reactions of others in an imaginary looking glass, derive a self-feeling, and then evaluate this self-feeling further; as the evaluation moves to this second level, the individual anticipates or even experiences varying degrees of pride, shame, or guilt. Once this second level of evaluation occurs during the process of weighing alternatives, selection of alternatives moves from calculations of utility or reinforcement, because each alternative is a valenced self-evaluation in terms of its potential to cause shame, guilt, and pride. These latter calculations or self-evaluations can often work against pursuing extrinsic reinforcement per se; and so, as self-evaluations measured against variants of pride, shame, or guilt become part of the calculus of decision making, these emotions work against selfishness that could disrupt social bonds and, as a consequence, direct individual decision making toward associative relations in order to experience pride, while avoiding shame or guilt. As a result, decision making becomes self-controlled in ways promoting social solidarity; without this ability to have a conception of self and to evaluate one's evaluation of self in light of potentials for experiencing pride, shame, or guilt, the kinds of solidarity built by human groupings would not be possible.

Such groups sustain the autonomy of self, as a compromise to our ape ancestry's individualism, but attach emotions to self in ways that encourage cooperative behavior. At times, of course, self becomes so highly subordinated to group imperatives that individuals lose their hard-wired propensity for autonomy—as is the case with many deviant groups, such as isolated religious sects—but far more typical of human groupings and certainly of the groupings among hunter-gatherers (the types of groups in which hominids evolved) is autonomy of self. This is a self, however, attuned to the responses of others and to moral codes in which self-regulation, more than external sanctioning, is the major means of social control. Such self-regulation is not possible without conceptions of self oriented to avoiding shame and guilt as well as to seeking pride.

THINKING AND DECISION MAKING

As Antonio Damasio (1994) and associates have emphasized, thinking and decision making cannot occur without emotions. And as I stressed in Chapter 2, the greater the repertoire of emotions that can be generated by body systems, the greater is the ability to tag cognitions with subtle and complex valences. For as the brain "thinks," it does so in configurations of linked and emotionally valenced images from past memories, from present circumstances, and from anticipated outcomes. To make a decision involves the activation of the integrative functions of the prefrontal cortex, as was briefly reviewed in the last chapter.

A great deal of social theory has reverted to utilitarian views of rational actors, weighing and assessing lines of conduct, and choosing that option which maximizes utility. Or, from a behavioristic point of view, organisms are seen to maximize their level of reinforcement by selecting behaviors that bring the most rewards and the least punishments. As Randall Collins (1993) has argued, "the common denominator" for these kinds of models is emotion. The notion of utility or reward, or conversely, of punishment, makes no sense without the ability to attach emotional tags to options.

As I emphasized in the last section, self is implicated in these processes in two senses. First, one must be self-aware to make conscious and deliberative decisions, although most decisions are made without fully conscious deliberation because of inputs from subcortical memories. Second, self is also an object of evaluation, and much of the utility or reinforcement value of emotionally tagged options revolves around evaluating self in terms of positive or negative emotions. Thus, utility does not just inhere in the reward-value of objects and options per se; it is part of a more inclusive process of self-evaluation. Many decisions and acts, however, are never focused on self because doing so would overwhelm an individual's attention span and clog working memory. One does not have to engage in self-evaluation in real or imagined looking glasses just to make a sandwich or drive a car, but these kinds of evaluations are never very far from what one does (as would be the case, for example, if the kind of sandwich reflected an evaluation of oneself as too heavy or too thin, or if the car driven is intended to present a particular self to others).

Thus, thinking and decision making are not only complicated by the range of variants for primary emotions and the repertoire of first- and second-order elaborations that can be used to tag cognitions, but they are also shaped by how emotions are used to evaluate self. True, pride, shame, and guilt are perhaps the most critical to such self-evaluations, but individuals still use many more emotional variants and elaborations in the evaluation of their selves, resulting in a much more complex process of thinking and decision making. We need, therefore, to argue beyond the view of emotions as a common denominator of rational choice (Collins 1993), as true as this point is, and to begin to examine the particular configurations of emotions used in this process that would be most salient to individuals as they make decisions. These salient emotions would bear, I believe, the marks of natural selection more than culture. But what might these be? The answer to this question follows from my earlier discussion, since we need to focus on how increased solidarity and continuity of groups were achieved among hominids. To organize more cohesive groups, natural selection would bias decision making in certain directions.

First, humans make decisions in order to avoid, if possible, shame and guilt in their self-evaluations, and are motivated to experience pride whenever they can. As noted earlier, these emotions are the key to integrating individuals into groups; thus it seems reasonable to suppose that the underlying neurology generating these emotions was subject to intense selection during hominid evolution. This powerful triad of shame, guilt, and pride dominates decisions, because these emotions place self in the middle of much "rational thought" as individuals seek options that allow them to experience some degree of pride and avoid either shame or guilt. Even if a decision does not directly relate to integration of self in groups, I believe that natural selection has biased all decision making toward self-evaluations through the crucible of pride, shame, and guilt. The activation of this triad is, therefore, a significant part of the emotional syntax that circumscribes the flow of thought. Thus, it can be hypothesized that most rational decisions, and particularly ones that are problematic and involve emotionally charged deliberations (from both conscious and unconscious memory systems) that make individuals self-aware, are very heavily biased by self-evaluation processes to experience pride and minimize shame and guilt.

Second, in addition to self-evaluation dynamics, decision making will be biased by those emotions most essential to maintenance of groups, because these emotions evolved among hominids to do just that: to maintain viable and more cohesive groups. Thus, even when individuals are exerting the independent-minded part of their ape ancestry, actively seeking to avoid "group think," their evolved emotional templates for making evaluations of options are neurologically biased toward emotions generating group cohesiveness, at least to some degree. That is, we are still an ape and seek to sustain some level of autonomy of self, but we are an ape whose brain underwent significant modification in order to generate more stable and cohesive groups. Thus, no matter how we may try, our neuroanatomy imposes on decision making syntaxes of emotions that are biased toward associative responses toward others. There is nothing new, of course, in this assertion, since philosophers have for hundreds years made various arguments about the innate sociality of humans. But we are now in a position, with the evolutionary story presented in this book, to make somewhat more informed speculation along these lines. Decisions will be biased toward those emotions that mobilize and channel emotional energy into attunement of responses, into positive and negative sanctioning, into reinforcing moral codes, and into sustaining cooperative exchanges. Again, even if a decision is not directly oriented to a group issue, the process of decision making is still oriented this way, since natural selection forced this neurological template on our ancestral line. In what ways, then, does our neurology force upon us group-oriented emotions.

With respect to satisfaction-happiness, individuals seek to make decisions and enact behaviors producing moderate levels of happiness. Higher-intensity forms of this emotion are hard to achieve if they are dependent on responses of others (and therefore involve greater risks), and moreover, high-voltage happiness is difficult to sustain and, in fact, usually produces a "come down" from an emotional high that can lead to activation of disappointment-sadness. For various first-order elaborations of happiness, pride is the most important for self-regulation, as noted above, while appeasement and calm help mitigate happiness tinged with anger, and hopefulness can mitigate against sadness accompanied by anger. Thus, as individuals make decisions over relative utilities, their decision making will be guided by the grammars organizing the production of moderate levels of happiness, first-order combinations like pride, appeased, and hopeful when mixed with, respectively, fear, anger, and sadness. If such speculations ring true, then humans are not happiness junkies, seeking the most intense forms of satisfaction-happiness. Rather, moderate-intensity happiness-satisfaction and various elaborations are likely to be activated, because of the solidarity-producing effects on positive sanctioning, on reducing the effects of fear and anger during negative sanctioning, on putting a positive emotional spin on sadness, and on promoting quiet pride. These kinds of emotions are the most likely to have promoted group solidarity in our ancestors, while allowing individuals to sustain some autonomy.

The low-end variants of aversion-anger, on the other hand, are used to organize decisions and orchestrate behavioral options. When high-intensity versions of this powerful emotion dominate thought and action, decisions and actions will generally yield lower utilities. Instead, the lower- and, at times, the moderate-intensity manifestation of variants and elaborations of fear are sufficient to mobilize energies in thought. And even if the higher-intensity end of the spectrum dominates thought, individuals generally try to move their behavioral responses to the lower and moderate ends of the spectrum, if they seek to gain utilities from others. Some of the power of anger is controlled by mixing anger with other emotions. Anger mixed with satisfaction-happiness produces emotions like snubbing, rudeness, and righteousness, which were perhaps selected during hominid evolution to be used as lower-key sanctions, whereas other first-order elaborations like appeased can signal that one's anger has been adequately compensated. Anger combined with aversion produces emotions like abhorrence, jealousy, and suspiciousness, none of which are particularly associative but do reduce the power of anger alone. Anger mixed with sadness produces emotions like bitterness, depression, and a sense of betrayal, all of which can serve as negative sanctions and, at the same time, as signals to offending parties that a breach exists that is in need of repair. Thus, as humans are forced to experience anger in making decisions and enacting behaviors, high-intensity anger will be mitigated by the implicit recognition that behavioral options guided by such anger will rarely be utility-maximizing and, in fact, may activate such negative reinforcers as shame and guilt. At a neurological level, then, it may be that the human brain always tries to mitigate against extreme anger because it is so disassociative; as is obvious, however, sometimes such cortical control breaks down, although it might be argued that the stresses generated in ever more complex societies since

the days of hunting-gathering have increased the incidence of anger beyond the neurological control of the brain. Still, even as this neurology is
taxed, it appears to systematically generate, not only second-order elaborations like shame and guilt, but first-order elaborations that reduce the
power of anger to disrupt thinking and associative responses. This kind of
neurological compensation can be seen as part of calculations about utilities (e.g., "If I get too angry or show my anger, I will not get what I want
and make everyone mad at me"), but my hypothesis is that such thoughts
are hard-wired in the way emotions are generated to reduce the disassociative effects of extreme anger.

As for aversion-fear in my schema, individuals experience this emotional
spectrum in order to become aware of disequilibrium with their environment and of the potential for negative reinforcers. Fear is an extremely
valuable emotion for weighing options and is a powerful behavioral cata-
lyst, but like anger, fear at extreme levels can disrupt thinking and produce
behavioral responses that also disturb social relations. Thus, moderate-
intensity fear or fear mixed with other emotions to lower its intensity will,
I believe, structure thinking, decision making, and behavior toward more
associative responses. When individuals experience and display in their demeanor such moderate levels of fear as anxiety, misgiving, alarm, and trepidation, these reduce the power of unmitigated fear to disrupt social relations and, instead, focus decision making in more constructive directions
and mobilize the energies of the person and those in his or her environment to repair those relations that have produced fear. Again, even if others are not directly involved in generating fear in a person through negative
sanctions, natural selection biased our hominid ancestors' neurology to organize fear responses in thought and action *as if* group integration were at
stake. As a result, when experiencing fear, neurological templates in the
brain of humans bias decisions toward associative responses in order to reduce or mitigate fear. When mixed with other emotions, fear can also generate associative responses. Fear coupled with happiness generates emotions
like awe, reverence, and veneration, which all have associative potential (as
would be the case if moral codes were imbued with any of these emotions).
Fear combined with anger can produce emotions like revulsion, repulsion,
and antagonism, which can act as moderate-level negative sanctions and,
potentially, serve to motivate others to repair breaches to the interaction or
moral order. And fear linked to sadness produces emotions like dread and

wariness, which alert individuals to the lack of reinforcers to be received and to the need to lower expectations. Fear is also an important component of shame and guilt (see Tables 3.4 and 4.1, pages 81 and 86); as such, it biases decision making toward the avoidance of fear, as individuals anticipate or seek to make amends for having behaved incompetently or for having failed to meet expectations. Thus, I believe that the brain is hardwired to mitigate the power of fear by constructing emotional reactions that move toward the moderate level of intensity as well as toward first- and second-order elaborations that lower the intensity of fear, thereby biasing decisions and behavior to repair breaches or to reconstitute associative relations.

For disappointment-sadness, the low to moderate end of these emotions is sufficient to guide individuals experiencing this spectrum of emotion and other individuals in their environment to attend to problems. Individuals who are moderately sad become mobilized to make decisions and pursue options that can reduce this emotional experience. In contrast, high levels of sadness are disruptive to social relations; generally, high-intensity sadness is only acceptable for specific events, such as the loss of a loved one and for the grieving associated with this loss. And typically, high-intensity sadness is guided by feeling rules and by rituals, which can be used as mechanisms to contain the potentially destructive effects of extreme sadness. High-voltage emotions like anguish, sorrow, and despondency are highly disruptive to social relations; they require too much interpersonal attention and effort by others over too long a period to promote associative responses, and indeed, they often arouse anger (and fear) in others if extreme sadness persists beyond the dictates of feeling rules and of rituals designed to channel and limit the production of sadness. Some of the linking of sadness with other emotions in first- and second-order elaborations can move sadness in more associative directions. Sadness is the dominant emotion, I believe, in shame and guilt; and as such, it dilutes the power of fear and anger in these emotions while operating as a powerful constraint on decisions and behaviors that might produce either shame or guilt. Sadness mixed with happiness produces a range of associative emotions such as acceptance and solace, although it can also produce moroseness and melancholy in which individuals actually seem to get some pleasure out of being sad. In this latter case, the sadness-happiness combination does not produce associative emotions, except to alert others to the need for some interpersonal attention to the melancholy individual and, perhaps, to signal to the individual that new directions in behavior must be pursued. Sadness combined with fear produces emotions that force individuals and others in his or her environment to make behavioral adjustments and to attend to the warning signs of regret, forlornness, remorse, and misery, although these emotions can also distort and disrupt a person's thinking, calculations of utilities, and behavioral options. Sadness linked with anger produces many emotions that are very effective in sanctioning, such as aggrievement, discontent, and dissatisfaction; and moreover, it creates less intense manifestations of sadness that signal to others and the individual the need for change, as is the case when individuals appear bored, aggrieved, and sullen. Thus, sadness is an emotion that signals to the person the need to make decisions and change behaviors so as to increase utilities, and it is the central emotion in such regulative emotions as shame and guilt. When combined with other emotions in first-order elaborations, the power of intense sadness is mitigated, calling attention to the need to make new decisions and to adjust responses in more associative ways; conversely, the power of anger and fear are also channelled in more associative directions by being mixed with extra doses of sadness.

Yet sadness is perhaps the most complex of the primary emotions because it is generated by the failure to activate diverse brain and body systems producing other emotions; as a result, the routes to its production are more complex than fear and anger, whose activation begins in discrete clusters of cells in the amygdala. Still, sadness and the anticipation of sadness, or elaborated versions of sadness like shame and guilt, are central to calculating utilities and selecting behavioral options; sadness alerts a person and those in his or her environment to the need to pursue more reinforcing options and to use more positive sanctions. In so doing, sadness has important integrative effects on groups, *if* not too intense or too profound; thus, we might consider the brain to have been wired by natural selection to create combinations of low to moderate variants as well as key first- and second-order elaborations of sadness that bias thinking, decision making, and behavior toward seeking associative options that can activate variants and elaborations of more positive emotions along the satisfaction-happiness spectrum.

In Chapter 3, I admitted to engaging in wide-eyed speculation, a danger that has only been compounded, of course, in this chapter. There are no data to bring to bear on the speculations here, but I believe that they are worth making, if only to stimulate thought and research on the topic. For if emotions have a kind of syntax—and I realize that this is indeed a big if—the ordering of emotions has a direction and pattern. My view is that the neurology of the brain is structured by templates, about which we know little, to use variants of primary emotions and elaborations of these emotions for group-bonding purposes, even when group integration is not the central issue as individuals calculate utilities and think about behavioral options. The brain has an emotional bias toward associative responses because it was necessary to mitigate the wiring of the ape brain for individual autonomy. In making decisions, individuals often feel empowered because it is they who are being active and efficacious; and in a society where individualism is also highly valued, we can get the illusion that we are really atomized actors making rational calculations. In fact we are often this, but the emotions that are used to load the relative values of pay-offs and utilities are themselves generated by a neurology already pushing emotions toward group-oriented responses.

STOCKS OF KNOWLEDGE, EMOTIONS, AND INTERACTION

In 1932, Alfred Schutz coined the phrase "stocks of knowledge at hand" to describe the amazing ability of humans to store rather vast amounts of information about appropriate behaviors in diverse contexts.[11] We now know some of the neurology behind this facility, as experiences move from the buffers of working memory to the hippocampus for contextualization and, eventually, to the neocortex for longer-term storage. It is the hippocampus that tags experiences with emotional valences and places them in a context, and it is probably the prefrontal cortex that operates as a switching station to integrate subcortical and cortical emotion systems so that stocks of knowledge can be stored and retrieved. The existence of subcortical memories adds an additional complication, however, because many of our responses to situations are initiated by emotions stored outside the direct purview of our neocortex.

As I have emphasized, the brain is more than an open-floor warehouse in which memories are stored, arrayed, and retrieved in order to guide behavior in particular contexts. Rather, it is a warehouse with entrances and exits, as well as internal partitions, that are the product of evolution as it worked on the ape neuroanatomy of hominids to produce the human brain. In many ways, this brain is still not all that different from that of other mammals and the great apes, except that the human brain has more storage and processing capacity and greater capacities to mobilize diverse emotions to tag cognitions for storage and for communicating needs, dispositions, and intentions toward others. These emotional abilities make the higher cognitive functions of humans possible, but they do more: they structure and order how our stocks of knowledge are housed. If, as I have speculated, the human brain is structured toward generating emotional configurations that lead to decisions and behaviors that are associative, then this structure must also determine how emotional memories are stored and retrieved for subsequent use (Gazzaniga, 1969, 1992). Our stocks of knowledge are "at hand" because they are emotionally tagged memories that are organized with a built-in bias toward using them in specific contexts. They already have a grammar that orders the configurations of emotions when they are taken from contexts, stored, and then retrieved to facilitate appropriate behavior in the same or similar context.

Even with the rather amazing capacities of the human brain, it would not be possible to store every bit of information as it might relate to every potential context, especially in a complex society where individuals constantly move about and find themselves in new contexts. Even if storage is possible, retrieval would take too long to be used effectively in face-to-face interactions or in decision making. There is not only a shorthand coding system storing for reactivation of memories, as Damasio (1994) argues, but there is also a neurologically based grammar that organizes the coding systems that regulate how memories are stored, retrieved, and used. We do not, in essence, have to search our memory as a computer might do as it scans a disk; the information is already "framed" and "chunked" in the way the emotions are generated and used to put valences on cognition that become part of our stocks of knowledge. As information is retrieved, it is once again processed by this neurology that automatically contextualizes the knowledge and orchestrates the configuration of emotions to be experienced and expressed. Associative responses in context are the way the brain is organized to generate the emotions that tag memories and thereby make them available for use, that order options during decision making, and that orchestrate feelings and appropriate demeanor in situations. There is a generative capacity for doing this kind of work, which is something that research on the brain should pursue—certainly as much as work along these lines has done for the "deep structures" of language. For if we desire to understand thinking and how humans use their stocks of knowledge, the answer may reside in the actual neurology of the brain and how its wiring was biased by natural selection in the ways that I have discussed in this book. This is, at the very least, a hypothesis that might be useful to pursue in research.

Cognitive science in psychology and in biology has explored this issue to a degree, but these efforts have not been as informed by sociology as they should be, nor have they considered the impact on the brain of natural selection working rapidly to make a low-sociality animal more social and thus more able to sustain enduring local group structures. It seems reasonable to assume that as natural selection altered the brain to make hominids more emotional, it also wired into our neurology not just the ability to generate and use a wide variety of emotions, but also a capacity to organize and configure them in ways promoting associative bonds. The templates involved in this process shape just about all interrelated aspects of human thinking: the maintenance of stocks of knowledge, the ability to retrieve them and bring them to bear both explicitly and implicitly on problems, the capacity to think and decide, and the propensity to feel and act in appropriate ways.

It is when we begin to address the issue of stocks of knowledge that human social structure and culture come into play. Stocks of knowledge are formed by an interplay between the operation of the brain and the structure of culture, society, and interpersonal forces; these sociological forces and neurological systems are compatible, I believe, for all the reasons that I have emphasized in this chapter, but I will close this book with a final speculation on how these cultural, structural, and interpersonal forces operate on human emotions.

CULTURE, SOCIAL STRUCTURE, AND
INTERPERSONAL NEEDS

Face-to-face interaction in an encounter is not shaped merely by the biases of the brain as it activates appropriate emotional responses from stocks of knowledge; there are also imperatives generated by culture, social structure, and interpersonal needs. For once a social structure exists, it circumscribes the flow of emotion in encounters. Thus, stocks of knowledge at hand always include information about cultural, structural, and interpersonal forces as these operate to constrain interaction, and indeed, I argue that humans are predisposed to seek out this information. Substantive knowledge about the particulars of various encounters, coded through the biases of human neurology, exists in these more general stocks of knowledge, but there are more generic and general stocks of knowledge that apply to all encounters. It is these that I wish to examine below.

Culture can be defined as systems of symbols that humans carry in their stocks of knowledge and that they use to order their responses in encounters. These stocks of cultural knowledge are arrayed along several basic dimensions. First, there is a value dimension in which highly abstract and general standards of good and bad are used to evaluate self and others. Second, there is a belief and ideology dimension that translates general values into more specific evaluative mandates for how self and others should and ought to act in a particular context. Third, there is a normative dimension along several fronts: (a) institutional norms indicating appropriate lines of conduct for activities of a certain type (e.g., work, play, sociality, family, etc.); (b) contextual norms specifying the appropriate ways to behave in a particular situation; and (c) feeling rules articulating the nature of the emotional configurations to be activated in a specific context within a broader institutional arena (Hochschild, 1975, 1979, 1983). Fourth, there are relevant technologies or knowledge about how to manipulate the material props of the situation. Fifth, there are appropriate texts or linguistic modes of representation (e.g., genres, ways of talking, modes of discourse, etc.) that are to be used in an encounter. These are outlined in Figure 5.1. And sixth, there are frames that, in accordance with values, beliefs, and norms, dictate what is to be included and excluded during the course of an interaction, and these vary along several basic dimensions listed in Figure 5.2. Together, these cultural forces constrain the flow of emotions in situations, and without clear guidelines from these cultural forces, it is difficult to maintain an interaction without awkwardness and constant breaches (producing embarrassment and forms of shame, anger, sadness, and other disassociative emotions).

Social structure can be defined as relations among different types of positions and the distribution of individuals across such positions. For interaction to proceed smoothly and for the appropriate emotions to be activated, individuals in an encounter pay attention to several features of social

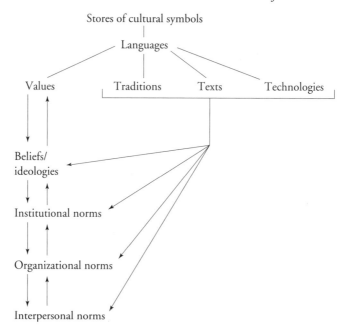

Figure 5.1.   Use of cultural systems during interaction.

structures. First, the demographics of an encounter with respect to (a) the number of individuals copresent; (b) the social categories of these individuals (e.g., age, gender, ethnicity); (c) the movement of different categories of individuals to and from the encounter over time; and (d) the distribution of different categories of individuals in space. Second, there is a positional dimension, revolving around (a) the level of prestige and authority of various positions (Kemper 1984) and (b) the attributes of individuals in such positions (e.g., diffuse status characteristics, style of demeanor, perceptions of self, etc.). And third, there is a network dimension revolving around such properties of ties, as (a) number, (b) directedness, (c) reciprocity, (d) transitivity, (e) density, (f) strength, (g) bridges, and (h) brokerage. All of these properties can be evident in interpersonal encounters, although given the nature of face-to-face interaction, the number, reciprocity, and density of ties are probably the most important in shaping the flow of emotions in an encounter.

Interpersonal needs vary, of course, for each individual, but there are more general transactional needs that individuals seek to meet in all situations (Turner 1987). These transactional needs are more generic and must

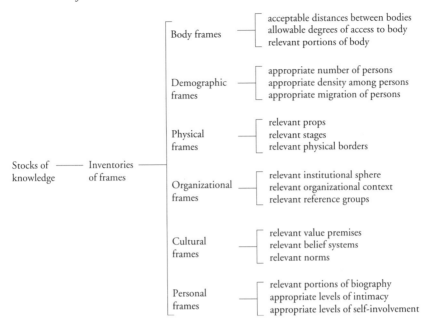

Body frames —
- acceptable distances between bodies
- allowable degrees of access to body
- relevant portions of body

Demographic frames —
- appropriate number of persons
- appropriate density among persons
- appropriate migration of persons

Physical frames —
- relevant props
- relevant stages
- relevant physical borders

Stocks of knowledge — Inventories of frames

Organizational frames —
- relevant institutional sphere
- relevant organizational context
- relevant reference groups

Cultural frames —
- relevant value premises
- relevant belief systems
- relevant norms

Personal frames —
- relevant portions of biography
- appropriate levels of intimacy
- appropriate levels of self-involvement

Figure 5.2.   Frames and framing dynamics. Adapted from J. H. Turner 1988.

first be met before more specific and idiosyncratic needs of particular individuals can be addressed. These transactional needs operate along several
dimensions. First, there are needs for exchange pay-offs of relevant resources and these pay-offs must exceed costs and investments in the situation. Second, there are needs for self-confirmation in which an individual's
self is evaluated by others in a manner consistent with this person's self-
evaluation. Third, there is a need for trust revolving around the perception
that others can be relied upon to do what they say they will do or what is
expected of them. Fourth, there is a need for predictability whereby the
actions of others can be anticipated. Fifth, there is a need for intersubjectivity, in which individuals perceive (however correctly or incorrectly)
that, for the purposes of the interaction, they share common experiences.
And sixth, there is a need for group inclusion revolving around the sense
that one is part of the flow of interaction. For an interaction to proceed
smoothly and for the appropriate emotions to be aroused, these needs
must be met.

    For all of these forces—cultural, structural, and transactional—there is, I
believe, a hard-wired basis. In any encounter, humans are predisposed to pay

attention to culture, structure, and transactional needs (both their own and those of others) because these are what make face-to-face interaction viable. If there is disagreement over relevant cultural symbols, over understandings about the social structural demography, positions or ties, and over meeting transactional needs, then interaction soon disintegrates, arousing potentially disassociative emotions like anger, fear, and sadness. When there is consensus over these forces, or at least perceived consensus, more associative emotions are activated revolving around variants and elaborations of satisfaction-happiness. Humans are thus predisposed in any encounter to understand the cultural constraints, the nature of positional networks and incumbents in these positions, and the transactional needs of others in all encounters. Our brains seek this information; and as our stocks of emotionally arrayed emotions are built up through experience in encounters, we become highly adept at reading the emotionally laden cues of others to secure the necessary information and, then, to activate the appropriate responses ordered in terms of the emotional syntax lodged in our neurology and in the way our neurology has stored stocks of knowledge and the manner in which such stocks are retrieved and made available for use in interaction.

Socialization and experience are critical, of course, in filling in these predispositions to seek relevant information about culture, structure, and transactional needs, but there is still a neurology involved because humans universally seek such information—and do so at a very young age. For without this cultural information, interaction becomes strained. Among our distant hominid ancestors, then, natural selection may have worked to wire into our neurology a predisposition to seek information along the dimensions discussed above; and these predispositions are a critical part of the grammar of emotions. That is, the way that emotional activation is configured for use is guided by humans' neurologically driven propensity to seek and use information about culture (values, beliefs, norms, technology, texts, and frames), structure (demography, positions, and relations), and transactional needs (for exchange pay-offs, self-confirmation, trust, predictability, and intersubjectivity).

Humans do not inevitably orient themselves in this direction; like spoken and emotional languages, the predisposition to seek information on culture, social structure, and transactional needs must be activated during a person's formative years—from birth to about twelve. If individuals' potential for this disposition is not stimulated through experiences in diverse encounters with others, then these individuals will always have problems, I suspect, perceiving the relevant cultural, structural, and transactional forces operating in a given situation. These individuals will always have difficulty in interaction, just as those who have never experienced language in their formative years have trouble learning it later. Even if such individuals know cognitively and rationally that they must pay attention to culture, structure, and transactional needs, they still have difficulty because their biography reveals a failure to activate the neurologically driven propensity to discover the most salient and relevant information on culture, structure, and transactional needs; as a result, they must consciously work at remaining attuned and must always be learning this information in diverse contexts. Interaction thus becomes very complicated and stressful for such individuals because their neurology cannot do the work for them automatically.

Conclusion

Humans use emotions with such ease and facility that structuring of internal experiences and of interactions with others cannot simply be the product of learning. True, learning is the key to activating humans' innate potential for using and understanding emotional syntax and to invoking the relevant emotionally ordered stocks of knowledge, but learning alone cannot explain humans' incredible facility with emotions. At the very least, the rather abstract "thought experiment" conducted in this last chapter might be worth considering as we try to extend our understanding of human emotions.

As has been my theme throughout this book, I do not believe that we can understand the emotional dynamics of human interaction without looking into the evolution of humans' emotional capacities as natural selection created a brain that could make our ancestors more social and group-oriented. It is a legitimate criticism to charge that I have constructed yet another speculative story about the evolution of human emotions, but I have tried to show how the story developed in earlier chapters is based upon some empirical data: namely, that apes are low-sociality animals who, if they were to survive as ecological changes forced them into niches of a new habitat, had to become better socially organized. Based on these facts, I have indeed told a highly speculative story. But I believe that my story better fits the conditions that hominids faced than others that I have read. The story in Chapter 2 about how imperatives for group solidarity channeled selection for a more emotional animal is plausible sociologically and, I believe, has not been told before. The story in Chapter 3 about the variants and first- and second-order emotional capacities is not my invention; in fact, many have told their own versions of this tale. My version can be considered a plausible variation on this narrative about how group imperatives operated to drive natural selection in certain directions. The story in Chapter 4 represents my best effort to extract some of the basic findings of neuroscience; it is not my own tale; rather, it is one told by others whose ideas I have adopted and adapted for my argument. The most speculative story is the one I have told in Chapter 5. But what is the point of telling a story if you do not reach a bit and seek to draw out potential implications?

Perhaps I sound defensive in this conclusion to my book, but from long experience as a general theorist, I have learned that most scholars do not like theoretically informed stories. They like findings based on empirical research, even if they are just findings not yet placed in a story. Speculative storytelling is not to everyone's taste, but a few researchers must venture into it if science is to advance. My sense is that sociology has just about gone as far as it can with its current crop of theories about human emotions; it needs knowledge and data from other fields to continue the burst of theoretical and empirical work that began a little over two decades ago. This book's goal has been to suggest new strategies for sociologists, and indeed, for others as well, that might be pursued to better understand the nature of human emotions. I invite those who do not like my story to tell a better one; out of this dialogue will come more interesting research and more robust theories.

NOTES

1. Primates in general can read a wide variety of cues visually, since they are visually dominant animals. Among chimpanzees, in particular, the reading is subtle and sophisticated, suggesting that there was something for selection to work on in our last common ancestor.

2. Female apes just tolerate each other. For chimpanzees, there is "GG rubbing" among female bonobos, but this is not a bonding mechanism as much as a

way to release tension and, thereby, allow for tolerance. There was, therefore, very little for selection to work on in creating strong female bonds in our last common ancestor to humans and apes.

3. Claude Lévi-Strauss was one of the first to make such arguments about culture; what I have in mind is more in line with Noam Chomsky's long-standing argument, but not to the same degree. Chomsky's (1965, 1980) position is too extreme, but it does address an important point. My view is that, whatever the merits of Chomsky's position, the neurological capacity for deep structures for language is built upon those for syntaxes of emotion.

4. All of the terms that I will use on this topic—templates, generative capacities, and the like—are vague. They are vague because I do not know what else to call them. My point is that the configurations and sequences of emotional cues that we experience and express are structured, to some degree, by the neurology of the brain, above and beyond the activation of the body systems that actually generate emotions. There is some kind of structure overriding body-system production of emotions, and this structure is lodged in the human brain. The operation of this structure orders emotional production into a syntax that is not cultural at its core, although culture obviously builds upon this syntax to generate feeling rules and other culture-specific modes of emotional expression. For language and, perhaps, for "emotional languages" as well, the "mental dictionary" and "mental grammar" may be lodged in different parts of the brain (Pinker 1997).

5. Emotions are communicated verbally via pacing and intonation of speech outputs. This ability to use voice to communicate subtle shades of emotional meanings could not have evolved first, since it depends upon such fine-grained control of the vocal apparatus, something that did not occur early on during hominid evolution. Thus, if selection favored more fine-tuned emotional responses among hominids, it had to work through the visual sense modality; only later, as ever greater control of the vocalizations was achieved, could the communication of subtle emotions occur through manipulations of "voice."

6. This habitat required gathering and hunting to produce food. A look at the ethnographies on hunter-gatherers reveals the basic structure which selection was creating. For representative analyses of hunting and gathering populations, see: Turner (1972, 1984, 1997a, 1997b); Lenski (1966); Maryanski and Turner (1992); Lenski, Nolan, and Lenski (1995); Roth (1890); Hose and McDougall (1912); Radcliffe-Brown (1914, 1930); Spencer and Gillen (1927); Linton (1936); Steward (1930); Holmberg (1950); Childe (1951); Clark (1952); Elkin (1954); Goldschmidt (1959); Davis and Reeves (1990); Goodhale (1959); Turnbull (1961); Washburn (1961); Service (1962, 1966); Clark and Piggott (1965); Lee and DeVore (1968, 1976); Sahlins (1968a, 1968b, 1972); Coon (1971); Bicchieri (1972); Earle and Ericson (1977); Rick (1978); Tonkinson (1978); Lee (1979); Winterhalder and Smith

(1981); Hayden (1981); Hultkrantz and Vorren (1982); Riches (1982); Schrire (1984); Johnson and Earle (1987); Hart, Pilling, and Goodhale (1988); Howell (1988).

7. The effort in Chapter 3 along these lines was only illustrative; here, I seek to be more systematic and to develop more clear-cut hypotheses.

8. I suspect that if videotapes were used more often in cross-cultural studies that the full syntax would be evident and that, as a result, the ability of individuals to read the emotions produced would be that much greater. What is amazing is that a snapshot at one time can produce such consensus over which emotions are involved. The reason for this is that we may be very attuned to the way muscles are contracted in producing emotions, and that on the basis of a configuration of muscle contractions and the production of an emotion, we can make very accurate assessments of the emotions being generated by a single snapshot.

9. For studies on the mirror tests on primates, see: Gallup (1982, 1991, 1994); Gallup et al. (1995); Heyes (1995); Swartz and Evans (1991); and Povinelli, Rulf, and Bierschwale (1994).

10. Surprisingly, except for Charles Horton Cooley's (1902) work, most early theories of self among sociologists did not include much analysis of emotions. Only recently have emotions been included in prominent interactionist theories. See Turner (1998: 374–448) for a review and references.

11. Schutz tended to have a verbal and linguistic view of stocks of knowledge, as implicit linguistic understandings. I doubt if this is the case, for the very reason that Schutz emphasized: stocks of knowledge are difficult to verbalize and make explicit, which suggests, I think, that they are stored in the brain's configurational and gestaltlike way of processing information.

Aggleton, J. P. 1992. *The Amygdala: Neurobiological Aspects of Emotion, Memory, and Mental Dysfunction.* New York: Wiley.

Agusti, J. P. Andrews, M. Fortelius, and L. Rook. 1998. "Hominoid Evolution and Environmental Change in the Neogene of Europe: A European Science Foundation Network." *Journal of Human Evolution* 34: 103–7.

Aiello, L. 1996. "Terrestriality, Bipedalism, and the Origins of Language." In *Evolution of Social Behavior Patterns in Primates and Man*, ed. W. G. Runciman, J. M. Smith, and R. I. M. Dunbar. Oxford: Oxford University Press for the British Academy.

Alexander, R. D. 1974. "The Evolution of Social Behaviours." *Annual Review of Ecological Systems* 5: 325–83.

Allman, J., and L. Brothers. 1994. "Faces, Fear, and the Amygdala." *Nature* 372: 613–14.

Andelman, S. 1986. "Ecological and Social Determinants of Cercopithecine Mating Patterns." In *Ecological Aspects of Social Evolution*, ed. D. Rubenstein and R. Wrangham. Princeton, N.J.: Princeton University Press.

Anderson, C. 1986. "Predation and Primate Evolution." *Primates* 27: 15–39.

Andrews, P. 1981. "Species Diversity and Diet in Monkeys and Apes During the Miocene." In *Aspects of Human Evolution*, ed. C. B. Stringer. London: Taylor and Francis.

———. 1989. "Palaeoecology of Laetoli." *Journal of Human Evolution* 18: 173–81.

———. 1992. "Evolution and Environment in the Hominoidea." *Nature* 360: 641–46.

———. 1995. "Ecological Apes and Ancestors." *Nature* 376: 555–56.

———. 1996. "Palaeoecology and Hominoid Palaeoenvironments." *Biological Review* 71: 257–300.

Andrews, P., and L. Martin. 1987. "Cladistic Relationships of Extant and Fossil Hominoids." *Journal of Human Evolution* 16: 101–18.

Ankel-Simons, F., J. G. Fleagle, and P. S. Chatrath. 1998. "Femoral Anatomy of *Aegyptopithecus zeuxis*, an Early Oligocene Anthropoid." *American Journal of Physical Anthropology* 106: 413–24.

Argyle, M. 1988. *Bodily Communication*. New York: International Universities Press.

Arieti, S. 1970. "Cognition and Feeling." In *Feelings and Emotions: The Loyola Symposium on Feelings and Emotions*, ed. M. B. Arnold. New York: Academic Press.

Arnold, M. B. 1960. *Emotion and Personality*. New York: Columbia University Press.

Asfaw, B., T. White, O. Lovejoy, B. Latimer, S. Simpson, and G. Suwa. 1999. *Science* 284: 629–35.

Axelrod, R., and D. Dion. 1988. "The Further Evolution of Cooperation." *Science* 242: 1385–90.

Baringaga, M. 1998. "Listening to the Brain." *Science* 280: 376–80.

Beard, C., L. Krishtalka, and R. Stucky. 1991. "First Skulls of the Early Eocene Primate *Shoshonius cooperi* and the Anthropoid-Tarsier Dichotomy." *Nature* 349: 64–67.

Begun, D. R. 1992. "Miocene Fossil Hominids and the Chimp-Human Clade." *Science* 257: 1929–33.

———. 1995. "Late Miocene European Orangutans, Gorillas, Humans, or None of the Above?" *Journal of Human Evolution* 29: 169–80.

Begun, D. R., C. Ward, and M. D. Rose. 1997. *Function, Phylogeny, and Fossils: Miocene Hominoid Evolution and Adaptations*. New York: Plenum Press.

Benefit, B. R., and M. L. McCrossin. 1995. "Miocene Hominoids and Hominid Origins." *Annual Review of Anthropology* 24: 237–56.

———. 1997. "Earliest Known Old World Monkey Skull." *Nature* 388: 368–70.

Bentivoglio, M., K. Kultas-Ilinsky, and I. Ilinsky. 1993. "Limbic Thalamus: Structure, Intrinsic Organization, and Connections." In *Neurobiology of Cingulate Cortex and Limbic Thalamus: A Comprehensive Handbook*, ed. B. A. Vogt and M. Gabriel. Boston: Birkhaüser.

Bicchieri, M. G., ed. 1972. *Hunters and Gatherers Today*. New York: Holt, Rinehart, and Winston.

Bickerton, D. 1990. *Language and Species*. Chicago: University of Chicago Press.

Birdwhistell, R. L. 1966. "Some Relations Between American Kinesics and Spoken American English." In *Communication and Culture*, ed. A. G. Smith. New York: Holt, Rinehart, and Winston.

Block, N. 1995. "On Confusion About a Function of Consciousness." *Behavior and Brain Sciences* 18: 227–87.

Bogen, J. E., and G. M. Bogen. 1969. "The Other Side of the Brain III: The Corpus Callosum and Creativity." *Bulletin of the Los Angeles Neurological Societies* 34: 191–220.

Bowers, K. S., and D. Meichenbaum. 1984. *The Unconscious Reconsidered.* New York: Wiley.

Bradshaw, J. L., and N. C. Nettleton. 1983. *Human Cerebral Asymmetry.* Englewood Cliffs, N.J.: Prentice-Hall.

Brewer, J. B., Z. Zhao, J. E. Desmond, G. H. Glover, and J. D. E. Gabrieli. 1998. "Making Memories: Brain Activity That Predicts How Well Visual Experience Will Be Remembered." *Science* 281: 1185–87.

Brothers, L. 1997. *Friday's Footprints: How Society Shapes the Human Mind.* New York: Oxford University Press.

Campbell, B. 1985. *Humankind Emerging.* Boston: Little, Brown.

Cartmill, M. 1974. "Rethinking Primate Origins." *Science* 184: 436–43.

Cerling, T., J. Harris, B. MacFadden, M. Leakey, J. Quade, V. Eisenmann, and J. Ehleringer. 1997. "Global Vegetation Change Through the Miocene/Bliocene Boundary." *Nature* 389: 153–58.

Cheney, D. 1984. "Category Formation in Vervet Monkeys." In *The Meaning of Primate Signals*, ed. R. Harre and V. Reynolds. Cambridge, Eng.: Cambridge University Press.

Cheney, D., R. Seyfarth, and B. Smuts. 1986. "Social Relationships and Social Cognition in Non-Human Primates." *Science* 234: 1361–66.

Childe, V. G. 1951. *Man Makes His Way.* New York: Mentor Books.

Chomsky, N. 1965. *Aspects of the Theory of Syntax.* Cambridge, Mass.: MIT Press.

———. 1980. *Rules and Representations.* New York: Columbia University Press.

Clark, G., and S. Piggott. 1965. *Prehistoric Societies.* New York: Knopf.

Clark, J. G. D. 1952. *Prehistoric Europe: The Economic Basis.* London: Methuen.

Clark, R. E., and L. R. Squire. 1998. "Classical Conditioning and Brain Systems: The Role of Awareness." *Science* 280: 77–81.

Cohen, N. J. 1993. *Memory, Amnesia, and the Hippocampal System.* Cambridge, Mass.: MIT Press.

Coleman, J. S. 1988. "Free-riders and Zealots: The Role of Social Networks." *Sociological Theory* 6: 52–57.

———. 1990. *Foundations of Social Theory.* Cambridge, Mass.: Belknap Press.

Collins. R. 1987. "Interaction Ritual Chains." In *The Micro-Macro Link*, ed. J. C. Alexander, B. Giesen, R. Munch, and N. J. Smelser. Berkeley: University of California Press.

———. 1988. *Theoretical Sociology.* San Diego: Harcourt Brace Jovanovich.

———. 1993. "Emotional Energy and the Common Denominator of Rational Action." *Rationality and Society* 5: 203–30.

Conroy, G. 1990. *Primate Evolution.* New York: W. W. Norton.

Conroy, G., G. W. Weber, H. Seidler, P. V. Tobias, A. Kane, and B. Brunsden.

1998. "Endocranial Capacity in Early Hominid Cranium from Sterxfontein, South Africa." *Science* 280: 1730–31.

Cooley, C. H. 1902. *Human Nature and the Social Order.* New York: Scribners.

———. 1916. *Social Organization: A Study of the Larger Mind.* New York: Scribners.

Coon, C. A. 1971. *The Hunting Peoples.* Boston: Little, Brown.

Corruccini, R. S., and R. L. Ciochon. 1983. "Overview of Ape and Human Ancestry: Phyletic Relationships of Miocene and Later Hominoidea." In *New Interpretations of Ape and Human Ancestry,* ed. R. L. Ciochon and R. Corruccino. New York: Plenum Press.

Corruccini, R., R. Ciochon, and H. McHenry. 1975. "Osteometric Shape Relationships in the Wrist Joint of Some Anthropoids." *Folia Primatologica* 24: 250–74.

Cosmides, L. 1989. "The Logic of Social Exchange: Has Natural Selection Shaped How Humans Reason?" *Cognition* 31: 187–276.

Courtney, S. M., L. Petit, J. M. Maisog, L. G. Ungerleider, J. V. Haxby. 1998. "An Area for Spatial Working Memory in Human Frontal Cortex." *Science* 279: 1347–50.

Covert, H. 1998. "Comment." *Current Biology* 8: 747.

Crompton, R. H., L. Yu, W. Weije, M. Günther, and R. Savage. 1998. "The Mechanical Effectiveness of Erect and 'Bent-hip, Bent knee' Bipedal Walking in *Australopithecus afarensis.*" *Journal of Human Evolution* 35: 55–74.

Damasio, A. R. 1994. *Descartes' Error: Emotion, Reason, and the Human Brain.* New York: G. P. Putnam.

———. 1997. "Towards a Neuropathology of Emotion and Mood." *Nature* 386: 769–70.

Darwin, C. 1872. *The Expression of Emotions in Man and Animals.* London: Watts.

Davis, K. 1940. "Extreme Social Isolation of a Child." *American Journal of Sociology* 45: 554–64.

———. 1947. "A Final Note on a Case of Extreme Isolation." *American Journal of Sociology* 52: 432–37.

Davis, L. B., and O. K. Reeves. 1990. *Hunters of the Recent Past.* Boston: Little, Brown.

deCharms, R. C., D. T. Blake, and M. M. Merzenich. 1998. "Optimizing Sound Features for Cortical Neurons." *Science* 280: 1439–43.

Devinski, O., and D. Luciano. 1993. "The Contributions of the Cingulate Cortex to Human Behavior." In *Neurobiology of Cingulate Cortex and Limbic Thalamus: A Comprehensive Handbook,* ed. B. A. Vogt and M. Gabriel. Boston: Birkhaüser.

De Waal, F. 1996. *Good Natured: The Origins of Right and Wrong in Humans and Other Animals.* Cambridge, Mass.: Harvard University Press.

Dewey, J. 1910. *How We Think.* Boston: D. C. Heath.

———. 1922. *Human Nature and Conduct.* New York: Henry Holt.

Drevets, W. C., J. L. Price, J. R. Simpson, Jr., R. D. Todd, T. Reich, M. Vannier, and M. E. Raichle. 1997. "Subgenual Prefrontal Cortex Abnormalities in Mood Disorders." *Nature* 386: 824–27.

Durkheim, É. 1912. *Elementary Forms of the Religious Life.* New York: Macmillan.

Earle, T., and J. Ericson, eds. 1977. *Exchange Systems in Prehistory.* New York: Academic Press.

Eccles, J. C. 1989. *Evolution of the Brain: Creation of Self.* London: Routledge.

Eichenbaum, H. 1997. "How Does the Brain Organize Memories?" *Science* 277: 330–31.

Eichenbaum, H., and T. Otto. 1992. "The Hippocampus: What Does It Do?" *Behavioral and Neural Biology* 57: 2–36.

Eichenbaum, H., T. Otto, and N. J. Cohen. 1994. "Two Functional Components of the Hippocampal Memory System." *Behavior and Brain Sciences* 17: 449–518.

Ekman, P. 1973a. *Darwin and Facial Expression.* New York: Academic Press.

———. 1973b. "Cross-cultural Studies of Facial Expressions." In *Darwin and Facial Expression,* ed. P. Ekman. New York: Academic Press.

———. 1982. *Emotions in the Human Face.* Cambridge, Eng.: Cambridge University Press.

———. 1984. "Expression and Nature of Emotion." In *Approaches to Emotion,* ed. K. Scherer and P. Ekman. Hillsdale, N.J.: Erbaum.

———. 1992a. "Are There Basic Emotions?" *Psychological Review* 99: 550–53.

———. 1992b. "Facial Expressions of Emotion: New Findings, New Questions." *Psychological Science* 3: 34–38.

———. 1992c. "An Argument for Basic Emotions." *Cognition and Emotion* 6: 169–200.

Ekman, P., and W. V. Friesen. 1975. *Unmasking Face.* Englewood Cliffs, N.J.: Prentice-Hall.

Ekman, P., W. V. Friesen, and P. Ellsworth. 1972. *Emotion in the Human Face.* New York: Pergamon Press.

Elkin, A. P. 1954. *The Australian Aborigines.* 3d ed. Sydney: Angus and Robertson.

Ember, C. 1978. "Myths About Hunter-Gatherers." *Ethnology* 17: 439–48.

Emde, R. N. 1980. "Levels of Meaning for Infant Emotions: A Biosocial View." In *Development of Cognition, Affect, and Social Relations: The Minnesota*

Symposium of Child Psychology, vol. 13, ed. W. A. Collins. Hillsdale, N.J.: Lawrence Erlbaum.

Emlen, J., and G. Schaller. 1960. "Distribution and Status of the Mountain Gorilla." *Zoologica* 45: 41–52.

Epstein, S. 1984. "Controversial Issues in Emotion Theory." In *Review of Personality and Social Psychology*, vol. 5, ed. P. Shaver. Beverly Hills, Calif.: Sage.

Falk, D. 1998. "Hominid Brain Evolution: Looks Can Be Deceiving." *Science* 280: 1714–15.

Fedigan, L. M. 1982. *Primate Paradigms: Sex Roles and Social Bonds.* St. Albans, Vt.: Eden Press.

Fehr, B., and J. A. Russell. 1984. "Concept of Emotion Viewed from a Prototype Perspective." *Journal of Experimental Psychology* 113: 464–86.

Fisher, R. A. 1930. *The Genetical Theory of Natural Selection.* Oxford: Clarendon Press.

Fiske, A. P. 1991. *Structures of Social Life: The Four Elementary Forms of Human Relations.* New York: Free Press.

Fleagle, J. 1988. *Primate Adaptation and Evolution.* New York: Academic Press.

Fleagle, J. G., J. T. Stern, W. L. Jungers, R. L. Susman, A. K. Vangor, and J. P. Wells. 1981. "Climbing: A Biomechanical Link with Brachiation and with Bipedalism." *Symposium of the Zoological Society of London* 48: 359–75.

Foley, R. A., and P. C. Lee. 1989. "Finite Social Space, Evolutionary Pathways, and Reconstructing Hominid Behavior." *Science* 243: 901–6.

Forbes, J., and J. King. 1982. "Vision: The Dominant Sense Modality." In *Primate Behavior*, ed. J. Forbes and J. King. New York: Academic Press.

Fossey, D. 1972. *Living with Mountain Gorillas.* Washington, D.C.: National Geographic Society.

Freides, D. 1974. "Human Information Processing and Sense Modality: Cross-Modal Functions, Information Complexity, Memory, and Deficit." *Psychological Bulletin* 81: 284–310.

Freud, S. 1900. *The Interpretation of Dreams.* London: Hogarth Press.

———. 1936 [1959]. "Inhibitions, Symptoms, and Anxiety." In *The Standard Edition of the Complete Psychological Works of Sigmund Freud*, vol. 20, ed. J. Strachey. London: Hogarth Press.

Fromme, D. K., and C. S. O'Brien. 1982. "A Dimensional Approach to the Circular Ordering of Emotions." *Motivation and Emotion* 6: 337–63.

Furuichi, T. 1989. "Social Interaction and the Life History of Female *Pan paniscus* in Wamba, Zaire." *International Journal of Primatology* 10: 173–97.

Gaeng, P. 1971. *Introduction to the Principles of Language.* New York: Harper and Row.

Galili, U., and P. Andrews. 1995. "Suppression of A-Galactosyl Epitopes Synthesis and Production of the Natural Anti-Gal Antibody: A Major Evolution Event in Ancestral Old World Primates." *Journal of Human Evolution* 29: 433–42.

Gallup, G. G. 1982. "Self-Awareness and the Emergence of Mind in Primates." *American Journal of Primatology* 2: 237–48.

———. 1991. "Toward a Comparative Psychology of Self-Awareness: Species Limitations and Cognitive Consequences." In *The Self: Interdisciplinary Approaches*, ed. J. Strauss and G. R. Goethals. New York: Springer-Verlag.

———. 1994. "Self-Recognition: Research Strategies and Experimental Design." In *Self-awareness in Animals and Humans*, ed. S. T. Parker, R. W. Mitchell, and M. L. Boccia. New York: Cambridge University Press.

Gallup, G. G., Jr., D. J. Povinelli, S. D. Suarez, J. R. Anderson, J. Lethmate, and E. W. Menzel, Jr. 1995. "Further Reflections on Self-Recognition in Primates." *Animal Behavior* 50: 1525–32.

Gannon, P. J., L. Holloway, D. C. Broadfield, and A. R. Braun. 1998. "Asymmetry of Chimpanzee Planum Temporale: Humanlike Patterns of Wernicke's Brain Language Area Homolog." *Science* 279: 220–22.

Gardner, R., B. Gardner, and T. Cantfort. 1989. *Teaching Sign Language to Chimpanzees.* Albany: State University of New York Press.

Garfinkel, H. 1966. *Studies in Ethnomethodology.* Englewood Cliffs, N.J.: Prentice-Hall.

Gazzaniga, M. S. 1969. *The Social Brain: Discovering the Networks of the Mind.* New York: Basic Books.

———. 1992. *Nature's Mind: The Biological Roots of Thinking, Emotions, Sexuality, Language, and Intelligence.* New York: Basic Books.

Gebo, D. L. 1992. "Plantigrady and Foot Adaptation in African Apes: Implications for Hominid Evolution." *American Journal of Physical Anthropology* 89: 29–58.

———. 1996. "Climbing, Brachiation, and Terrestrial Quadrupedalism: Historical Precursors of Hominid Bipedalism." *American Journal of Physical Anthropology* 101: 55–92.

Gebo, D., L. MacLatchy, R. Kityo, A. Deino, J. Kingston, and D. Pilbeam. 1997. "A Hominoid Genus from the Early Miocene of Uganda." *Science* 276: 401–4.

Geschwind, N. 1965a. "Disconnection Syndromes in Animals and Man, Part I." *Brain* 88: 237–94.

———. 1965b. "Disconnection Syndromes in Animals and Man, Part II." *Brain* 88: 585–644.

———. 1970. "The Organization of Language and the Brain." *Science* 170: 940–44.

Geschwind, N., and A. Damasio. 1984. "The Neural Basis of Language." *Annual Review of Neuroscience* 7: 127–47.

Gibbons, A. 1998. "New Study Points to Eurasian Ape as Great Ape Ancestor." *Science* 281: 622–23.

Gibbons, A., and E. Culotta. 1997. "Miocene Primates Go Ape." *Science* 276: 355–56.

Gingerich, P. 1990. "African Dawn for Primates." *Nature* 346: 411.

Gingerich, P., and M. Uhen. 1994. "Time of Origin of Primates." *Journal of Human Evolution* 27: 443–45.

Glanz, J. 1998. "Magnetic Brain Imaging Traces: A Stairway to Memory." *Science* 280: 37.

Gloor, P. 1997. *The Temporal Lobe and Limbic System.* New York: Oxford University Press.

Goffman, E. 1967. *Interaction Ritual: Essays on Face-to-Face Behavior.* Garden City, N.Y.: Anchor Books.

———. 1974. *Frame Analysis: An Essay on the Organization of Experience.* Boston: Northeastern University Press.

Goldschmidt, W. 1959. *Man Makes His Way: A Preface to Understanding Human Society.* New York: Holt, Rinehart, and Winston.

Goodall, J. 1986. *The Chimpanzees of Gombe.* Cambridge, Mass.: Belknap Press.

Goodhale, J. 1959. "The Tiwi Women of Melville Island." Ph.D. diss., University of Pennsylvania.

Gouldner, A. W. 1960. "The Norm of Reciprocity." *American Sociological Review* 25: 161–78.

Gray, J. A. 1982. *The Neuropsychology of Anxiety: An Enquiry into the Functions of the Septo-Hippocampal System.* New York: Oxford University Press.

Greenwood, P. J. 1980. "Mating Systems, Philopatry, and Dispersal in Birds and Mammals." *Animal Behavior* 28: 1140–62.

Gross, C., and J. Sergeant. 1992. "Face Recognition." *Current Opinion in Neurobiology* 2: 156–61.

Groves, C. 1998. "Comment." *Current Biology* 8: 747.

Hall, K. R. L. 1967. "Social Interactions of the Adult Male and Adult Females of a Patas Monkey Group." In *Social Communication Among Primates,* ed. S. Altmann. Chicago: University of Chicago Press.

Hammond, M. 1990. "Affective Maximization: A New Macro-Theory in the Sociology of Emotions." In *Research Agendas in the Sociology of Emotions,* ed. T. O. Kemper. Albany: State University of New York Press.

Haoenigswalk, H. 1950. "The Principal Step in Comparative Grammar." *Language* 26: 357–64.

Harcourt, A. 1977. "Social Relationships of Wild Mountain Gorillas." Ph.D. diss., Cambridge University.

———. 1979. "Social Relationships Among Adult Female Mountain Gorillas." *Animal Behavior* 27: 251–64.

Harrison, T., and L. Rook. 1997. "Enigmatic Anthropoid or Misunderstood Ape? The Phylogenetic Status of *Oreopithecus bambolii* Reconsidered." In *Function, Phylogeny, and Fossils: Miocene Hominoid Evolution and Adaptations,* ed. David Begun, Carol Ward, and Michael Rose. New York: Plenum Press.

Hart, C. W. M., A. Pilling, and J. Goodhale. 1988. *The Tiwi of North Australia.* Chicago: Holt, Rinehart, and Winston.

Hass, M. 1966. "Historical Linguistics and the Genetic Relationship of Languages." *Current Trends in Linguistics* 3: 113–53.

Hayden, B. 1981. "Subsistence and Ecological Adaptations of Modern Hunter-Gatherers." In *Omnivorous Primates,* ed. R. Harding and G. Teleki. New York: Columbia University Press.

Hechter, M. 1987. *Principles of Group Solidarity.* Berkeley: University of California Press.

Heimer, L. 1995. *The Human Brain and Spinal Cord: Functional Neuroanatomy and Dissection Guide.* New York: Springer-Verlag.

Hennig, W. 1966. *Phylogenetic Systematics.* Urbana: University of Illinois Press.

Hewes, G. W. 1973. "Primate Communication and the Gestural Origin of Language." *Current Anthropology* 14: 5–12.

Heyes, C. M. 1995. "Self-Recognition in Primates: Further Reflections Create a Hall of Mirrors." *Animal Behavior* 50: 1533–42.

———. 1998. "Theory of Mind in Nonhuman Primates." *Brain and Behavioral Science* 21: 101–21.

Hill, A. 1972. "On the Evolutionary Foundations of Language." *American Anthropologist* 74: 308–15.

———. 1998. "Causes of Perceived Faunal Change in the Late Neogene of East Africa." *Journal of Human Evolution* 16: 583–96.

Hinde, R. 1983. *Primate Social Relationships.* Oxford: Blackwell.

Hochschild, A. R. 1975. "The Sociology of Feelings and Emotions." In *Another Voice,* ed. M. Millman and R. M. Kanter. Garden City, N.Y.: Doubleday.

———. 1979. "Emotion Work, Feeling Rules, and Social Structure." *American Journal of Sociology* 85: 551–75.

———. 1983. *The Managed Heart: Commercialization of Human Feeling.* Berkeley: University of California Press.

Holloway, R. W. 1968. "The Evolution of the Primate Brain: Some Aspects of Quantitative Relations." *Brain Research* 7: 121–72.

Holmberg, A. 1950. *Nomads of the Long Bow: The Siriono of Eastern Bolivia.* Institute for Anthropology, no. 10. Washington, D.C.: Smithsonian Institution.

Hopkins, W. D., and D. A. Leavens. 1998. "Hand Use and Gestural Communication in Chimpanzees (*Pan troglodytes*)." *Journal of Comparative Psychology* 112: 95–99.

Hose, C., and W. McDougall. 1912. *The Pagan Tribes of Borneo.* London: Macmillan.

Howell, N. 1988. "Understanding Simple Social Structures: Kinship Units and Ties." In *Social Structures: A Network Approach*, ed. B. Wellman and S. D. Berkowitz. Cambridge, Eng.: Cambridge University Press.

Hultkrantz, A., and O. Vorren. 1982. *The Hunters.* Oslo: Universitets-Forlaget.

Hunt, K. 1991. "Positional Behavior in the Hominoidea." *International Journal of Primatology* 12: 95–118.

———. 1994. "The Evolution of Human Bipedality: Ecology and Functional Morphology." *Journal of Human Evolution* 26: 183–202.

Hunt, K. P., and M. H. Hodge. 1971. "Category-Item Frequency and Category-Name Meaningfulness: Taxonomic Norms for 83 Categories." *Psychonomic Monograph Supplements.* Vol. 466, no. 54. N.p.

Imanishi, K. 1965. "The Origins of the Human Family: Primalogical Approach." In *Japanese Monkeys: A Collection of Translations*, ed. S. A. Altmann. Atlanta: S. A. Altmann.

Isbell, L. A., and T. P. Young. 1996. "The Evolution of Bipedalism in Hominids and Reduced Group Size in Chimpanzees: Alternative Responses to Decreasing Resource Availability." *Journal of Human Evolution* 30: 389–97.

Isbell, L., J. Pruetz, M. Lewis, and T. Young. 1998. "Locomotor Activity Differences Between Sympatric Patas Monkeys (*Erythrocebus patas*) and Vervet Monkeys (*Cercopithecus aethiops*): Implication for the Evolution of Long Hindlimb Length in *Homo*." *American Journal of Physical Anthropology* 105: 199–207.

Izard, C. 1971. *The Face of Emotion.* New York: Appleton-Century-Crofts.

———. 1977. *Human Emotions.* New York: Plenum Press.

———. 1992a. "Basic Emotions, Relations Among Emotions, and Emotion-Cognition Relations." *Psychological Review* 99: 561–65.

———. 1992b. "Four Systems for Emotion Activation: Cognitive and Noncognitive." *Psychological Review* 100: 68–90.

Jackson, C. D., and J. S. Duncan. 1996. *MRI Neuroanatomy: A New Angle on the Brain.* New York: Churchill Livingston.

Jeffers, R., and I. Lehiste. 1979. *Principles and Methods for Historical Linguistics.* Cambridge, Mass.: MIT Press.

Johnson, A. W., and T. Earle. 1987. *The Evolution of Human Societies: From Foraging Group to Agrarian State.* Stanford, Calif.: Stanford University Press.

Johnson-Laird, P. N., and K. Oatley. 1992. "Basic Emotions, Rationality, and Folk Theory." *Cognition and Emotion* 6: 201–23.

Jolly, A. 1985. *The Evolution of Primate Behavior.* New York: Macmillan.

Jones, E. 1990. "Modulatory Events in the Development of Evolution of Primate Neocortex." In *Cerebral Cortex,* ed. E. Jones and A. Peters. New York: Plenum Press.

Jones, M. 1976. "Time, Our Lost Perception: Towards a New Theory of Perception, Attention, and Memory." *Psychological Review* 83: 323–55.

Kaada, B. R. 1951. "Somato-motor, Autonomic, and Electrocorticographic Responses to Electrical Stimulation of Rhinencephalic and Other Structures in Primates, Cat, and Dog." *Acta Physiologica Scandinavia* 23, suppl. 83: 1–285.

Kaas, J., and T. P. Pons. 1988. "The Somatosensory System of Primates." In *Neurosciences,* ed. H. Steklis and J. Erwin. New York: Alan R. Liss.

Kandel, E. R., J. H. Schwartz, T. M. Jessell. 1995. *Essentials of Neural Science and Behavior.* Norwalk, Conn.: Appleton and Lange.

Kay, R., and P. Ungar. 1997. "Dental Evidence for Diet in Some Miocene Catarrhines with Comments on the Effects of Phylogeny on the Interpretation of Adaptation." In *Function, Phylogeny, and Fossils: Miocene Hominoid Evolution and Adaptations,* ed. D. Begun, C. Ward, and M. Rose. New York: Plenum Press.

Kemper, T. D. 1981. "Social Constructionist and Positivistic Approaches to the Sociology of Emotions." *American Journal of Sociology* 87: 336–62.

———. 1984. "Power, Status, and Emotions: A Sociological Contribution to a Psychophysiological Domain." In *Approaches to Emotion,* ed. K. R. Scherer and P. Ekman. Hillsdale, N.J.: Lawrence Erlbaum.

———. 1987. "How Many Emotions Are There? Wedding the Social and Autonomic Components." *The American Journal of Sociology* 93: 263–89.

———. 1990. *Social Structure and Testosterone.* New York: Wiley.

Kendon, A. 1972. "Some Relationships Between Body Motion and Speech." In *Studies in Dyadic Communication,* ed. A. Siegman and B. Pope. New York: Pergamon Press.

———. 1980. "Gesticulation and Speech: Two Aspects of the Process of Utterance." In *The Relationship of Verbal and Nonverbal Communication,* ed. M. R. Key. The Hague: Mouton.

———. 1988. "How Gestures Become Like Words." In *Cross Cultural Perspectives in Nonverbal Communication,* ed. F. Poyatos. Toronto: Hogrefe.

Kety, S. S. 1972. "Norepinephrine in the Central Nervous System and Its Correlations with Behavior." In *Brain and Behavior*, ed. A. G. Karczman and J. D. Eccles. New York: Springer-Verlag.

Khanna, S., and J. Tonndorf. 1978. "Physical and Physiological Principles Controlling Auditory Sensitivity in Primates." In *Sensory Systems of Primates*, ed. C. Noback. New York: Plenum Press.

Killcross, S., T. W. Robbins, and B. J. Everitt. 1997. "Different Types of Fear-Conditioned Behaviour Mediated by Separate Nuclei with Amygdala." *Nature* 388: 377–80.

Kingston, J. D., B. D. Marino, and A. Hill. 1994. "Isotopic Evidence for Neogene Hominid Paleoenvironments in the Kenya Rift Valley." *Science* 264: 955–59.

Knapp, M. L., and J. A. Hall. 1992. *Nonverbal Communication in Human Interaction*. 3d ed. Fort Worth, Tex.: Harcourt Brace.

Kohlberg, L. 1976. "Moral Stages and Mobilization: The Cognitive Development Approach." In *Moral Development and Behavior: Theory, Research, and Social Issues*. New York: Holt, Rinehart, and Winston.

Köhler, M, and S. Moyá-Solá. 1997. "Paleoanthropology—Fossil Muzzles and Other Puzzles." *Nature* 388: 327–28.

Kramer, M. S., N. Cutler, J. Feighner, R. Shrivastava, J. Carman, J. J. Sramek, S. A. Reines, G. Lin, D. Snavely, E. Wyatt-Knowles, J. J. Hale, S. G. Mills, M. MacLoss, C. J. Swain, T. Harrison, R. G. Hill, F. Hefti, E. M. Scolnick, M. A. Cascieri, G. G. Chicchi, S. Sadowski, A. R. Williams, L. Hewson, D. Smith, E. J. Carlson, R. J. Hargreaves, N. M. J. Rupniak. 1998. "Distinct Mechanism for Antidepressant Activity by Blockade of Substance P Receptors." *Science* 281: 1640–44.

Latimer, B., and C. O. Lovejoy. 1990. "Metatarsophalangeal Joints of Australopithecus Afarensis." *American Journal of Physical Anthropology* 83: 13–23.

Lawler, E. J., and J. Yoon. 1993. "Power and the Emergence of Commitment Behavior in Negotiated Exchange." *American Sociological Review* 58: 465–81.

———. 1996. "Commitment in Exchange Relations: A Test of a Theory of Relational Cohesion." *American Sociological Review* 61: 89–108.

Leakey, M. G., C. S. Feibel, I. McDougall, and A. Walker. 1995. "New Four-Million-Year-Old Hominid Species from Kanapoi and Allia Bay, Kenya." *Nature* 376: 565–71.

———. 1998. "New Specimens and Confirmation of an Early Age for *Australopithecus anamensis*." *Nature* 393: 62–66.

Le Doux, J. 1987. "Emotion." In *Handbook of Physiology*, vol. 5, ed. F. Plum. Bethesda, Md.: American Physiological Society.

————. 1991. "Neuroscience Commentary: Emotion and the Brain." *Journal of NIH Research* 3: 49–51.

————. 1993a. "Emotional Networks of the Brain." In *Handbook of Emotions*, ed. M. Lewis and J. M. Haviland. New York: Guilford Press.

————. 1993b. "Emotional Memory Systems in the Brain." *Behavioural Brain Research* 58: 69–79.

————. 1996. *The Emotional Brain: The Mysterious Underpinnings of Emotional Life.* New York: Simon and Schuster.

Lee, R. 1979. *The !Kung San.* Cambridge, Eng.: Cambridge University Press.

Lee, R., and I. DeVore, eds. 1968. *Man the Hunter.* Chicago: Aldine.

————, eds. 1976. *Kalahari Hunter-Gatherers.* Cambridge, Eng.: Cambridge University Press.

Leighton, D. 1987. "Gibbons: Territoriality and Monogamy." In *Primate Societies*, ed. B. Smuts, D. Cheney, R. Seyfarth, R. Wrangham, and T. Struhsaker. Chicago: University of Chicago Press.

Lenski, G. 1966. *Power and Privilege.* New York: McGraw-Hill.

Lenski, G., P. Nolan, and J. Lenski. 1995. *Human Societies: An Introduction to Macrosociology.* New York: McGraw-Hill.

Lewis, H. B. 1971. *Shame and Guilt in Neurosis.* New York: International Universities Press.

Lieberman, P. 1984. *The Biology and Evolution of Language.* Cambridge, Mass.: Harvard University Press.

Lieberman, P., and E. S. Crelin. 1971. "On Speech of Neanderthal Man." *Linguistic Inquiry* 11: 203–22.

Lieberman, P., E. S. Crelin, and D. H. Klatt. 1972. "Phonetic Ability and Related Anatomy of the Newborn and Adult Human, Neanderthal Man, and the Chimpanzee." *American Anthropologist* 74: 287–307.

Linton, R. 1936. *The Study of Man.* New York: Appleton-Century.

Maas, P. 1958. *Textual Criticism.* Oxford: Oxford University Press.

MacLean, P. D. 1990. *The Triune Brain in Evolution: Role of Paleocerebral Functions.* New York: Plenum Press.

————. 1993. "Introduction: Perspective on Cingulate Cortex in the Limbic System." In *Neurobiology of Cingulate Cortex and Limbic Thalamus: A Comprehensive Handbook*, ed. B. A. Vogt and M. Gabriel. Boston: Birkhaüser.

Malatesta, C. Z., and J. M. Haviland. 1982. "Learning Display Rules: The Socialization of Emotion Expression in Infancy." *Child Development* 53: 991–1003.

Malone, D. 1987. "Mechanisms of Hominoid Dispersal in Miocene East Africa." *Journal of Human Evolution* 16: 469–81.

Martin, R. D. 1990a. *Primate Origins and Evolution: A Phylogenetic Reconstruction.* London: Chapman and Hall.

———. 1990b. "Some Relatives Take a Dive." *Nature* 345: 291–92.

Maryanski, A. 1987. "African Ape Social Structure: Is There Strength in Weak Ties?" *Social Networks* 9: 191–215.

———. 1992. "The Last Ancestor: An Ecological-Network Model on the Origins of Human Sociality." *Advances in Human Ecology* 2: 1–32.

———. 1993. "The Elementary Forms of the First Proto-Human Society: An Ecological/Social Network Approach." *Advances in Human Ecology* 2: 215–41. Greenwich, Conn.: JAI Press.

———. 1996a. "Was Speech an Evolutionary Afterthought?" In *Communicating Meaning: The Evolution and Development of Language*, ed. B. M. Velichkousky and D. M. Rumbaugh. Hillsdale, N.J.: Lawrence Erlbaum.

———. 1996b. "African Ape Social Networks: A Blueprint for Reconstructing Early Hominid Social Structure." In *The Archaeology of Human Ancestry*, ed. James Steele and Stephen Shennan. London: Routledge.

———. 1997a. "African Ape Social Networks: A Blueprint for Reconstructing Early Hominid Social Structure." In *The Archaeology of Human Ancestry*, ed. J. Steele and S. Shennan. London: Routledge.

———. 1997b. "Primate Communication and the Ecology of Language." In *Nonverbal Communication: Where Nature Meets Culture*, ed. V. Segerstrale and P. Molnar. Hilldale, N.J.: Lawrence Erlbaum.

Maryanski, A., and J. H. Turner. 1992. *The Social Cage: Human Nature and The Evolution of Society.* Stanford, Calif.: Stanford University Press.

Masterton, B. 1992. "Role of the Central Auditory System in Hearing: The New Direction." *Trends in Neurosciences* 15: 280–85.

Masterton, B., and I. Diamond. 1973. "Hearing: Central Neural Mechanisms." In *Handbook of Perception*, vol. 3, ed. E. Carterrette and M. Friedman. New York: Academic Press.

Mauss, M. 1925. *The Gift.* Trans. I. Cunnison. New York: Free Press.

McKee, J. 1996. "Faunal Turnover Patterns in the Pliocene and Pleistocene of Southern Africa." *South African Journal of Science* 92: 111–12.

Mead, G. H. 1934. *Mind, Self, and Society.* Chicago: University of Chicago Press.

Mehrabian, A., and S. R. Ferris. 1967. "Inference of Attitudes from Nonverbal Communication in Two Channels." *Journal of Counseling Psychology* 13: 37–58.

Melnick, D., and M. Pearl. 1987. "Cercopithecines in Multimale Groups: Genetic Diversity and Population Structure." In *Primate Societies*, ed. B. Smuts, D. Cheney, R. Seyfarth, R. Wrangham, and T. Struhsaker. Chicago: University of Chicago Press.

Meltzoff, A. N., and M. K. Moore. 1983a. "Newborn Infants Imitate Adult Facial Gestures." *Child Development* 54: 702–9.

———. 1983b. "The Origins of Imitation in Infancy: Paradigm, Phenomena, and Theories." In *Advances in Infancy Research*, vol. 2. Norwood, N.J.: Ablex.

Menzel, E. W. 1971. "Communication About the Environment in a Group of Young Chimpanzees." *Folia Primatologica* 15: 220–32.

Mesulam, M. M. 1983. "The Functional Anatomy and Hemispheric Specialization for Direct Attention." *Trends in Neurosciences* 6: 384–87.

Miller, G. 1972. "Linguistic Communication as a Biological Process." In *Biology and the Human Sciences*, ed. J. W. S. Pringle. Oxford: Clarendon Press.

Miyamoto, M., and T. Young. 1988. "Comment." *Current Biology* 8: 745–46.

Mlot, C. 1998. "Probing the Biology of Emotion." *Science* 280: 1005–7.

Moore, J. 1984. "Female Transfer in Primates." *International Journal of Primatology* 5: 537–89.

Morgan, L. H. 1877. *Ancient Society.* New York: Henry Holt.

Moyá-Solá, S., and M. Köhler. 1996. "A Dryopithecus Skeleton and the Origins of Great-Ape Locomotion." *Nature* 379: 156–59.

Murdock, G. 1967. *Ethnographic Analysis.* Pittsburgh: University of Pittsburgh Press.

Nakatsukasa, M., A. Yamanaka, Y. Kunimatsu, D. Shimizu, and H. Ishida. 1998. "A Newly Discovered Kenyapithecus Skeleton and Its Implications for the Evolution of Positional Behavior in Miocene East African Hominoids." *Journal of Human Evolution* 34: 657–64.

Napier, J. R., and P. H. Napier. 1985. *The Natural History of the Primates.* Cambridge, Mass.: MIT Press.

Needham, C. 1982. *The Principles of Cerebral Dominance: The Evolutionary Significance of the Radical Deduplication of the Human Brain.* Springfield, Ill.: Thomas.

Negus, V. E. 1929. *The Mechanism of the Larynx.* London: Heinemann Medical Books.

O Scalaidhe, S. P., F. A. W. Wilson, and P. S. Goldman-Rakic. 1997. "Areal Segregation of Face-Processing Neurons in Prefrontal Cortex." *Science* 278: 1135–38.

Osgood, C. E. 1966. "Dimensionality of the Semantic Space for Communication via Facial Expressions." *Scandinavian Journal of Psychology* 7: 1–30.

Panksepp, J. 1982. "Toward a General Psychobiological Theory of Emotions." *Behavioral and Brain Sciences* 5: 407–67.

———. 1998. *Affective Neuroscience: The Foundations of Human and Animal Emotions.* Oxford: Oxford University Press.

Piaget, J. 1932. *The Moral Judgment of the Child.* New York: Free Press.

Pilbeam, D. 1997. "Research on Miocene Hominoids and Hominid Origins: The Last Three Decades." In *Function, Phylogeny and Fossils: Miocene Hominoid Evolution and Adaptations,* ed. D. Begun, C. Ward, and M. Rose. New York: Plenum Press.

Pinker, S. 1997. "Words and Rules in the Human Brain." *Nature* 387: 547–48.

Platnick, N., and H. D. Cameron. 1977. "Cladistic Method in Textual, Linguistic, and Phylogenetic Analysis." *Systematic Zoology* 26: 380–85.

Plutchik, R. 1962. *The Emotions: Facts, Theories, and a New Model.* New York: Random House.

———. 1980. *Emotion: A Psychoevolutionary Synthesis.* New York: Harper and Row.

Povinelli, D. J., and T. M. Preuss. 1995. "Theory of Mind: Evolutionary History of Cognitive Specialization." *Trends in Neuroscience* 18: 418–24.

Povinelli, D. J., A. B. Rulf, and D. T. Bierschwale. 1994. "Absence of Knowledge Attribution and Self-Recognition in Young Chimpanzees." *Journal of Comparative Primatology* 108: 74–80.

Prevschoft, H., D. Chivers, W. Brockelman, and N. Creel. 1984. *The Lesser Apes.* Edinburgh: Edinburgh University Press.

Pusey, A., and C. Packer. 1987. "Dispersal and Philopatry." In *Primate Societies,* ed. B. Smuts, D. Cheney, R. Seyfarth, R. Wrangham, and T. Struhsaker. Chicago: University of Chicago Press.

Radcliffe-Brown, A. R. 1914. *The Andaman Islanders.* New York: Free Press.

———. 1930. "The Social Organization of Australian Tribes." *Oceana* 1: 44–46.

Radinsky, L. B. 1970. "The Fossil Evidence of Prosimian Brain Evolution." *American Journal of Physical Anthropology* 41: 15–28.

———. 1974. "The Fossil Evidence of Anthropoid Brain Evolution." *American Journal of Physical Anthropology* 41: 15–28.

———. 1975. "Primate Brain Evolution." *American Scientist* 63: 656–63.

———. 1977. "Early Primate Brains: Facts and Fiction." *Journal of Human Evolution* 6: 79–86.

Reynolds, V. 1966. "Open Groups in Hominid Evolution." *Man* 1: 441–52.

Rhine, R. J., P. Boland, and L. Lodwick. 1985. "Progressions of Adult Male Chocma Baboons (*Papio ursinus*) in the Moremi Wildlife Reserve." *International Journal of Primatology* 6: 116–22.

Riches, D. 1982. *Northern Nomadic Hunter-Gatherers.* London: Academic Press.

Rick, J. 1978. *Prehistoric Hunters of the High Andes.* New York: Academic Press.

Rodieck, R. W. 1988. "The Primate Retina." In *Neurosciences,* vol. 4, ed. H. Steklis and J. Erwin. New York: Alan Liss.

Rodman, P. S., and H. M. McHenry. 1980. "Bioenergetics and the Origin of Hominid Bipedalism." *American Journal of Physical Anthropology* 52: 102–6.

Rodman, P. S., and J. Mitani. 1987. "Orangutans: Sexual Dimorphism in a Solitary Species." In *Primate Societies*, ed. B. Smuts, D. Cheney, R. Seyfarth, R. Wrangham, and T. Struhsaker. Chicago: University of Chicago Press.

Rolls, E. T. 1995. "Learning Mechanisms in the Temporal Lobe Visual Cortex." *Behavioral Brain Research* 66: 177–85.

Rose, K. D., and J. G. Fleagle. 1987. "The Second Radiation-Prosimians." In *Primate Evolution and Human Origins*, ed. R. L. Ciochon and J. Fleagle. New York: Aldine de Gruyter.

Rose, M. 1993. "Locomotor Anatomy of Miocene Hominoids." In *Postcranial Adaptation in Nonhuman Primates*, ed. D. Gebo. DeKalb: Northern Illinois University Press.

———. 1997. "Functional and Phylogenetic Features of the Forelimb in Miocene Hominoids." In *Function, Phylogeny, and Fossils: Miocene Hominoid Evolution and Adaptations*, ed. D. Begun, C. Ward, and M. Rose. New York: Plenum Press.

Roth, H. L. 1890. *The Aborigines of Tasmania*. London: Kegan, Paul, Trench, and Trubner.

Ruff, C. B., E. Trinkaus, and T. W. Holliday. 1997. "Body Mass and Encephalization in Pleistocene Homo." *Nature* 387: 173–76.

Rugg, M. D. 1998. "Memories Are Made of This." *Science* 281: 1151–52.

Sahlins, M. 1968a. *Tribesmen*. Englewood Cliffs, N.J.: Prentice-Hall.

———. 1968b. "Notes on the Original Affluent Society." In *Man the Hunter*, ed. R. Lee and I. DeVore. Chicago: Aldine.

———. 1972. *Stone Age Economics*. Chicago: Aldine.

Sanghera, M. F., E. T. Rolls, and A. Roper-Hall. 1979. "Visual Response of Neurons in the Dorsolateral Amygdala of the Alert Monkey." *Experimental Neurology* 63: 61–62.

Savage-Rumbaugh, E. S., D. Rumbaugh, and K. McDonald. 1985. "Language Learning in Two Species of Apes." *Neuroscience and Biobehavioral Reviews* 9: 653–65.

Savage-Rumbaugh, E. S., J. Murphy, R. Seveik, D. Brakke, S. Williams, and D. Rumbaugh. 1993. *Language Comprehension in the Ape and Child*. Monographs of the Society for Research in Child Development, vol. 58. Chicago: University of Chicago Press.

Schacter, D. L. 1998. "Memory and Awareness." *Science* 280: 59–60.

Schaller, G. 1962. "The Ecology and Behavior of the Mountain Gorilla." Ph.D. diss., University of Wisconsin.

Scheff, T. J. 1988. "Shame and Conformity: The Deference-Emotion System."
    American Sociological Review 53: 395–406.

———. 1990a. *Microsociology: Discourse and Social Structure.* Chicago:
    University of Chicago Press.

———. 1990b. "Socialization of Emotion: Pride and Shame as Causal Agents."
    In *Research Agendas in the Sociology of Emotions*, ed. T. D. Kemper. Albany:
    State University of New York Press.

Scheff, T. J., and S. M. Retzinger. 1991. *Emotions and Violence: Shame and Rage
    in Destructive Conflicts.* Lexington, Mass.: Lexington Books.

Schrire, C., ed. 1984. *Past and Present in Hunter-Gatherer Studies.* Orlando, Fla.:
    Academic Press.

Schubert, G., and R. Masters, eds. 1991. *Primate Politics.* Carbondale: Southern
    Illinois University Press.

Schultz, A. 1933. "Die Korperpoportionen der Catarrhinen Primaten, mit
    spezieller Berucksichtigung der Menschenaffen." *Anthropologischer Anzeiger*
    10: 240–60.

Schutz, A. H. 1932 [1967]. *The Phenomenology of the Social World.* Evanston, Ill.:
    Northwestern University Press.

Science. 1998. "Anthropologists Probe Genes, Brains at Annual Meetings."
    Science 280: 380.

Scott, J. P. 1980. "The Function of Emotions in Behavioral Systems: A Systems
    Theory Analysis." In *Emotion: Theory, Research, and Experience*, vol. 1,
    ed. R. Plutchik and H. Kellerman. New York: Academic Press.

Semendeferi, K., H. Damasio, R. Frank, and G. W. Van Hoesen. 1997. "The
    Evolution of the Frontal Lobes: A Volumetric Analysis Based on Three-
    Dimensional Reconstructions of Magnetic Resonance Scans of Human and
    Ape Brains." *Journal of Human Evolution* 32: 375–88.

Service, E. 1962. *Primitive Social Organization: An Evolutionary Perspective.*
    New York: Random House.

———. 1966. *The Hunters.* Englewood Cliffs, N.J.: Prentice-Hall.

Shepherd, G. M. 1994. *Neurobiology.* 3d ed. New York: Oxford University Press.

Shott, S. 1979. "Emotion and Social Life: A Symbolic Interactionist Analysis."
    American Journal of Sociology 84: 1317–34.

Simons, E. L. 1990. "Discovery of the Oldest Known Anthropoidean Skull from
    the Paleogene of Egypt." *Science* 247: 1567–69.

Simons, E. L., and E. Delson. 1978. "Cercopithecidae and Parapithecidae." In
    Evolution of African Mammals, ed. V. Magio and H. B. S. Cooke. Cambridge,
    Mass.: Harvard University Press.

Smith, C. A., and R. S. Lazarus. 1990. "Emotion and Adaptation." In *Handbook
    of Personality: Theory and Research*, ed. L. A. Pervin. New York: Guilford Press.

Smith, T. S., and G. T. Stevens. 1997a. "Comfort Regulation as a Morphogenetic Principle." *Advances in Group Processes* 14: 113–55.

———. 1997b. "The Architecture of Small Networks: Strong Interaction and Dynamic Organization in Small Social Systems." Paper presented at American Sociological Association Meeting, Toronto, Canada.

Smuts, B., D. Cheney, R. Seyfarth, R. Wrangham, and T. Struhsaker. 1987. *Primate Societies*. Chicago: University of Chicago Press.

Snowdon, C. 1990. "Language Capacities of Non-Human Animals." *Yearbook of Physical Anthropology* 33: 215–43.

Spencer, B., and F. J. Gillen. 1927. *The Arunta: A Study of a Stone Age People*. London: Macmillan.

Spencer, H. 1874–96 [1898]. *The Principles of Sociology*. New York: Appleton-Century.

Sperry, R. W. 1982. "Some Effects of Disconnecting the Cerebral Hemispheres." *Science* 217: 1223–26.

Spoor, F., B. Wood, and F. Zonneveld. 1994. "Implications of Early Hominid Labyrinthine Morphology for Evolution of Human Bipedal Locomotion." *Nature* 369: 645–48.

Sroufe, L. A. 1979. "Socioemotional Development." In *Handbook of Infant Development*, ed. J. D. Osofsky. New York: Wiley.

Steklis, H. 1985. "Primate Communication, Comparative Neurology, and the Origin of Language Re-Examined." *Journal of Human Evolution* 14: 157–73.

Stephan, H. 1983. "Evolutionary Trends in Limbic Structures." *Neuroscience and Biobehavioral Reviews* 7: 367–74.

Stephan, H., and O. J. Andy. 1969. "Quantitative Comparative Neuroanatomy of Primates: An Attempt at Phylogenetic Interpretation." *Annals of the New York Academy of Science* 167: 370–87.

———. 1977. "Quantitative Comparison of the Amygdala in Insectivores and Primates." *Acta Antomica* 98: 130–53.

Stephan, H., G. Baron, and H. Frahm. 1988. "Comparative Size of Brains and Brain Components." In *Neurosciences*, vol. 5, ed. H. Steklis and J. Erwin. New York: Alan R. Liss.

Stern, J. T. 1972. "Functional Myology of the Hip and Thigh of Cebid Monkeys and Its Implications for the Evolution of Erect Posture." In *Biblioteca Primatologica*. Vol. 14. Karger: Basel.

———. 1975. "Before Bipedality." *Yearbook of Physical Anthropology* 19: 58–68.

Steward, J. H. 1930. "The Economic and Social Basis of Primitive Bands." In *Essays on Anthropology in Honor of Alfred Louis Kroeber*, ed. R. Lowie. Berkeley: University of California Press.

Stewart, C., and T. Disotell, 1998. "Primate Evolution—In and Out of Africa." *Current Biology* 8: 582–88.

Strasser, E., and E. Delson. 1987. "Cladistic Analysis of Cercopithecid Relationships." *Journal of Human Evolution* 16: 81–99.

Swartz, K., and S. Evans. 1991. "Not All Chimpanzees Show Self-Recognition." *Primates* 32: 483–96.

Swartz, S. 1989. "Pendular Mechanics and Kinematics and Energetics of Brachiating Locomotion." *International Journal of Primatology* 10: 387–418.

Tattersall, I. 1998. *Becoming Human: Evolution and Human Uniqueness.* New York: Harcourt Brace.

Tattersall, I., E. Delson, and J. van Couvering. 1988. *Encyclopedia of Human Evolution and Prehistory.* New York: Garland Publishing.

Temerin, A., and J. Cant. 1983. "The Evolutionary Divergence of Old World Monkeys and Apes." *The American Naturalist* 122: 335–51.

Terrace, H. S., L. A. Petitto, R. J. Sanders, and G. Bever. 1979. "Can an Ape Create a Sentence?" *Science* 206: 891–96.

Tonkinson, R. 1978. *The Marduojara Aborigines.* New York: Holt, Rinehart, and Winston.

Trevarthen, C. 1984. "Emotions in Infancy: Regulators of Contact and Relationship with Persons." In *Approaches to Emotion*, ed. K. R. Scherer and P. Ekman. Hillsdale, N.J.: Lawrence Erlbaum.

Trivers, R. L. 1971. "The Evolution of Reciprocal Altruism." *Quarterly Review of Biology* 46: 35–57.

Turnbull, C. 1961. *The Forest People.* New York: Simon and Schuster.

Turner, J. H. 1972. *Patterns of Social Organization: A Survey of Social Institutions.* New York: McGraw-Hill.

———. 1984. *Social Stratification: A Theoretical Analysis.* New York: Columbia University Press.

———. 1987. "Toward a Sociological Theory of Motivation." *American Sociological Review* 52: 15–27.

———. 1988. *A Theory of Social Interaction.* Stanford, Calif.: Stanford University Press.

———. 1992. "The Production and Reproduction of Solidarity: A Synthesis of Two Rational Choice Theories." *Journal for the Theory of Social Behavior* 22: 311–23.

———. 1995. "Roles and Interaction Processes: Toward a More Robust Theory." In *Self, Collective Action, and Society*, ed. G. Platt and C. Gordon. Greenwich, Conn.: JAI Press.

———. 1996a. "The Evolution of Emotions in Humans: A Darwinian-Durkheimian Analysis." *Journal for the Theory of Social Behaviour* 26: 1–34.

————. 1996b. "Cognition, Emotion, and Interaction in the Big-Brained Primate." In *Social Processes and Interpersonal Relations*, ed. K. M. Kwan. Greenwich, Conn.: JAI Press.

————. 1997a. "The Nature and Dynamics of the Social Among Humans." In *The Mark of The Social*, ed. J. D. Greenwood. New York: Rowman and Littlefield.

————. 1997b. "The Evolution of Emotions: The Nonverbal Basis of Human Social Organization." In *Nonverbal Communication: Where Nature Meets Culture*, ed. U. Segerstrale and P. Molnar. Hillsdale, N.J.: Lawrence Erlbaum.

————. 1998. "The Evolution of Moral Systems." *Critical Review* 11: 211–32.

————. 1999a. "Toward a General Sociological Theory of Emotions." *Journal for the Theory of Social Behavior* 29: 133–62.

————. 1999b. "The Neurology of Emotions: Implications for Sociological Theories of Interpersonal Behavior." In *The Sociology of Emotions*, ed. D. Franks. Greenwich, Conn.: JAI Press.

Turner, R. H. 1962. "Role Taking: Process Versus Conformity." In *Human Behavior and Social Processes*, ed. A. Rose. Boston: Houghton Mifflin.

Tuttle, R. 1986. *Apes of the World: Their Social Behavior, Communication, Mentality, and Ecology*. Park Ridge, Ill.: Noyes.

————. 1988. "What's New in African Paleoanthropology?" *Annual Review of Anthropology* 17: 391–426.

Tylor, E. B. 1868. "On the Origins of Language." *Fortnightly Review* 1: 25–37.

————. 1871 [1958]. *Primitive Culture* (reissued as *The Origins of Culture*). New York: Harper and Row.

Ungar, P. 1996. "Dental Microwear of European Miocene Catarrhines: Evidence for Diets and Tooth Use." *Journal of Human Evolution* 31: 335–66.

Ungar, P., and R. Kay. 1995. "The Dietary Adaptations of European Miocene Catarrhines." *Proceedings of the National Academy of Sciences of the United States* 92: 5479–81.

Van Der Merwe, N. J., and J. F. Thackeray. 1997. "Stable Carbon Isotope Analysis of Plio-Pleistocene on Gulate Teeth from Sterkfontein, South Africa." *South African Journal of Science* 93: 194.

Vargha-Khadem, F., D. G. Gadian, K. E. Watkins, A. Connelly, W. Van Paesschen, and M. Mishkin. 1997. "Differential Effects of Early Hippocampal Pathology on Episodic and Semantic Memory." *Science* 277: 376–80.

Vogt, B. A. 1993a. "Structural Organization of Cingulate Cortex." In *Neurobiology of Cingulate Cortex and Limbic Thalamus*, ed. B. A. Vogt and M. Gabriel. Berlin: Birkhaüser.

————. 1993b. "Structural Organization of Cingulate Cortex: Areas, Neurons, and Somatodentritic Transmitter Receptors." In *Neurobiology of Cingulate*

Cortex and Limbic Thalamus: A Comprehensive Handbook, ed. B. A. Vogt and M. Gabriel. Berlin: Birkhäuser.

Wahlestedt, C. 1998. "Reward for Persistence in Substance Research." *Science* 281: 1624–25.

Wallace, A. R. 1895. "Expressiveness of Species' Mouth Gesture as a Factor in the Origin of Language." *Fortnightly Review* 64: 528–43.

Ward, C. 1993. "Torso Morphology and Locomotion in Proconsul nyanzae." *American Journal of Physical Anthropology* 92: 291–328.

———. 1998. "Comment." *Current Biology* 8: 746.

Ward, C., D. Begun, and M. Rose 1997. "Function and Phylogeny in Miocene Hominoids." In *Function, Phylogeny, and Fossils: Miocene Hominoid Evolution and Adaptations*, ed. David Begun, Carol Ward, and Michael Rose. New York: Plenum Press.

Warren, R., and R. Warren. 1976. "Auditory Illusions and Confusions." In *Recent Progress in Perception*, ed. R. Held and W. Richards. San Francisco: Freeman.

Washburn, S. L., ed. 1961. *Social Life of Early Man*. Chicago: Aldine.

———. 1968. "Speculations on the Problem of Man's Coming to the Ground." In *Changing Perspectives on Man*, ed. B. Rothbatt. Chicago: University of Chicago Press.

Whalen, P. J., S. L. Rauch, N. L. Etcoff, S. C. McInerney, M. B. Lee, and M. A. Jenike. 1998. "Masked Presentations of Emotional Facial Expressions Modulate Amygdala Activity Without Explicit Knowledge." *Journal of Neuroscience* 18: 411–18.

Wheeler, P. E. 1993. "The Influence of Stature and Body Form on Hominid Energy and Water Budgets: A Comparison of *Australopithecus* and *Homo* Physiques." *Journal of Human Evolution* 24: 13–28.

White, T., and G. Suwa. 1987. "Hominid Footprints at Laetoli: Facts and Interpretations." *American Journal of Physical Anthropology* 72: 485–514.

White, T. D., G. Suwa, and B. Asfaw. 1994. "*Australopithecus ramidus*: A New Species of Early Hominid from Aramis, Ethiopia." *Nature* 371: 280–81.

Winterhalder, B., and E. A. Smith, eds. 1981. *Hunter-Gatherer Foraging Strategies*. Chicago: University of Chicago Press.

Wood, B. 1994. "The Oldest Hominid Yet." *Nature* 371: 280–81.

Wrangham, R. 1980. "An Ecological Model of Female-Bonded Primate Groups." *Behaviour* 74: 262–99.

———. 1987. "The Significance of African Apes for Reconstructing Human Social Evolution." In *Evolution of Human Behavior: Primate Models*, ed. W. Kinzey. Albany: State University of New York Press.

Wrangham, R., W. C. McGrew, F. de Waal, and P. Heltne. 1994. *Chimpanzee Cultures.* Cambridge, Mass.: Harvard University Press.

Wundt, W. 1916. *Elements of Folk Psychology: Outlines of a Psychological History of the Development of Mankind.* London: George Allen.

Yamagiwa, J. 1983. "Diachronic Changes in Two Eastern Lowland Gorilla Groups (*gorilla gorilla graueri*) in the Mt. Kahuze Region, Zaire." *Primates* 25: 174–83.

Zihman, A., and J. Lowenstein. 1998. "Comment." *Current Biology* 8: 746.